"I have ever deemed it fundamental for the United States never to take active part in the quarrels of Europe. Their political interests are entirely distinct from ours. Their mutual jealousies, their balance of power, their complicated alliances, their forms and principles of government, are all foreign to us. They are nations of eternal war."

— Thomas Jefferson, 1823

..."a passionate attachment of one nation for another produces a variety of evils. Sympathy for the favorite nation, facilitating the illusion of an imaginary common interest in cases where no real common interest exists, and infusing into one the enmities of the other, betrays the former into a participation in the quarrels and wars of the latter, without adequate inducement or justification. It leads also to concession to the favorite nation of privileges denied to others, which is apt doubly to injure the nation making the concessions; by unnecessarily parting with what ought to have been retained; and by exciting jealousy, ill-will and a disposition to retaliate, in the parties from whom equal privileges are withheld. And it gives to ambitious, corrupted or deluded citizens (who devote themselves to the favorite nation) facility to betray, or sacrifice the interests of their own country, without odium, sometimes even with popularity .... Against the insidious wiles of foreign influence, (I conjure you to believe me fellow-citizen) the jealousy of a free people ought to be constantly awake."

— George Washington
WASHINGTON'S FAREWELL ADDRESS, 1796

"Never was so much false arithmetic employed on any subject, as that which has been employed to persuade nations that it is in their interest to go to war."

— Thomas Jefferson, 1782

About the Uncle Eric Series

The Uncle Eric series of books is written by Richard J. Maybury for young and old alike. Using the epistolary style of writing (using letters to tell a story), Mr. Maybury plays the part of an economist writing a series of letters to his niece or nephew. Using stories and examples, he gives interesting and clear explanations of topics that are generally thought to be too difficult for anyone but experts.

Mr. Maybury warns, "beware of anyone who tells you a topic is above you or better left to experts. Many people are twice as smart as they think they are, but they've been intimidated into believing some topics are above them. You can understand almost anything if it is explained well."

The series is called UNCLE ERIC'S MODEL OF HOW THE WORLD WORKS. In the series, Mr. Maybury writes from the political, legal and economic viewpoint of America's Founders. The books can be read in any order, and have been written to stand alone. To get the most from each one, however, Mr. Maybury suggests the following order of reading:

Uncle Eric's Model
of How the World Works

Uncle Eric Talks About Personal, Career, and Financial Security

Whatever Happened to Penny Candy?

Whatever Happened to Justice?

Are You Liberal? Conservative? or Confused?

Ancient Rome: How It Affects You Today

Evaluating Books: What Would Thomas Jefferson Think About This?

The Money Mystery

The Clipper Ship Strategy

The Thousand Year War in the Mideast

World War I: The Rest of the Story and How It Affects You Today

World War II: The Rest of the Story and How It Affects You Today

(Study guides available or forthcoming for above titles.)

An Uncle Eric Book

World War II

The Rest of the Story
and How It Affects You Today
1930 to September 11, 2001

Revised Edition

Part two of a two-part series about the World Wars

by Richard J. Maybury
(Uncle Eric)

published by
Bluestocking Press
www.BluestockingPress.com

Cover illustrations by Bob O'Hara, Georgetown, CA
Cover design by Brian C. Williams, El Dorado, CA
Edited by Jane A. Williams
       Library of Congress Cataloging-in-Publication Data
Maybury, Rick.
     World War II : the rest of the story and how it affects you today,
1930 to September 11, 2001 / by Richard J. Maybury ; [edited by Jane
A. Williams].-- Rev. ed.
       p. cm. -- (An Uncle Eric book)
"Part two of a two-part series about the World Wars."
Summary: An examination of the ideas and events that led to World
War II, events during the war, and how they led to subsequent wars,
including the "war on terror," written as a series of letters from a man
to his niece or nephew.
Includes bibliographical references and index.
    ISBN-13: 978-0-942617-43-6
    ISBN-10: 0-942617-43-6 (alk. paper)
   1. World War, 1939-1945--Juvenile literature. 2. World War,
1939-1945--Influence--Juvenile literature. 3. World politics--1945---
Juvenile literature. 4. Protracted conflicts (Military science)--Juvenile
literature. 5. Terrorism--Juvenile literature. [1. World War, 1939-
1945. 2. World politics--1945-] I. Title: World War 2, the rest of the
story and how it affects you today, 1930 to September 11, 2001. II.
Title: World War Two, the rest of the story and how it affects you
today, 1930 to September 11, 2001. III. Williams, Jane A., 1950- IV.
Title. V. Series.
D743.7.M364 2003
940.53--dc22   2003016765
     Published by Bluestocking Press • P.O. Box 1014
            Placerville, CA 95667-1014
        web site: www.BluestockingPress.com

To Robert Meier
A great friend
An honorable man
And the finest researcher I have ever met.

Uncle Eric's Model
of How the World Works

What is a model? In his book UNCLE ERIC TALKS ABOUT PERSONAL, CAREER, AND FINANCIAL SECURITY, Richard Maybury (Uncle Eric) explains that one of the most important things you can teach children or learn yourself is:

"Models are how we think, they are how we understand how the world works. As we go through life we build these very complex pictures in our minds of how the world works, and we're constantly referring back to them — matching incoming data against our models. That's how we make sense of things.

"One of the most important uses for models is in sorting incoming information to decide if it's important or not.

"In most schools, models are never mentioned because the teachers are unaware of them. One of the most dangerous weaknesses in traditional education is that it contains no model for political history. Teachers teach what they were taught — and no one ever mentioned models to them, so they don't teach them to their students.

"For the most part, children are just loaded down with collections of facts that they are made to memorize. Without good models, children have no way to know which facts are important and which are not. Students leave school thinking history is a senseless waste of time. Then, deprived of the real lessons of history, the student is vulnerable."

The question is, which models to teach. Mr. Maybury says, "The two models that I think are crucially important for everyone to learn are economics and law."

WHATEVER HAPPENED TO PENNY CANDY? explains the economic model, which is based on Austrian economics, the most free-market of all economic models. WHATEVER HAPPENED TO JUSTICE? explains the legal model and shows the connection between rational law and economic progress. The legal model is the old British Common Law — or Natural Law. The original principles on which America was founded were those of the old British Common Law.

These two books, PENNY CANDY and JUSTICE, provide the overall model of how human civilization works, especially the world of money.

Once the model is understood, read ARE YOU LIBERAL? CONSERVATIVE? OR CONFUSED? This book explains political philosophies relative to Uncle Eric's Model — and makes a strong case for consistency to that model, no exceptions.

Next, read ANCIENT ROME: HOW IT AFFECTS YOU TODAY, which shows what happens when a society ignores Uncle Eric's Model and embraces fascism—an all too common practice these days, although the word fascism is never used.

To help you locate books and authors generally in agreement with these economic and legal models, Mr. Maybury wrote EVALUATING BOOKS: WHAT WOULD THOMAS

JEFFERSON THINK ABOUT THIS? This book provides guidelines for selecting books that are consistent with the principles of America's Founders. You can apply these guidelines to books, movies, news commentators, and current events — to any spoken or written medium.

Further expanding on the economic model, THE MONEY MYSTERY explains the hidden force affecting your career, business, and investments. Some economists refer to this force as velocity, others to money demand. Whichever term is used, it is one of the least understood forces affecting your life. Knowing about velocity and money demand not only gives you an understanding of history that few others have, it prepares you to understand and avoid pitfalls in your career, business, and investments. THE MONEY MYSTERY is the first sequel to WHATEVER HAPPENED TO PENNY CANDY? It provides essential background for getting the most from THE CLIPPER SHIP STRATEGY.

THE CLIPPER SHIP STRATEGY explains how government's interference in the economy affects business, careers, and investments. It's a practical nuts-and-bolts strategy for prospering in our turbulent economy. This book is the second sequel to WHATEVER HAPPENED TO PENNY CANDY? and should be read after THE MONEY MYSTERY.

THE THOUSAND YEAR WAR IN THE MIDEAST: HOW IT AFFECTS YOU TODAY explains how events on the other side of the world a thousand years ago can affect us more than events in our own hometowns today. In the last quarter of the 20th century, the Thousand Year War has been the cause of great shocks to the investment markets — the oil embargoes, the Iranian hostage crisis, the Iraq-Kuwait war, the Caucasus Wars over the Caspian Sea oil basin, and the September 11th attack — and it is likely to remain so for decades to come. Forewarned is forearmed. You must understand where this war is leading to manage your career, business, and investments.

The explosion of the battleship Maine in Havana Harbor in 1898 was the beginning of a chain reaction that eventually led to the destruction of the World Trade Center. In his two-part World War series Richard Maybury explains that an unbroken line leads directly from the Spanish-American War through World War I, World War II, the Korean and Vietnam Wars, the Iraq-Kuwait War, and the "War on Terror" that began September 11, 2001. Mr. Maybury explains the other side of the story, the side you are not likely to get anywhere else, in this two-part World War series: WORLD WAR I: THE REST OF THE STORY AND HOW IT AFFECTS YOU TODAY and WORLD WAR II: THE REST OF THE STORY AND HOW IT AFFECTS YOU TODAY.

Uncle Eric's Model of How the World Works

These books can be read in any order and have been written to stand alone. But to get the most from each one, Mr. Maybury suggests the following order of reading:

Book 1. UNCLE ERIC TALKS ABOUT PERSONAL, CAREER, AND FINANCIAL SECURITY.
Uncle Eric's Model introduced. Models (or paradigms) are how people think; they are how we understand our world. To achieve success in our careers, investments, and every other part of our lives, we need sound models. These help us recognize and use the information that is important and bypass that which is not. In this book, Mr. Maybury introduces the model he has found most useful. These are explained in WHATEVER HAPPENED TO PENNY CANDY? WHATEVER HAPPENED TO JUSTICE? and THE CLIPPER SHIP STRATEGY.

Book 2.   WHATEVER HAPPENED TO PENNY CANDY? A FAST, CLEAR, AND FUN EXPLANATION OF THE ECONOMICS YOU NEED FOR SUCCESS IN YOUR CAREER, BUSINESS, AND INVESTMENTS. The economic model explained. The clearest and most interesting explanation of economics around. Learn about investment cycles, velocity, business cycles, recessions, inflation, money demand, and more. Contains "Beyond the Basics" which supplements the basic ideas in the book and is included for readers who choose to tackle more challenging concepts. Recommended by former U.S. Treasury Secretary William Simon and many others.
(Study Guide available.)

Book 3.   WHATEVER HAPPENED TO JUSTICE?
The legal model explained. Explores America's legal heritage. Shows what is wrong with our legal system and economy, and how to fix it. Discusses the difference between higher law and man-made law, and the connection between rational law and economic prosperity. Introduces the Two Laws: 1) Do all you have agreed to do. 2) Do not encroach on other persons or their property.

Book 4.   ARE YOU LIBERAL? CONSERVATIVE? OR CONFUSED?
Political labels. What do they mean? Liberal, conservative, left, right, democrat, republican, moderate, socialist, libertarian, communist — what are their economic policies, and what plans do their promoters have for your money? Clear, concise explanations. Facts and fallacies.

Book 5.   ANCIENT ROME: HOW IT AFFECTS YOU TODAY.
This book explains what happens when a society
ignores the model. Are we heading for fascism
like ancient Rome? Mr. Maybury uses historical
events to explain current events, including the wars
in the former Soviet Empire, and the legal and
economic problems of America today. With the
turmoil in Russia and Russia's return to fascism,
you must read this book to understand your future.
History does repeat.

Book 6.   EVALUATING BOOKS: WHAT WOULD THOMAS JEFFERSON
THINK ABOUT THIS?
Most books, magazines, and news stories are
slanted against the principles of America's
Founders. Often the writers are not aware of it,
they simply write as they were taught. Learn how
to identify the bias so you can make informed
reading, listening, and viewing choices.

Book 7.   THE MONEY MYSTERY: THE HIDDEN FORCE AFFECTING
YOUR CAREER, BUSINESS AND INVESTMENTS.
The first sequel to WHATEVER HAPPENED TO PENNY
CANDY? Some economists refer to velocity, others
to money demand. However it is seen, it is one of
the least understood forces affecting our
businesses, careers, and investments — it is the
financial trigger. This book discusses precautions
you should take and explains why Federal Reserve
officials remain so afraid of inflation. THE MONEY
MYSTERY prepares you to understand and avoid
pitfalls in your career, business, and investments.

Book 8. THE CLIPPER SHIP STRATEGY: FOR SUCCESS IN YOUR CAREER, BUSINESS, AND INVESTMENTS.
The second sequel to WHATEVER HAPPENED TO PENNY CANDY? Conventional wisdom says that when the government expands the money supply, the money descends on the economy in a uniform blanket. This is wrong. The money is injected into specific locations causing hot spots or "cones" such as the tech bubble of the 1990s. Mr. Maybury explains his system for tracking and profiting from these cones. Practical nuts-and-bolts strategy for prospering in our turbulent economy.

Book 9. THE THOUSAND YEAR WAR IN THE MIDEAST: HOW IT AFFECTS YOU TODAY.
Mr. Maybury shows that events on the other side of the world a thousand years ago can affect us more than events in our hometowns today. This book explains the ten-century battle the U.S. has entered against the Islamic world. It predicted the events that began unfolding on September 11, 2001. It helps you understand the thinking of the Muslims in the Mideast, and why the coming oil war will affect investment markets around the globe. In the last three decades this war has been the cause of great shocks to the economy and investment markets, including the oil embargoes, the Iranian hostage crisis, the Iraq-Kuwait war, the Caucasus Wars over the Caspian Sea oil basin, and the September 11th attack — and it is likely to remain so for decades to come. Forewarned is forearmed. To successfully manage your career, business, and investments, you must understand this war.

Book 10. WORLD WAR I: THE REST OF THE STORY AND HOW IT AFFECTS YOU TODAY, 1870 TO 1935.

The explosion of the battleship Maine in Havana Harbor in 1898 was the beginning of a chain reaction that continues today. Mr. Maybury presents an idea-based explanation of the First World War. He focuses on the ideas and events that led to World War I, events during the war, and how they led to World War II. Includes the ten deadly ideas that lead to war.

Book 11. WORLD WAR II: THE REST OF THE STORY AND HOW IT AFFECTS YOU TODAY, 1935 TO SEPTEMBER 11, 2001.

An idea-based explanation of the war. Focuses on events in the Second World War and how our misunderstanding of this war led to America's subsequent wars, including the Korean and Vietnam Wars, the Iraq-Kuwait War, and the "War on Terror" that began September 11, 2001.

Study Guides and/or Tests
are available or forthcoming
for the "Uncle Eric" books.

Maps

Note to Reader

Throughout the book when a word that appears in the glossary is introduced in the text, it is displayed in **bold typeface.**

Study Guide Available

A BLUESTOCKING GUIDE: WORLD WAR II

by Jane A. Williams

— based on Richard J. Maybury's book —

WORLD WAR II: THE REST OF THE STORY
AND HOW IT AFFECTS YOU TODAY

Includes: 1) chapter-by-chapter comprehension questions and answers for WORLD WAR II: THE REST OF THE STORY, 2) research activities, 3) a list of World War I films, 4) thought questions, and 5) final exam.

Order from your favorite book store or direct from the publisher: Bluestocking Press (see order information on last page of this book).

Study Guides and/or Tests
are available or forthcoming
for other "Uncle Eric" books.

Contents

Author's Disclosure

For reasons I do not understand, writers today are supposed to be objective. Few disclose the viewpoints or opinions they use to decide what information is important and what is not, or what shall be presented or omitted.

I do not adhere to this standard and make no pretense of being objective. I am biased in favor of liberty, free markets, and international neutrality and proud of it. So I disclose my viewpoint, which you will find explained in detail in my other books.[1]

For those who have not yet read these publications, I call my viewpoint Juris Naturalism (pronounced *jur*-es *nach*-e-re-liz-em, sometimes abbreviated JN) meaning the belief in a natural law that is higher than any government's law. Here are six quotes from America's Founders that help to describe this viewpoint:

> ...all men are created equal, that they are endowed by their Creator with certain unalienable rights.
> — Declaration of Independence, 1776

> The natural rights of the colonists are these: first, a right to life; second to liberty; third to property; together with the right to support and defend them in the best manner they can.
> — Samuel Adams, 1772

---

[1] See Richard Maybury's other Uncle Eric books (see pgs. 6-13), published by Bluestocking Press, web site: www.BluestockingPress.com.

It is strangely absurd to suppose that a million of human beings collected together are not under the same moral laws which bind each of them separately.
— Thomas Jefferson, 1816

A wise and frugal government, which shall restrain men from injuring one another, which shall leave them otherwise free to regulate their own pursuits of industry and improvement, and shall not take from the mouth of labor the bread it has earned. This is the sum of good government.
— Thomas Jefferson, 1801

Not a place on earth might be so happy as America. Her situation is remote from all the wrangling world, and she has nothing to do but to trade with them.
— Thomas Paine, 1776

The great rule of conduct for us, in regard to foreign nations, is, in extending our commercial relations, to have with them as little political connection as possible.
— George Washington, 1796

George
Washington

Cast of Characters
and Important Terminology

Allies. Enemies of the Axis, led by Britain, United States, Russia.

Axis. Enemies of the Allies, led by Germany, Italy, Japan.

Chiang Kai-Shek. Leader of Kuomintang in China. Ally of U.S. Government.

Churchill, Winston. Prime Minister of Britain in World War II. A close friend of Franklin Roosevelt.

Eastern Front. The war in East Europe. Mostly involved Russia and Germany.

Eisenhower, General Dwight. Allies' supreme commander in Europe.

European Theater. The war in Europe. Mostly involving Germany, Italy, Britain, France, Russia, and the United States. Mostly land and air battles.

FDR. President Franklin Delano Roosevelt.

Harris, Air Marshall A.T. Commander of British bomber forces. "Bomber Harris."

Hitler, Adolph. German dictator, chief of Nazi Germany in World War II.

Johnson, Lyndon B. U.S. President, 1963-1969, including during the Vietnam War.

Kai-Shek. See Chiang Kai-Shek.

Kennedy, John F. U.S. President, 1961-1963.

Kimmel, Admiral Husband E. Navy commander at Pearl Harbor, Hawaii 1941.

Kuomintang. Chinese regime led by Chiang Kai-Shek. Ally of the United States Government (USG).

MacArthur, General Douglas. Allies' supreme commander in the Pacific.

Mussolini, Benito. Italian dictator, chief of fascist Italy in World War II.

Pacific Theater. The war in the Pacific. Mostly between the U.S. and Japan, and mostly naval and island battles.

Richardson, Admiral James O. Commander of Pacific Fleet before Kimmel.

Roosevelt, President Franklin Delano. FDR. U.S. President 1933-1945. Ally of Stalin and Churchill.

Short, General Walter C. Army and Army Air Corps commander at Pearl Harbor, Hawaii 1941.

Stalin, Joseph. Soviet dictator, 1924-1953, including during World War II. A former bank robber, responsible for the murder of tens of millions. Ally of President Roosevelt.

Stark, Admiral Harold R. Chief of Naval Operations in Washington, D.C. 1941.

Tojo, Hideki. Japanese premier and dictator in World War II.

Truman, Harry S. U.S. President 1945-1953.

USG. United States Government.

Timeline

1929	Stock market crash. Global Great Depression begins.
1931	Japanese attack Manchuria.
1933	Hitler becomes chancellor of Germany.
1935	Italians attack Ethiopia.
1936	Spanish Civil War. Hitler explains desire for lebensraum (living space) in east Europe.
1937	In China, U.S. gunboat Panay sunk by Japanese.
1939	Russians, Germans attack Poland.
1940	Russians attack Finland. Germans attack west Europe. Battle of Britain ends, British win. Hitler turns east.
1941	Hitler attacks Stalin. FDR begins aid to Stalin. FDR cuts off Japan's oil supply. Russian winter strikes Germans. Japanese attack Pearl Harbor.
1943	Germans lose Battle of Stalingrad; now clearly losing war. FDR calls for Unconditional Surrender.
1944	Allies invade Normandy.
1945	A-bombs. War ends. Rebellion against Stalin begins to fade.
1946	Churchill: an "Iron Curtain" has descended across Europe.

Part One

Who Were The Good Guys?

1

The Main Theater of the War

Dear Chris,

War is about death and destruction.

In my previous set of letters about World War I[2] I stated that the number of innocent people murdered seems one of the most revealing ways to measure evil. I said that in a future letter I would look at the body counts of the various players in World War II.

This is that letter, it will give you a look at the grimmest of the statistics.

No one is sure how many were killed or wounded in the Second World War. We do know this war was much worse than any other in all of world history. The ENCYCLOPEDIA BRITANNICA says estimates of the dead range from 35 million to 60 million.

The death estimates that BRITANNICA gives for the chief powers in World War II between 1939 and 1945 are listed in the chart that follows.

This is also a revealing list of the chief powers of the two sides, the **Allies** and the **Axis**. I suggest you read down the list, locating each country on a globe or world map, so that

---

[2] Uncle Eric is referring to Richard J. Maybury's book WORLD WAR I: THE REST OF THE STORY AND HOW IT AFFECTS YOU TODAY which is part one of his two-part series on the World Wars, published by Bluestocking Press, web site: www.BluestockingPress.com.

World War II Death Estimates

NATION	DEATHS
Chief Allied Powers	
Belgium	88,000
Brazil	1,000
British Empire	
Australia	24,000
Britain	357,000
Canada	38,000
India	24,000
New Zealand	10,000
South Africa	7,000
Other colonies	7,000
China	1,310,000
Czechoslovakia	225,000
Denmark	4,000
France	563,000
Greece	413,000
Netherlands	208,000
Norway	10,000
Poland	5,800,000
Philippines	118,000
USA	298,000
USSR	18,000,000
Yugoslavia	1,505,000
Chief Axis Powers	
Bulgaria	20,000
Finland	84,000
Germany	4,200,000
Hungary	490,000
Italy	395,000
Japan	1,972,000
Romania	500,000
Total Allied dead:	**29,010,000**
Total Axis dead:	**7,661,000**
Total dead:	**36,671,000**

U.S. dead as a portion of total dead: 0.8%.
U.S. dead as a portion of Soviet dead: 1.7%.

you gain an understanding for who was fighting and who suffered the worst losses.

Chris, please take a moment to think about the fact that these are not just statistics. Each was a living, breathing man, woman, or child, and each was loved by someone who felt the loss very deeply.

Also, remember that the Old World has given mankind thousands of wars, this was only the worst of them.

Very important: Which of the Allies suffered the most deaths? Which of the Axis?

Check the statistics. World War II was mostly a battle between Germany and the **U.S.S.R.**,[3] with Poland caught between them. My letters will deal a lot with this part of the conflict called the **Eastern Front**. More than 28 million were killed on the Eastern Front. This was three-quarters of all the deaths in the war.

Other major fronts included the Pacific Theater, Western Front, North Africa, the Italian Campaign, Southeast Asia, and the Balkans. Americans generally focus on the **Western Front** and the Pacific Campaign and have the impression that these were the main areas of the conflict. Not so, the main event by far was the Eastern Front; everything else was sideshows.

So few Americans have been taught about the Eastern Front that I wonder how many today even know Germany and the U.S.S.R. were enemies in World War II.

My letters will give you a lot of information about the Eastern Front, so you will *understand* a lot more about World War II than almost anyone else you know.

---

[3] USSR: Union of Soviet Socialist Republics. The Russian Empire. Headquarters, the Kremlin in Moscow.

Again, Chris, the Eastern Front was three-quarters of the war.

Uncle Eric

P.S. Chris, if you have trouble envisioning where the war was fought and the extent of the losses, try this. Spread out a world map; on each nation's capital city, pile matchsticks to represent bodies. Let each matchstick represent 100,000 dead.

P.P.S. Also, Chris, I encourage you to examine the footnotes in this set of letters. You will find the research is not from esoteric sources that you cannot check. It's from material that has been freely available to the general public and to historians for years.

All I have done is rearrange and highlight the facts according to my "Uncle Eric Model" which is based on the two laws explained in my previous set of letters on law [WHATEVER HAPPENED TO JUSTICE?] — especially, Do not encroach on other persons or their property. This causes the facts to paint a picture much different than the one commonly accepted.

2

Good Guys Against Bad Guys

Dear Chris,

Thanks for your letter — and your questions.

You said you have heard that German military power has been vastly exaggerated, but you are sure there can be no exaggerating the German evil. You also said that you believe Hitler and his Nazis were the most horrible gang of cutthroats ever seen on earth — they killed six million Jews — and America had to get into the war to keep them from conquering the whole world.

Chris, I will write about the capabilities of the German armed forces in future letters. As you might expect, we will get into the economics of the war. When you understand the economics, you will see that what you have heard is true, the German war machine was not so mighty as is generally thought.

In this and the next few letters, I will write about the most important part of the war, the ethics.

Were the Nazis really so evil?

Yes, but focusing on them keeps us from seeing the rest of the picture, and when you do see the rest, you may be shocked. So let's get started.

World War II was the biggest event in all of history, and throughout my life I have been deluged with stories about it. The stories always paint the war as if it were a Hollywood movie, good guys against bad guys. Even in scholarly history books written by the most respected historians, the war is usually shown as **white hats against black hats**.[4]

We are led to believe that Americans were fighting for good and against evil, but this was simply not the case. Americans *thought* they were fighting for good against evil because their government told them so, and they trusted their government. The facts say otherwise.

Chris, here, as in my previous set of letters about Word War I, I want to emphasize that the government and the country are not the same thing. I love America and would not want to live anywhere else, and I am dedicated to the principles on which America was founded. But the government is a different matter entirely.

I will be saying some harsh things about the government. Please do not take these as criticisms of America, or of the individual men and women who served in the armed forces. There was a lot the government was doing that the people in uniform knew nothing about.

Most, I am sure, still believe what the government taught them. It certainly crops up a lot in current writing. In a WALL STREET JOURNAL article, for instance, the writer says,

What gives a special dimension of glory to the Americans who fought in World War II, what makes their history compelling beyond most tales of courage, was not simply that these men were brave and fought together, but that they were defending the core values of modern civilization. World War II was not only about which side was handier in combat or most firmly

---

[4] White hats against black hats: An expression from early western movies in which the good guys wore white hats and the bad guys wore black hats.

bonded on the battlefield. It was also a mighty struggle
of philosophies — pitting freedom against tyranny.[5]

In a popular book about World War II, the author, a highly
respected historian, says to a World War II veteran, "Thanks
for what you did to help win the victory, and thus save the
world."[6]
Save the world?
Freedom against tyranny?
This is what nearly everyone believes, so in my next letter we will take a close look at it.

Uncle Eric

P.S. Chris, for the rest of these letters I will be writing a lot
about the United States Government. In referring to a
national government, writers often use the name of the capital
city to show they see a distinction between the government
and the country. For example, writers will refer to Moscow
instead of Russia, or Washington instead of the United States
of America.

When I write about Washington, I am not referring to
George Washington unless I make it clear that I am. When I
write about the United States Government I might refer to
Washington D.C., or I will frequently use a more precise term
that you may not have seen before: **USG**, meaning United
States Government. Officials in the government often use
this term in their internal correspondence to show that they
mean the government, not the country.

---

[5] "TV: Hollywood Blurs the Battle Lines," by Claudia Rosett, WALL STREET JOURNAL, August 27, 2001, p.A13.

[6] THE WILD BLUE, by Stephen E. Ambrose, Simon & Schuster, 2001, p.262.

3

Not Six Million

Dear Chris,

Yes, the Nazis were evil. Estimates of the number of Jews murdered by them run as high as six million.

Few realize that Hitler and his Nazis killed others, too. In the excellent book DEATH BY GOVERNMENT, R.J. Rummel gives his extensive research on the much broader question, how many people have governments murdered? All governments. Rummel did a lot of research.

Let me emphasize, we are talking here about murder, not warfare. Rummel's research is concerned not with soldiers killed in battle but with innocent men, women, and children murdered, as the Nazis murdered the Jews.

Hitler's death toll is really 20.9 million. In addition to Jews, reports Rummel, the Nazis murdered prisoners of war, the aged, the sick, homosexuals, Slavs, Serbs, Czechs, Italians, Poles, Ukrainians, and many others including, of course, anyone they thought might be plotting against them.[7] Rummel looked into the whole sorry catastrophe, not just the Jewish Holocaust.

Again, the body count for the Nazis is not 6 million, it is 20.9 million.[8]

---

[7] DEATH BY GOVERNMENT, by R.J. Rummel, Transaction Publishers, New Brunswick, NJ, 1994, p.111.

[8] DEATH BY GOVERNMENT, by R.J. Rummel, p.8.

In my opinion, the **Jewish Holocaust**[9] gets the publicity because it is regarded as the justification for Jews to have a Jewish state (Israel) in the Mideast. The Jewish state gets billions of dollars from the USG and from individual donors in the U.S., so it and its supporters continually remind us of the six million. But Hitler and his followers murdered another 14.9 million. These get little mention. The reason? I don't know. A good book about non-Jewish victims is THE OTHER VICTIMS: FIRST-PERSON STORIES OF NON-JEWS PERSECUTED BY THE NAZIS[10] by Ina R. Friedman. I suggest you read it.

Chris, it is also important to note that Germans usually get the blame for all 20.9 million murders, but they had plenty of enthusiastic help. **Fascism** was popular all over Europe, not just in Germany. Fascism is, after all, the original Roman philosophy that still has strong appeal, although it is no longer called fascism.

The allies of Germany — Romanians, Hungarians, Austrians, French, Croatians, and others — murdered millions. Often the victims were not just executed; they were tortured to death.

Of course, Hitler was the chief leader, the Axis honcho, so he should get more blame than anyone else.

Surely, you say, this makes Hitler the most evil person the world has ever seen, and something had to be done to stop him; 20.9 million murders is a mind-boggling atrocity.

It certainly is, and this reasoning is what led millions of Americans to support aid to Stalin, who was fighting Hitler.

---

[9] The Jewish Holocaust refers to the systematic murder of Jews by Hitler and his followers during World War II.

[10] THE OTHER VICTIMS: FIRST-PERSON STORIES OF NON-JEWS PERSECUTED BY THE NAZIS by Ina R. Friedman, Houghton Mifflin Co., Boston, MA 1990.

But Stalin was twice the demon that Hitler was, if we are measuring evil by body count.

Stalin murdered 42.7 million.[11]

This is saving the world? This is freedom against tyranny?

Chris, I think you can see where I am headed with this. How could the Allies be the good guys if Stalin, an Ally, murdered twice as many people as Hitler?

On June 24, 1941, President Franklin Roosevelt announced that he would begin sending aid to Stalin. The strangest thing about this is that in 1941, Hitler was still new at **genocide**. The Allies had only vague information about Hitler's death camps and other atrocities, while millions of Stalin's murders were well known.

More than ten million murders had happened before 1936,[12] and millions of these were widely reported.[13] Says THE ECONOMIST magazine:

> Even Hitler's armies of snoopers, his 95 Germans a day convicted of political crimes in 1933-39, his political murders, concentration camps and killings of Jews and left-wingers in that period, cannot match Stalin's record. Russia had traditions of secrecy and violence; but the isolation, paranoia and terror that kept the Soviet people in thrall for so long exceeded anything comparable, anywhere, ever.[14]

---

[11] DEATH BY GOVERNMENT, by R.J. Rummel, Transaction Publishers, New Brunswick, NJ, 1994, p.8.

[12] DEATH BY GOVERNMENT, by R.J. Rummel, Transaction Publishers, New Brunswick, NJ, 1994, p.83.

[13] THE PENGUIN BOOK OF LIES, edited by Philip Kerr, Viking Penguin, NY, 1990, p.334-338.

[14] "The Heights of Evil," THE ECONOMIST, December 31, 1999, p.39.

In WHY THE ALLIES WON, historian Richard Overy reports that, "Few even moderately informed Britons or Americans could have been unaware of the political complexion of their Soviet ally, although it was true that information from the Soviet Union was difficult to obtain. During the period when Hitler and Stalin were in temporary alliance, the Soviet and Nazi systems were treated by much western opinion as varieties of the same warped totalitarianism."[15]

On August 16, 1941, Stalin, a former bank robber, issued his famous Order #270. This said all Soviet troops taken prisoner would be considered traitors and shot, and their wives would be sent to **labor camps.** This was Stalin's way of making sure all his troops fought to the death. In effect, he made his whole army into a suicide army.

Yet President Franklin Delano Roosevelt (FDR) backed Stalin.

Why? We cannot read FDR's mind. My guess is that it was because Stalin was socialist.

Socialism was the hot new philosophy in the U.S. and FDR had strong socialist leanings.

Again, we are talking here not about soldiers killed in battle but of innocent men, women, and children exterminated, as Hitler exterminated the Jews. The score for Stalin, FDR's ally, was 42.7 million.

It is generally believed that Hitler was trying to take over the whole world, but I have never seen any evidence that would support this assumption. He intended to take most or all of Europe, which totals 6.6 percent of the earth's land surface,[16] but that was as far as his true intentions went, at

---

[15] WHY THE ALLIES WON, by Richard Overy, W. W. Norton & Co., NY, 1995, p.296.

[16] Europe defined as the area from Iceland to the Ural Mountains.

least according to the evidence I have seen. Fascists issued bloodcurdling propaganda about taking over the world, but as for serious plans to do so, I have never seen any.

The Soviet Socialists, on the other hand, had earnest plans to conquer the world, and they were working hard at it long before Hitler came along. Read the works of Lenin and Marx, written more than four decades earlier, and you will have no doubt that world domination was the goal.

Marx's COMMUNIST MANIFESTO was published clear back in 1848. It ended with the famous rallying cry, "The workers have nothing to lose but their chains. They have the world to win. Workers of all lands, unite!"

This was taken very seriously in the Soviet Union and everyone knew it.

Compared to the Soviet Socialists, the German Nazis were amateurs. At the maximum extent of his reach, in 1942, Hitler controlled about 4 percent of the world,[17] and through most of the war less than 2 percent.[18] This while the Soviet Socialists had already conquered 16 percent (and the USG's other ally, London, had conquered 22 percent).[19]

Chris, do the math. Who do *you* think was the greater threat to America, the Allies or the Axis?

Look at it this way. When the war started, the Kremlin alone had already taken four *times* as much of the world as Hitler ever would, and they fully intended to take the entire world, and every educated person knew it.

---

[17] TIMES ATLAS OF WORLD HISTORY, Hammond Inc., Maplewood, NJ, 1986, p.272, 273.

[18] TIMES ATLAS OF WORLD HISTORY, Hammond Inc., p.272, 273.

[19] TIMES ATLAS OF WORLD HISTORY, Hammond Inc., p.244. Calculations exclude Antarctica.

We have been taught that the Allies were the white hats and the Axis the black hats. Here are the statistics on the number of people murdered by the worst of the cutthroats on the two sides:

Murders by Worst Governments of World War II[20]

Allies

U.S.S.R. (Stalin)	42,672,000
China (Chiang Kai-Shek)	10,214,000
Allied total	**52,886,000**

Axis

Germany (Hitler)	20,946,000
Japan (Tojo)	5,964,000
Axis total	**26,910,000**

So, Chris, who would you judge to be the white hats, the Allies or the Axis?

Neither side was the good guys, unless we define "good" as the side that murders the fewest millions. In that case, the Axis would have been the good guys, which would mean America was on the wrong side.

---

[20] DEATH BY GOVERNMENT, by R.J. Rummel, Transaction Publishers, New Brunswick, NJ, 1994, p.4,8.

In my opinion, it is much more realistic to call the neutral Swiss the good guys; they stayed out of the war. Through it all, living in the center of the chaos, the neutral Swiss kept their rifles loaded and sadly watched the massacres, shaking their heads as they had so many times before.[21] Chris, you might want to reread the recent letters I sent you in my previous correspondence about World War I on Swiss **neutrality**.[22]

Again, the only ethical choice in either world war was to stay out of them.

Incidentally, Chris, all told, before the Kremlin's Empire collapsed in the 1990s, the Soviet Socialists murdered 61.9 million.[23]

That is Rummel's estimate. Another highly credible estimate puts Soviet Socialist murders at between 85 million and 100 million,[24] but I will go with Rummel's more conservative estimate because I am using his figures for other regimes and I want to stay consistent for purposes of comparison.

---

[21] Not all the Swiss were neutral and some did profit from the war, but no human behavior corrupts as much as war does, and the Swiss, through no fault of their own, were caught in the exact center of the worst war in history. Most were doing their best to hold both sides at bay, but some Swiss cities were bombed by accident by both sides. If you are in the mood to compare ethics, compare those of the neutral Swiss to those of any nation in the war including the U.S.

[22] Uncle Eric is referring to Chapters 20 and 21 of Richard J. Maybury's book WORLD WAR I: THE REST OF THE STORY AND HOW IT AFFECTS YOU TODAY, published by Bluestocking Press, web site: www.BluestockingPress.com.

[23] DEATH BY GOVERNMENT, by R.J. Rummel, Transaction Publishers, New Brunswick, NJ, 1994, p.79.

[24] "Teflon Totalitarianism," by Anne Applebaum, WALL STREET JOURNAL, January 16, 1998.

I think you can see that by no stretch of the imagination were the German Nazis as great a threat as the Soviet Socialists. Hitler was evil, but not the worst evil.

And — look back at body counts — Tojo in Japan was doing the world a favor by attacking Chiang Kai-Shek in China.

Chris, now look back at the ENCYCLOPEDIA BRITANNICA's statistics on the number of people killed on the Eastern Front. Note that Soviet losses are reported as 18 million. Maybe this is correct, but given the Soviet Socialists' penchant for mass murder, I would not be surprised if the Socialists killed many of these 18 million and then pinned the blame on the German Nazis.

Why so many murders — 61.9 million — in the Union of Soviet Socialist Republics?

My guess is **central planning.** Under socialism, government "experts" develop a plan for the production of goods and services, and for nearly everything else the people do. These authorities decide what will be produced and who shall produce it, what prices will be charged, and what jobs the workers will do. Then they order the citizens to follow the plans.

This leads to the question, what do you do with someone who wants to live his life his own way and refuses to obey the plans?

The Soviet answer was, throw them in prison, and when the prisons are full, kill them.

Incidentally, Chris, all governments that do central planning face the same question about people who do not want to follow the plans: Do we spend millions of dollars building and operating a prison, or do we buy a box of ten-cent bullets?

Stalin and Hitler opted for the bullets.

Chris, the mass murder by both sides in World War II is shocking, but it should not be surprising. In the Old World, this kind of behavior has always been common, and still is. In my next letter I will give you the awful details. Please prepare yourself, this will not be pretty.

And remember that when you see those World War II films showing piles of bodies in the Nazi death camps, you are not shown the bodies of people killed by Stalin and his Soviet Socialists; the Socialist piles were twice as high as the Nazi piles.

Bodies in China, another ally of the USG, were counted in the millions, too.

Also of no small importance is the fact that the Kremlin's victory in World War II soon led to the nuclear arms race that could have incinerated us all. No one is sure how many atomic bombs the Kremlin had — or maybe still has — aimed at the U.S., but it is generally estimated in the thousands and maybe tens of thousands.

Yes, Nazi Germany was a threat — and horribly evil. But, by any measure I know, the USG's ally, the Kremlin, was a much bigger threat and much more evil. This is what the evidence clearly pointed to before the war, and after the war it was still the case if we judge by the total of 61.9 million murdered by the Soviet Socialists and the thousands of atomic bombs aimed at the U.S. by the Kremlin.

Summarizing, Chris, the Eastern Front battle between Adolph Hitler and Joseph Stalin was the main event, three-quarters of the war, and all else was sideshows. By helping Stalin beat Hitler, the U.S. Government claimed to be saving the world, but was this the truth?

Was this a war between good and evil?

Was this a fight for freedom against tyranny?

Now that you have heard the other side of the story, Chris, what do you think?

Uncle Eric

4

World War II Was Nothing New

Dear Chris,

Okay, if World War II was not a war between good and evil, or between freedom and tyranny, what was it? In my opinion, the answer is easy to see if you read R.J. Rummel's DEATH BY GOVERNMENT. Rummel gives a stomach-churning look at the Old World, a look few Americans know anything about.

Statistics on killings before the 20th century are hard to come by, but here are a few estimates reported by Rummel. They show that the World Wars really were not anything new.

Tamerlane, who lived in the 14th century, killed an estimated 17 million.[25]

Kublai Kahn, the Mongol leader who lived in the 13th century, killed an estimated 18.4 million.[26]

The Mongols as a group are thought to have killed about 30 million.[27]

Over the past five centuries, slave traders in Europe, Africa, and Asia are thought to have murdered somewhere between 17 million and 65 million.[28]

---

[25] "A Kinder, Gentler Tamerlane," WORLD PRESS REVIEW, March 1998, p.38.

[26] DEATH BY GOVERNMENT, by R.J. Rummel, Transaction Publishers, New Brunswick, NJ, 1994, p.51.

[27] DEATH BY GOVERNMENT, by R.J. Rummel, p.51.

[28] DEATH BY GOVERNMENT, by R.J. Rummel, p.48.

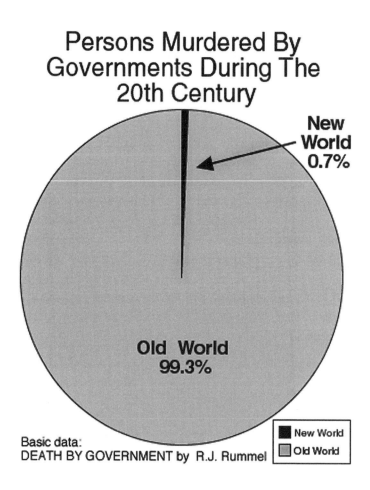

Persons Murdered By Governments During The 20th Century

New World 0.7%

Old World 99.3%

Basic data:
DEATH BY GOVERNMENT by R.J. Rummel

■ New World
☐ Old World

Few Americans realize how bloody the Old World is and always has been. This chart does not show troops or civilians killed in battle, it shows only the unarmed men, women, and children deliberately murdered.

In China during the third century, the population was estimated at 50 million before the transition to the Three Kingdom period, and 7 million after.[29]

In the war-torn period from 1626 to 1655 in China, the population reportedly decreased from 51 million to 14 million.[30]

During the 30 Years War in Europe, 1618-1648, the population in the region we now call Germany may have been decreased by 7.5 million.[31]

We do not know how many were killed in the Crusades, but it was certainly millions.

In the half-century since World War II, the slaughter has continued. In Yugoslavia under Tito, an estimated 1.07 million were murdered.[32]

In Pakistan between 1958 and 1987, an estimated 1.5 million were murdered.[33]

In Poland between the end of the Second World War and 1948, almost 1.6 million were murdered.[34]

In Cambodia between 1975 and 1979, two million were sent to their deaths.[35]

In China between 1949 and 1987, an estimated 35.2 million were murdered.[36]

In Indonesia, in 1965 and 1966, a half-million were murdered.[37]

---

[29] DEATH BY GOVERNMENT, by R.J. Rummel, Transaction Publishers, New Brunswick, NJ, 1994, p.52.

[30] DEATH BY GOVERNMENT, by R.J. Rummel, p.52.

[31] DEATH BY GOVERNMENT, by R.J. Rummel, p.54.

[32] DEATH BY GOVERNMENT, by R.J. Rummel, p.4.

[33] DEATH BY GOVERNMENT, by R.J. Rummel, p.4.

[34] DEATH BY GOVERNMENT, by R.J. Rummel, p.10.

[35] DEATH BY GOVERNMENT, by R.J. Rummel, p.4.

[36] DEATH BY GOVERNMENT, by R.J. Rummel, p.4.

[37] DEATH BY GOVERNMENT, by R.J. Rummel, p.10.

No one knows how many people were massacred in the Rwanda-Burundi-Congo fighting during the 1990s. The lowest estimate I have seen is 800,000.

In Vietnam between 1945 and 1987, an estimated 1.7 million were murdered.[38]

During the era of its Soviet Empire, for seven decades after World War I, the Kremlin sat on much of the Old World like a lid on a pressure cooker. Then after the fall of the Empire in the early 1990s, the lid blew off. Since then, more than 100 conflicts have erupted, killing more than five million.[39] The United Nations estimates that two million were children.[40]

Chris, as I mentioned in my previous set of letters, in 1984, the Norwegian Academy of Sciences and University of Oslo calculated that since the year 3,600 B.C., there have been more than 14,000 wars.[41] The vast majority of wars have been in the Old World, and they have killed an estimated 3.6 billion — not 3.6 million, 3.6 *billion*. [42]

The Old World is a nasty place and always has been. Hitler was horrible, but he was not unusual. The idea that he was the worst person who ever lived and had to be stopped at any cost is a terribly misleading exaggeration.

Among rulers of the Old World, Hitler was depressingly ordinary.

---

[38] DEATH BY GOVERNMENT, by R.J. Rummel, Transaction Publishers, New Brunswick, NJ, 1994, p.4.

[39] "A New Kind Of War," by Jeffrey Boutwell and Michael T. Klare, SCIENTIFIC AMERICAN, June 2000, p.48.

[40] "Fairly Holy Innocents," THE ECONOMIST, December 23, 2000, p.77.

[41] DIRTY LITTLE SECRETS, by James F. Dunnigan and Albert A. Nofi, Quill/William Morrow, 1990, p.419.

[42] DIRTY LITTLE SECRETS, by James F. Dunnigan and Albert A. Nofi, Quill/William Morrow, 1990, p.419.

He may have been more efficient than some, and his uniform was spiffy — he certainly looked impressive in the newsreels — but that is about all that made him different.

Painting Hitler as something vastly worse than the hundreds of other tyrants who have been responsible for the deaths of the other 3.4 *billion* draws attention away from those 3.4 *billion* and thereby diminishes the importance of those 3.4 *billion*.

In DEATH BY GOVERNMENT, Rummel reports that during the 20th century alone, an estimated...

...170 million men, women, and children have been shot, beaten, tortured, knifed, burned, starved, frozen, crushed, or worked to death; buried alive, drowned, hung, bombed, or killed in any other of the myriad ways governments have inflicted death on unarmed, helpless citizens and foreigners. The dead could conceivably be nearly 360 million people. It is as though our species has been devastated by a modern Black Plague. And indeed it has, but a plague of Power, not germs.[43]

Chris, we are continually reminded that Hitler murdered six million Jews. The horrible truth of the matter is that in the Old World, six million dead is hardly noticeable unless someone draws our attention to it while ignoring the other 164 million. During the 1990s, five million were killed,[44] but you probably did not read anything about it; it was not

---

[43] DEATH BY GOVERNMENT, by R.J. Rummel, Transaction Publishers, New Brunswick, NJ, 1994, p.9.

[44] "A New Kind Of War," by Jeffrey Boutwell and Michael T. Klare, SCIENTIFIC AMERICAN, June 2000, p.48.

considered important enough to report. That's the Old World. It is why Thomas Jefferson and George Washington advised us to never have political or military connections with the Old World.

Chris, even though we are dealing with statistics, and the word millions rolls easily off the tongue, always remember that each of these people was a living, breathing human being with feelings, just like you and me and the people we love. Each death caused great suffering for the families and friends who were left alive.

The New World has rarely seen anything like the massacres that are common in the Old World. And most of the butchery we know of in the New World was perpetrated by Old World regimes that had invaded the New World. An example is the Spanish conquest of the Aztecs and Incas. This is not to say the native rulers of the New World have been nice guys, but the scale of their atrocities has not been anything like those in the Old World.

Chris, you might have heard someone argue that in giving aid to Hitler's enemy, Stalin, USG officials were not really helping Stalin, they were helping the ordinary Russian people.

Think about that for a minute.

Does this mean the ordinary Russian people were good and the ordinary German people bad? Under this logic, did the ordinary German people not deserve U.S. aid, while the ordinary Russian people did? And if so, why?

Here is a trick often used in propaganda. When arguing for a fight *against* another nation, show the evil done by that nation's rulers. When arguing to fight *for* another nation, show the harm done to the innocent civilians; say nothing about what the rulers are doing to civilians on the other side.

In short, if it is an ally, focus on the suffering of the ally civilians; if it is an enemy, focus on the atrocities committed by the rulers.

You will see this in films about why the USG had to support the U.S.S.R. against Germany. The atrocities by Stalin and his Soviet Socialists are conveniently omitted, while the suffering of the Russian people under the Germans is given detailed attention. An especially good example of this type of propaganda film is WHY WE FIGHT directed by Frank Capra.

So, if the Second World War was not about good versus evil, or freedom versus tyranny, what was it about?

I think on both sides it was about the joy of power, the fun of beating people into submission.

In other words, World War II was nothing unusual, it was what governments in the Old World have been doing for thousands of years.

Uncle Eric

5

Millions

Dear Chris,

Looking back over statistics in previous letters, in the Pacific Theater of the war, the number of people murdered by the Japanese regime was 5,964,000.

Those murdered by Japan's enemy, the Chinese Kuomintang led by Chiang Kai-Shek, was 10,214,000.

President Roosevelt sided with Chiang Kai-Shek.

This turned out to be a study in what can happen when the USG gets into other people's wars.

With the USG's help, the Kuomintang won. But they were so brutal that the Chinese people rebelled against them and supported the Red Chinese, who took over China in 1949. (Red means Socialist).

The Red Chinese then murdered 35 million.

If Roosevelt had not helped the Kuomintang, the Japanese likely would have beaten the Kuomintang. The Kuomintang were poorly equipped and trained, while the Japanese were the best fighting force in the East.

But, compared to other Old World regimes, the Japanese were amateurs at the game of murder and conquest, and they had to operate at the end of a long, vulnerable supply line that stretched across the Sea of Japan. It is hard to believe they could have killed as many Chinese as the new Red Chinese government eventually did.

Chris, again, these are not statistics for soldiers killed in battle, they are the statistics for civilian men, women, and children murdered. The numbers are not in dozens, hundreds or thousands; they are in millions.

As I said in my last letter, the word millions rolls off the tongue too easily. Each of these people was a living, breathing human being with feelings, just like you and me. Each death caused great suffering for the families and friends who were left alive.

Imagine if your parents or other members of your family were hauled away and killed. How would you feel? Now try to imagine this happening to *millions*.

It is very important to keep these deaths from being face-less, nameless statistics. A million deaths is an unimaginable horror.

The 62 million by Stalin and his henchmen were even more so.

And remember, President Roosevelt backed Stalin as well as Chiang Kai-Shek.

Some say it was necessary to back Stalin because Hitler's Germany was geographically closer to America than the Soviet Union; it was better for the United States that the more distant Stalin should win.

Look at a globe. The Soviet Union stretched all the way to the Bering Strait, where it was only 55 miles from the U.S. territory of Alaska.

So, in terms of both geographic location and brutality, the Soviet Union was by far the greatest threat to America.

What about the British? They were Allies, too, and they deserve several letters all to themselves, which I will send shortly. For now, suffice to say that the rulers of Britain were not choirboys, either.

Uncle Eric

P.S. Chris, here is another interesting calculation about the war in the East. The only two significant powers in the East were China and Japan. With the creation of the Flying Tigers in August 1941 (before the Japanese attack on Pearl Harbor) the USG sided with China's government, so Americans were told China's government was the good guys and Tokyo the bad guys. (I'll tell you more about the Flying Tigers in a future letter.)

China's Kuomintang murdered 10 million, and was followed by the Red Chinese who murdered another 35 million, for a total Chinese murder count of 45 million.

Tokyo murdered 6 million.

Therefore, in the East the so-called good guys eventually murdered seven times more people than the bad guys.

6

Britain Was A White Hat?

Dear Chris,

During the Battle of Britain, which occurred in the summer and fall of 1940, radio news broadcasts and movie newsreels showed the British fight against German bombers.

The bombs falling on London and the heroic efforts of Londoners to save historic landmarks such as St. Paul Cathedral gave Americans the impression that Britain was an innocent victim of German aggression.

This was exactly the impression the British government wanted them to have.

Newsreels and broadcasts did not come from Germany, the Germans did not speak English, so no one told the rest of the story.

Few wanted to face what British (and other) rulers had done to the Germans under the Treaty of Versailles. The fact that British rulers had set their people up for the **Blitz**[45] — that they had, in effect, asked for it — went almost completely unmentioned.

Due to radio and movies, no prior war had ever before been brought to Americans so clearly and dramatically. This coverage galvanized American opinion in favor of the British.

---

[45] Blitz: The German bombing of England. The meaning is often restricted only to the German bombing of London in 1940.

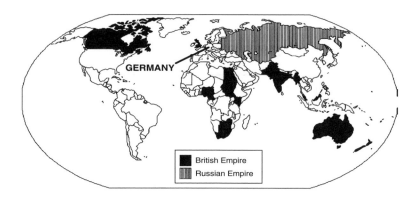

This map highlights the Russian Empire, the chief nations of the British Empire, and their enemy Germany. Russia and Britain were allied against Germany.

By World War II, Britain had been attacking other countries for 800 years and had conquered 22% of the world.

Russia had been conquering for more than 1,000 years and had taken 16%.

Germany did not become a nation until 1871, and in 1939 had no empire at all. Its land area comprised 0.035% of the world. This was a bit larger than Britain's colony of Rhodesia (now Zimbabwe) in Africa, and far smaller than Texas.

The war was Germany's attempt to copy the British and Russians by stealing some of what the British and Russians had stolen. Neither giant had any intentions of permitting this.

By July 1941, in a fit of collective insanity, midget Germany had attacked the two largest titans on earth and was sandwiched between them. How could anyone have doubted the outcome?

But, Chris, from my previous set of letters about World War I,[46] you know about the brutal treatment of the Germans by the British and their allies, so you have a better foundation of knowledge about the causes of World War II than most Americans did then, or do today.

Millions of Americans in 1940 jumped to the conclusion that the eruption of bloodshed in the Old World was a strange new kind of global crisis, and America had to do something to save innocent Britain.

Today this affection for "innocent Britain" is so deeply engrained in American culture that it is never questioned. So, let's question it. Let's look at the rest of the story.

London had been building its global empire for at least eight centuries. By 1940, London had conquered 22% of the world.

If we count other areas that London had held at one time or another — America before 1776 would be an example — then London conquered at least a fourth of the world.

This was the meaning of the old saying, "the sun never sets on the British Empire." London held stolen territories around the globe, so somewhere in the British Empire it was always daylight.

The British did not get control of 22% of the world by being nice guys. The old British Common Law may have been one of the greatest gifts ever bestowed on the world, but outside Britain the government rarely obeyed it.

The American Revolutionaries who made their stand on the green at Lexington were not risking their lives to fight *for* the British government; they were fighting against it.

---

[46] Uncle Eric is referring to Richard J. Maybury's book WORLD WAR I: THE REST OF THE STORY AND HOW IT AFFECTS YOU TODAY, published by Bluestocking Press, web site: www.BluestockingPress.com.

In DEATH BY GOVERNMENT, Rummel reports that during the 20th century the government of Britain was responsible for the murder of 816,000.[47] This may not sound important compared to the body counts of Stalin, Hitler, and many other Old World rulers, but this is only because most British conquests happened in earlier centuries before deaths were systematically counted.

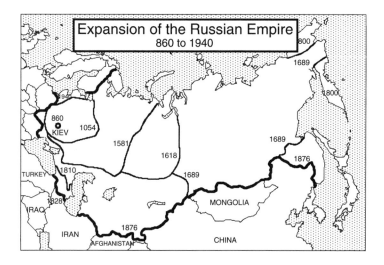

The Russian Empire began in Kiev around the year 860. The Russians conquered neighboring people until, by 1689, they held much of Europe and Asia all the way to the Pacific. At the end of World War I, the Russian Empire became the Soviet Empire, or the Union of Soviet Socialist Republics, and continued the killing and conquering.

---

[47] DEATH BY GOVERNMENT, by R.J. Rummel, Transaction Publishers, New Brunswick, NJ, 1994, p.4.

Also, most British conquests happened before war had become industrialized. For most of its rampage, the British government did not have machine guns or other highly efficient weapons. If they had owned them, we can be sure they would have used them, and London might have chalked up a larger body count than even Stalin. The Kremlin, after all, held "only" 16% of the world in 1940; Britain's empire was the largest the world has ever seen except perhaps for that of the Mongols.

The British defeated much of Africa and all of India using the Brown Bess musket of American Revolution fame. This musket was the most important weapon in the building of the British Empire. It was invented around 1720 and remained in service for 120 years.[48] This gives you a taste of how early the British got into the game of conquest and how long they were at it. Their global empire was established centuries before Germany was a nation.

The British were in Ireland in the 12th century, and some of the Irish are still trying to throw them out.

The only reason the German armed forces posed a threat to Britain in 1940 was that London enabled them to pose it. The British navy was vastly more powerful than the German navy, and more than adequate to keep the Germans from crossing the English Channel — if the navy had been used for defense of Britain.

Much of the British navy was not available for defense because it was scattered all over the world trying to hang onto all the nations London had conquered.

Chris, when the British warships *Repulse* and *Prince of Wales* were sunk in the South China Sea in December 1941,

---

[48] STORY OF THE GUN, by Ian V. Hogg, St. Martin's Press, 1996, p.29.

and when the British army was beaten at Hong Kong and Singapore, Americans considered these great disasters. Instead, Americans should have been asking, what right did the British army and navy have to be in those far corners of the globe in the first place?

The British lust for conquest had not ended. In April 1941, the Iraqis tried to throw off the British, and London sent in troops to reconquer them and retain control of Iraq's oil.[49]

In August 1941, both the British and Russians invaded Iran and divided it and its oil between them.[50]

These British troops in the Mideast were far from home and unable to defend their own families in Britain.

In my next letter I will give you some examples of how the British Empire was built and maintained. Until then, Chris, remember that in the effort to rally the American people behind the English and French against the Germans, few paid much attention to the fact that the British and French were reaping what they had sown in the Treaty of Versailles.

Uncle Eric

---

[49] WORLD WAR II DAY BY DAY, by Donald Sommerville, Dorset Press, 1989, p.71.

[50] WORLD WAR II DAY BY DAY, by Donald Sommerville, p.93.

7

British Conquests

Dear Chris,

British rulers conquered more of the earth than anyone except perhaps the Mongols, but I have been unable to find any useful statistics on their total body count, other than Rummel's estimate of 816,000 murdered during the 20th century. The British Empire was nearly complete by the 20th century, so the 816,000 can be seen as just a residual number — the people killed during the British mopping up.[51]

Again, let me remind you, Chris, that Rummel's numbers do not include soldiers killed in battle, these are innocent men, women, and children murdered. I will explain more about the British murders shortly.

As you know, my line of work requires me to travel and learn about other countries. I have visited 40 countries, and I hope you someday get to do the same. One thing you will learn when you talk with persons in other countries is that, with the possible exception of the Russians, no one is hated more than the British. The British conquered more countries than anyone else and left more messes behind when they withdrew.

But the British were members of the Allies, and the Allies won both World Wars. There is an old saying, history books are written by the victors. We have abundant statistics on the

---

[51] DEATH BY GOVERNMENT, by R.J. Rummel, Transaction Publishers, New Brunswick, NJ, 1994, p.14.

number of people murdered by the German, Italian, and Japanese governments (the Axis), but not the British government. History books regard the Allies as the good guys, so we all have limited information about what the British government really did to the world.

Probably the people who have suffered most at the hands of British rulers were the Irish. The British first invaded Ireland in 1170, and the fighting still goes on today. Think about it, Chris, after *eight centuries,* British troops are still in Ireland fighting with the Irish.

The Irish have never invaded England; it's always been the British invading Ireland. I suggest that you listen to some Irish folk songs. I have a CD copyrighted in 1999 called THE IRISH TENORS, who are John McDermott, Anthony Kearns, and Ronan Tynan. Nothing gives a better feel for what the British government has done to the Irish (and much of the rest of the world) than the songs "Only Our Rivers Run Free," "Grace," and "The Town I Loved So Well."

Chris, please listen to that CD, it will give you a much more profound understanding of the British Empire than my words ever will.

For the Irish killed in the British conquest of Ireland, I have read estimates as high as five million. This five million includes deaths from starvation and disease as well as direct attack. In destroying farms and businesses, war erases a person's ability to take care of his or her family, so in most wars, deaths from starvation and disease have greatly outnumbered those from battle.

Five million appears high to me, although the British have been pounding the Irish for eight centuries, so it is within the realm of possibilities. But let's be very conservative and reduce the estimate to a "mere" 100,000.

Then consider that Ireland is only 32,588 square miles; this made it less than 0.3% of the British Empire in 1940.

Using the conservative rate of three British-caused deaths per square mile, the total deaths for the entire British Empire would be 32,588,000.

British Empire builders had to do most of their killing with single-shot muskets, not machine guns, so this estimate may still be too high, but you get the idea. For eight centuries, British rulers were cut from the same mold as Hitler and Stalin.

The British are justifiably proud of their ancient Common Law heritage, but in the minds of British rulers, the Common Law stopped at the British coast, just as the U.S. Constitution and Bill of Rights stop at the borders of the United States. British rulers were allowed to do anything they pleased to the rest of the world.

In my next letter, I'll tell you more about London's cruelty.

Uncle Eric

P.S. Chris, let me emphasize that all my indictments in these letters are of the governments, not the people. I have met many British and Germans who are fine people. Wars bring great secrecy and much lying. The British and German people had little knowledge of what their governments were doing in the World Wars. Even if they had known, I doubt they could have done anything about it. To resist the actions of a government after it is in a war is to set oneself up for charges of treason and a firing squad. This is why it is so important to avoid getting into wars. A war is the easiest thing in the world to get into — and the hardest to get out of.

8

P.T. Barnum Knew

Dear Chris,

Britain is a land of contradictions. While the British government has been one of the most brutal the world has ever seen, the British people have given the world two of the most wonderful gifts ever.

The British people, as opposed to the British government, developed the old British Common Law (see my previous set of letters called WHATEVER HAPPENED TO JUSTICE?[52]) and the Industrial Revolution, which grew out of this law. The two together created our civilization today.

In nations with legal systems that are most faithful to the fundamental principles of Common Law, economic advancement has been so swift that our average life span is decades longer than that of our ancestors. We do not fear famine, cholera, winter, or any of the other killers that wiped out so many millions in previous centuries.

The British Common Law and its offspring, the Industrial Revolution, have been wonderful; the British government has been unimaginably evil. When I visited history museums in Sydney, Australia, I discovered an example. Here is the story.

When I say British rulers conquered a fourth of the world, what do I mean by "conquer"?

---

[52] Uncle Eric is referring to Richard J. Maybury's book WHATEVER HAPPENED TO JUSTICE? published by Bluestocking Press, web site: www.BluestockingPress.com.

To get a visual impression of the grim truth, watch four movies: QUIGLEY DOWN UNDER starring Tom Selleck (1990), ZULU starring Michael Caine (1964), BRAVEHEART starring Mel Gibson (1995), and KHARTOUM starring Charlton Heston (1966).

The movies are not perfectly accurate, but for Hollywood efforts they are not bad.

As you watch, continually remind yourself of the question, what right did the British have to be in these people's homelands? Who was the invader?

In ZULU, notice the number of Africans killed by the superior British arms.

To my mind, the most important of the three movies is QUIGLEY DOWN UNDER. That movie is a dramatization of what I learned in Australia.

The British in Australia once hunted Aborigines the way Americans commonly hunt rabbits and squirrels. They pursued this "sport" so enthusiastically that it became ingrained in British-Australian culture, and when the government reversed course in the 20th century and tried to stop it, officials had a difficult time of it.

Australian court records show that mass-murders of "blacks" (Aborigines) — meaning the killing of scores of men, women and children at a time — was still happening in Southeast Australia in 1926, only 13 years before World War II.[53]

How long it went on after 1926, we don't know. The last record I could find of the authorities catching someone was in 1926. That was, however, a large incident, two police

---

[53] "Genocide In Australia," by Colin Tatz, a research paper published by the Australian Institute of Aboriginal and Torres Strait Islander Studies, 1999; GPO Box 553, Canberra ACT 2601. ISBN 0 85575 345 5. ISSN 1323-9422

officers allegedly shot as many as 100 Aborigines and burned the bodies. I suspect smaller, covert incidents were still happening years later, but I could find no evidence. Even today, most of Australia is a vast wilderness where a great many sins could be hidden and never discovered.

The officers were acquitted and then promoted.[54] Yes, promoted. Maybe they committed the crime and maybe not, but someone certainly did. Acquittals in cases of whites massacring Aborigines were not unusual.

Again, this was only seven years before the first German **concentration camp** was erected at Dachau in 1933. I know an elderly white Australian who still pines for the days when hunting dark-skinned people was great sport. It was a form of **varmint** hunting.

This man is very old, and in no way representative of Australians or British today, but when he was young his casual brutality was quite typical of the master race that ran the British Empire. The movie QUIGLEY DOWN UNDER shows this brutality without exaggeration.

What Berlin was doing in the 1930s and '40s — genocide — London had been at for *eight centuries* before Hitler penned the first Nazi swastika. Yet, in my entire life, I have never heard anyone point this out. This is how effective the USG's war propaganda was. In both World Wars, Britain was painted as an innocent victim, a bastion of freedom, and few Americans today question this.

In his 1981 book GREAT BRITAIN, GREAT EMPIRE, W. Ross Johnston reports that:

---

[54] "Genocide In Australia," by Colin Tatz, a research paper published by the Australian Institute of Aboriginal and Torres Strait Islander Studies, 1999; GPO Box 553, Canberra ACT 2601. ISBN 0 85575 345 5. ISSN 1323-9422

From the beginning the English blithely assumed that they had a certain superiority; this in itself gave them a kind of impetus to assert themselves and their way of life over the different peoples that they encountered. ... only exceptionally did a band of Englishmen negotiate and arrange fair land transfers with people of a different race; usually the English claimed whatever they wanted by right of first discovery (meaning first white, Christian discovery), occupation, cheap sales or conquest. ... although the Aborigines put up some resistance they could not match the firepower of their foes. ... In the first century of contact the number of Australian Aborigines dropped from about 300,000 to about 75,000. Guns, poison and punitive raids quickly took their toll.[55]

Chris, does that sound any different than what German Nazis did to Jews?

The English did not wear the nifty black uniforms that the Nazi **SS** did, they had the sense not to stage huge political rallies boasting of their white supremacy. They didn't even give speeches about their intent to exterminate other races, so they have never looked as threatening on film as the German Nazis did. They just went out and killed anyone who got in their way, and no one ever said much about it.

In Australia's National History Museum in Sydney, I learned something fascinating about P.T. Barnum.

The Barnum & Bailey Circus ran from 1871 to 1907, and was famous for its sideshows featuring people from other lands such as Australia, Borneo, Tasmania, and Africa. These

---

[55] GREAT BRITIAN, GREAT EMPIRE, by W. Ross Johnston, University of Queensland Press, St. Lucia, Queensland, 1981, p.18 & 87.

people would appear in their native dress so that Americans could meet them and see what they were like.

I used to wonder what would induce a person to leave his family and friends — to leave everything he had ever known — and travel thousands of miles to work in a circus in a land where he did not even know the language. In Australia's National History Museum I found the answer.

Barnum told his agents to follow the British army around the world. After the British had swept through a region, killing all who resisted — and often even those who did not resist — the agents would search the area.

If Barnum's men could find a survivor, they would make him or her an offer. They would say, your home has been destroyed and your family, your friends, everyone you ever knew is dead. You can stay here, or you can come with us to America and work in our circus. If you come with us, you will have food, shelter, medical care, and clothing. And friends. If you stay here, you will be alone.

Chris, try to imagine what these survivors must have felt when they looked around and saw the bodies of everyone they loved. It gives you a small taste of what the British Empire was all about.

The character of the German Nazi government depicted in World War II movies — brutal, arrogant, racist — was a fact, but this is also what the British government had been for centuries. It is why the early Americans rebelled against their British rulers.

In fact, Chris, it is not at all an exaggeration to say that when it comes to ruthless butchery, few have ever done it better than London. Those few might include the Kremlin, Beijing, and Kublai Kahn. Can you think of any others?

As I said in an earlier letter, in the Old World six million dead is hardly noticeable, sad but true.

Uncle Eric

9

British Area Bombing

Dear Chris,

The belief that in the World Wars the British were fighting for liberty and justice for all is ridiculous. They were fighting for liberty and justice for the British, and for continued British domination over hundreds of millions of others.

There was a day when London's desire to conquer the world was well understood in America. After all, the U.S. had been a colony of Britain and had fought a war to gain independence, plus another war against Britain in 1812. The warship *Constitution* — "Old Ironsides" — drew its fame from battles against the British in 1812.

In the 1920s, Winston Churchill (then Britain's Chancellor of the Exchequer) warned the British cabinet of possible war with America,[56] and the USG had drawn up precautionary war plans, including a naval blockade of Britain. Churchill had said, "No doubt it is quite right to go on talking about war with the U.S. being unthinkable. But everyone knows this is not true."[57]

In the early 1930s — less than a decade before World War II — the British government was still considered the number one threat to America; the U.S. Army Air Corps was making plans to repel a British attack.[58]

---

[56] "Rome, DC," THE ECONOMIST, July 28, 1980, p.71.

[57] AN OCEAN APART, PBS TV documentary.

[58] "Defense Plans Lack Foresight," by Loren B. Thompson, AIR FORCE TIMES, June 19, 2000, p.47.

Chris, notice this was years *after* the USG had come to London's aid in World War I. What does this tell you about how U.S. officials judged the British government's character?

The British government's ruthlessness can be seen in the way it bombed Germany in World War II.

Bombing in daylight was highly dangerous. Antiaircraft gunners and pilots of fighter planes could see the bombers.

Night flying was safer but the bombardiers could not see their targets.

Americans usually bombed military targets — oil refineries, ports, rail yards, arms factories, etc. — in daylight and suffered the losses.[59]

The British bombed at night and went after big, easy-to-hit residential areas where German families were sleeping.

This was called **area bombing**. The British justified it by pointing to the fact that Hitler was doing it to them.[60]

Interesting logic, Chris. If Hitler does it, that makes it okay.

This is why most films showing the bombing of Germany shows American bombers. The British flew at night, bombing housing areas, so cameras could not see their planes.

After the war, the eminent British historian B.H. Liddell Hart wrote, "terrorization became without reservation the definite policy of the British government."[61] He refers to "terrorization" of German civilians as "a prime aim," and says "the British pursued area-bombing long after they had any reason, or excuse, for such indiscriminate action."[62]

---

[59] HISTORY OF THE SECOND WORLD WAR, by B.H. Liddell Hart, Perigee Books, NY, 1982, Chapter 33.

[60] HISTORY OF THE SECOND WORLD WAR, B.H. Liddell Hart, Chapter 33.

[61] HISTORY OF THE SECOND WORLD WAR, B.H. Liddell Hart, p.596.

[62] HISTORY OF THE SECOND WORLD WAR, B.H. Liddell Hart, p.609.

One of the more infamous examples of this terrorization came in 1945. One night in February, Air Marshall A.T. Arthur Harris — known as Bomber Harris — ordered British aircrews to hit the German city of Dresden. Harris told the crews to ignore the factories and rail center, and bomb residential areas.

The British planes burned the entire city and its people,[63] killing an estimated 100,000. This body count put Dresden in the same league as Hiroshima and Nagasaki, which the U.S. hit with atomic bombs.

Harris did it at the request of Stalin. Afterward, Churchill was shocked and questioned the policy of "bombing German cities simply for the sake of increasing the terror." He referred to the bombings as "mere acts of terror and wanton destruction."[64]

When the British burned Hamburg, they killed over 40,000 and left a million homeless; the fire could be seen 120 miles away.[65]

The British were remarkably scientific about area bombing. They calculated that, on average, one ton of bombs could burn 200 German homes. An Avro Lancaster Type One bomber could carry 11 tons of bombs, so British calculations showed that each attack by each Lancaster could burn 2,200 homes, and the men, women, and children sleeping in them.

It is important to understand, Chris, the aircrews had been ordered to do this, and some were not happy about it. As one

---

[63] HISTORY OF THE SECOND WORLD WAR, by B.H. Liddell Hart, Perigee Books, NY, 1982, p.610.

[64] "Dresden: Time to Say We're Sorry," by Simon Jenkins, WALL STREET JOURNAL, February 14, 1995.

[65] WHY THE ALLIES WON, by Richard Overy, W. W. Norton & Co., NY, 1995, p.119.

British airman put it, "To whom could you express doubts?...What would have been the result? Court martial!"[66]

Chris, the British government was exterminating Germans just as the German government was exterminating Jews. For reasons I do not understand, using concentration camps and gas chambers to commit murder is frowned upon, while using airplanes to drop bombs on houses is considered legitimate warfare.

Remember, the victors write the history books.

This is not to say the Americans were innocent. In some cases they also bombed housing areas, especially in Japan. There can be no justification for this, but we can point out that the American objective in doing so was to win the war. The British objective was not only to win but to exterminate, to kill Germans simply for the sake of killing Germans. Indeed, London could have ended the war months earlier by bombing military targets, but British officials traded this opportunity away to continue bombing German families.[67]

Were the British the good guys in World War II? What do you think, Chris?

Uncle Eric

P.S. Speaking of concentration camps, Chris, the Germans were not the first to use them. In its conquest of South Africa

---

[66] THE NEW DEALERS' WAR, by Thomas Fleming, Basic Books, NY, 2001, p.276.

[67] See HISTORY OF THE SECOND WORLD WAR, by B.H. Liddell Hart, Perigee Books, NY, 1982, page 612. A foremost British military historian, Hart writes on page 612 that, "There is ample evidence to show that the war could have been shortened, several months at least, by better concentration on oil and communications targets," instead of housing areas. He refers to London's "disregard for basic morality."

during the Boer War, the British government set up concentration camps for Dutch men, women and children. By the end of the war in 1902, 20,000 of the 120,000 Dutch in these camps had died of disease and neglect.[68]

---

[68] OUR TIMES, edited by Lorraine Glennon, Turner Publishing, Atlanta, 1995, p.16.

10

Two Questions

Dear Chris,

Thanks for your letter. You asked two questions. The first was, why did the British and other European Empires end after World War II?

It is hard to know for sure, my guess is photography. World War II was the most photographed war in history, and, by 1945, experienced combat photographers with good equipment were in every corner of the globe. This made it impossible for European governments to suppress uprisings in their colonies the way they had in the past. Each time an officer gave an order to exterminate a village, he knew a photographer would soon show up to film the bodies.

The European Empires began to fall apart. One example happened in Palestine. When Jews began fighting the British after World War II, the British did not massacre them, they just gave up and left.

One after another, the colonies of the European conquerors declared independence. By 1970, all the European Empires were mere shadows of their former selves.

The British government still fights the Irish, and in 1982 they fought Argentina to retain control of the Falkland Islands off the coast of Argentina. So the British government's ruthlessness is not entirely dead yet, but it is close, thanks, I believe, to the effectiveness of news cameras.

Chris, the pen may be mightier than the sword but the camera is mightier than both of them. It is hard to exaggerate the fear governments have of cameras and the effect of cameras on every government's foreign policy. In World War II, the USG was so terrified photographs would undermine support for the war that in the first 21 months after the Pearl Harbor attack, censors forbade publication of any photograph of a dead American.[69]

The British and French Empires were mostly complete before cameras became widespread, so the horrific reality of what those governments did has never been grasped by Americans.

After cameras were everywhere, these governments were afraid to continue doing what was necessary to hold the territories they had conquered.

Your second question was, why did the USG side with Britain in both World Wars?

This is easier to answer. The German Nazis were not the only people with hallucinations about racial superiority. History books are written by the victors, few Americans today know that before 1945 there was a movement called Anglo-Saxonism. The Anglo-Saxonists believed that the white British and Americans were natural allies, superior to others and entitled to rule the world.

In my previous set of letters about World War I, I told you about Rudyard Kipling's poem "The White Man's Burden." That poem was a popular justification for Anglo-Saxonism.

Anglo-Saxonism, or the White Man's Burden, was used to justify London's slaughter of millions in the building of

---

[69] THE NEW DEALERS' WAR, by Thomas Fleming, Basic Books, NY, 2001, p.128.

the British Empire, and it was used to justify the USG's slaughter of Native Americans ("Indians") and Filipinos. The majority of America's East Coast leaders believed in Anglo-Saxonism. These included President Theodore Roosevelt, his Secretary of State Elihu Root, and Franklin Roosevelt's Secretary of War Henry L. Stimson.[70] Many of these East Coast leaders admired the British Empire and saw it as a model for how the whole world should be run.[71] To these officials, siding with Britain was a natural and reasonable idea, and they looked forward to British-American domination of the world.

I should also point out that the Soviet Socialists in the Kremlin talked a good game about the brotherhood of the world's workers, but they had little good to say about the dark-skinned people in the southern parts of the Soviet Union. They killed millions of them, and today the Russian belief in the superiority of whites remains quite strong.

So, Chris, when you read a book or see a movie about the beliefs of the German Nazis, bear in mind that Nazis did not have a monopoly on racism, or on mass murder. The Anglo-Saxonists and Russians were at it centuries before the first swastika appeared in Germany.

Uncle Eric

---

[70] "Benjamin Strong, the Federal Reserve, and the Limits to Interwar American Nationalism," by Priscilla Roberts, FEDERAL RESERVE BANK OF RICHMOND ECONOMIC QUARTERLY, Vol. 86/2, Spring 2000, p.61-66.

[71] "Benjamin Strong, the Federal Reserve, and the Limits to Interwar American Nationalism," by Priscilla Roberts, p.61-66.

Part Two

First Rumblings

11

When Did The War Begin?

Dear Chris,

Ask any American when World War II began and I think most will say December 7, 1941, when the Japanese attacked Pearl Harbor. More knowledgeable ones might say September 1, 1939, when the Germans invaded Poland.

Actually, the shooting started in 1931, and then increased gradually until the war was fully developed at the end of 1941.

In previous letters I have given a lot of attention to Germany because it was a special case due to the Treaty of Versailles. A quick summary:

In World War I, the Allied and **Central Powers** had fought each other to a standstill by 1917, triggering mutiny and desertion among their demoralized troops.

The war was in danger of going out of business when President Wilson abandoned neutrality, jumped in and saved it. U.S. forces helped the Allies break out and crush the Germans.

Backed by this awesome U.S. firepower, the Allies were then able to impoverish and humiliate the Germans with the Treaty of Versailles.

The German hunger for revenge became World War II.

Nice work. The U.S. Government's ability to turn small wars into big ones borders on the miraculous.

In the 1930s, Germany became the central player in the Axis, and the most brutal of the Axis powers. (Russia was the most brutal of the Allied powers.)

However, while a special case, Germany was also typical. In my previous set of letters about World War I,[72] I told you about the Usual Suspects. These are the nine governments that have been behind most of the worst wars since the Middle Ages. In alphabetical order they are Beijing, Berlin, London, Moscow, Paris, Rome, Tokyo, Vienna, and Washington D.C.

By the 1930s, older members of the Usual Suspects — London, Paris, and Moscow — had been conquering other lands and forcing them into their empires for centuries. They were the Allies.

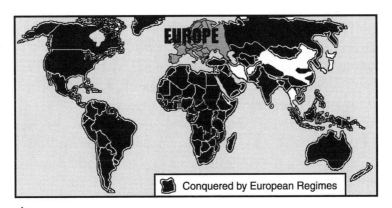

Conquered by European Regimes

Europe is only 6.6% of the earth's land surface, but Europeans inherited the Roman lust for one world government. The first to acquire advanced weapons produced by the industrial revolution, Europeans attacked and conquered all the rest of the globe, with only five exceptions. Persia (Iran), Afghanistan, Thailand, Japan, and most of China were able to beat them off, but only Japan escaped terrible death and destruction.

---

[72] Uncle Eric is referring to Chapter 31 "The Usual Suspects" in Richard J. Maybury's book WORLD WAR I: THE REST OF THE STORY AND HOW IT AFFECTS YOU TODAY, published by Bluestocking Press, web site: www.BluestockingPress.com.

Younger members of the group — primarily Rome,[73] Tokyo, and Berlin — were jealous. They had gotten a late start and were working hard to catch up. They were the Axis. In other words, during the two decades between the World Wars, the Usual Suspects were conducting business as usual. They were trying to dominate the world, and Berlin had joined this game.

Remember the deadly idea called the Pax Romana?[74] This desire to emulate the old Roman Empire was carried to such extremes that in Italy, Mussolini adopted the German goose step for his soldiers and renamed it the Roman step.[75]

The problem the younger members of the Usual Suspects ran up against is that the older ones had already taken most of the world, so the only way for the younger ones to build their empires was to steal what the older ones had stolen.

The older ones regarded this as aggression.

The first grab by one of the younger Usual Suspects was in the Orient by Tokyo. You may remember that in the Russo-Japanese War in 1904-05, the Japanese beat the Russians and pushed them out of Manchuria.

Russia was forced to recognize Japanese dominance in the area, and Tokyo got Port Arthur and the Liaodong (Liaotung) Peninsula, plus the southern half of Sakhalin Island.

---

[73] Rome is an ancient city, but did not amount to much for centuries after the Roman Empire fell. In the Middle Ages, Italy fragmented into small kingdoms, and was not reunited into the country we see on maps today until 1870.

[74] The Pax Romana is discussed in Richard J. Maybury's book ANCIENT ROME: HOW IT AFFECTS YOU TODAY. Pax Romana as a deadly idea that leads to war was discussed in Chapter 9 of Richard J. Maybury's book WORLD WAR I. Both books are published by Bluestocking Press, web site: www.BluestockingPress.com.

[75] WORLD WAR II, by C.L. Sulzberger, AMERICAN HERITAGE, 1966, p.39.

In 1931, Tokyo decided to take the rest of Manchuria. The Chinese fought, but lost, and in early 1932 the battle was over, the better-armed Japanese had moved in. Later they began to gradually take parts of China's East Coast.

The beginning of the shooting in World War II is usually regarded as the September 1, 1939, German invasion of Poland. In my opinion, the 1931 Japanese invasion of Manchuria was the real beginning. Tokyo, a younger member of the Usual Suspects, had begun dominating areas formerly thought to be the **bailiwick**[76] of Beijing and Moscow.

In the late 1800s, Rome had begun taking parts of Somaliland (now Somalia). By 1927 the conquest of Italian Somaliland was complete. Rome then began to look toward neighboring Abyssinia (now Ethiopia).

In October 1935, Rome attacked Abyssinia, and in May 1936, that massacre ended with the Italian annexation of the African country.

The younger members of the Usual Suspects were on a roll.

Two months later, in July, the Spanish Civil War began. The leftist government of Spain had been trying to reduce the power of the army, and of the Catholic Church and aristocracy. The army, led by the fascist Francisco Franco, revolted.

Fascist Rome, led by Mussolini, sent about 70,000 ground troops to aid the rebels, and Nazi Germany provided planes, pilots, arms, and technicians.

Socialist (leftist) Moscow sent weapons and advisors to the Spanish government. The Comintern, or Communist International, was a global organization of Communist parties under the leadership of Moscow. It organized thousands of

---

[76] Bailiwick: domain.

leftists from 53 foreign countries — especially France — into volunteer International Brigades to fight the fascist rebels.

The Spanish Civil War thus became a preview of the conflict between fascism and socialism that would eventually be played out between Germany and Russia on the Eastern Front.

The Spanish Civil War also served as a proving ground for new weapons and tactics, especially the fast moving tank-and-aircraft **blitzkrieg** that Germany would soon use.

In short, the Spanish Civil War was a dress rehearsal for World War II. It ended on March 28, 1939, when Madrid fell to the fascists.

A very important point to remember, Chris, is that World War II is painted as a battle between freedom and tyranny. But, as we saw in earlier letters, the main event of the war was the Eastern Front, everything else was small compared to that, and that was a battle between Hitler's German Nazis and Stalin's Soviet Socialists. The Spanish Civil War was a preview of this.

In other words, Chris, World War II was mostly a battle between two forms of tyranny — fascism and socialism — and the USG sided with the worst of the two, Stalin's Soviet Socialists. The fact that events were leading toward this historic duel between fascism and socialism was already apparent in 1936 with the Spanish Civil War.

Now can you see why I say that the war had little to do with good versus evil? It was evil versus evil. It reminds me of a friend's recent comment about the Arab-Israeli war: "All the leaders on both sides are corrupt, and everyone else is cannon fodder." Chris, this is an excellent description of nearly every war I have ever studied, especially the World Wars.

Uncle Eric

12

Appeasement and Comparative Brutality

Dear Chris,

While Tokyo and Rome were expanding their empires, trying to catch up with London, Paris, and Moscow, the Nazi regime in Berlin was doing the same.

First the Germans took land that had originally belonged to them, the Rhineland along the border between France and Germany. In March 1936, German troops moved in.

The British and French governments protested, but did nothing. This was the beginning of what would be called "appeasement" — the idea that if the German Nazis and Italian Fascists were allowed to take a small amount of territory, then they would be satisfied and would not try to take huge ones, as the governments of Britain, France, and Moscow had for centuries.

Why anyone would assume the young upstarts would not be as power hungry as the old ones, I don't know, but the old ones did jump to that conclusion.

Chris, when talking about the face-off between the young and old Usual Suspects, some people compare the brutality of the Japanese, Italian, and German conquests with the much more gentle French and British administrations of their territories.

Notice they compare conquest with administration.

Administration happens only after conquest is complete.

The argument is that the British and French were white hats because they treated their subjects well, even helping them develop their industries and raise their standards of living, while the Japanese, Italians, and Germans slaughtered their victims by the millions.

The Japanese, Italians, and Germans were just beginning to build their empires. Back in the days when the British and French were in their early stages, they were every bit as brutal.

In the 1930s, the British and French governments were able to be much more kind because the people who had been resisting them had been killed. British and French rulers were being kind to the survivors.

The main reason Britain and France were vulnerable to Germany was that Britain and France had their armies, navies, and air forces scattered all over the world controlling the people they had conquered.

Interesting point to think about: On September 11, 2001,[77] the USG had troops in more than 100 countries.

Uncle Eric

---

[77] On September 11, 2001, in an attack against the United States, over 3000 civilians were murdered. The World Trade Center in New York was destroyed, as well as a portion of the Pentagon. Four civilian airliners were destroyed, including their passengers and crew. This attack is also referred to as Sept. 11, Sept. 11 Attack, and 9-11.

13

Carving Up Central Europe

Dear Chris,

After the Nazis got away with occupying the Rhineland, they were more confident about trying other conquests. In January 1937, Hitler gave a speech in which he formally declared an end to the Treaty of Versailles. Then in March 1938, the German Nazis annexed Austria. This sad event would someday become the backdrop to one of America's favorite movies, THE SOUND OF MUSIC.

In May 1938, the Czechs heard reports of German preparations to take Czechoslovakia. The Czechs **mobilized**. London and Paris warned Berlin not to do it, and Hitler backed down temporarily.

A **fasces**, symbol of the ancient Roman philosophy of fascism.

Czechoslovakia had a population of 14,000,000, of which 3,000,000 were German. The Germans lived mostly in the Sudetenland bordering Germany. In October 1938, Hitler's troops invaded the Sudetenland.

At the same time, Poland's government grabbed the Teschen area from the Czechs.

In November 1938, the Hungarian government joined the game and took a chunk of Czechoslovakia.

Chris, the Polish and Hungarian moves on Czechoslovakia are two important events that are often forgotten in the desire to see World War II as a battle between good guys and bad guys. It was not just the Germans who were carving up Central Europe.

In March 1939, Berlin took the rest of Czechoslovakia, except for another section taken by Hungary.

Despite their earlier warnings to Hitler, the governments of Britain and France did nothing. So, later in the month, the Germans also took a portion of Lithuania.

Like the other two upstarts, Tokyo and Rome, Berlin was on a roll.

Moscow was a major power, it had long ago taken everything from Poland to the Pacific, and Hitler knew the Soviets could cause him big trouble. He made a deal.

In August 1939, Berlin and Moscow agreed to the Soviet-German Nonaggression Pact. This said that Berlin would get a large part of Poland for its new empire, and Moscow could have the rest of Poland, plus Finland, Estonia, Latvia, and Lithuania.

The Hollywood version of history says Hitler's September 1, 1939, attack on Poland was the trigger for war, and the Axis powers were the black hats and the Allies the white hats.

Few Americans realize that only 16 days after Hitler's attack, Stalin, who was an Ally, also invaded Poland. And, on November 30th, Stalin attacked Finland.[78]

Then on June 17, 1940, Stalin invaded and conquered Latvia, Lithuania, and Estonia.[79]

---

[78] WORLD WAR II DAY BY DAY, by Donald Sommerville, Dorset Press, 1989, p.18-20.

[79] CHRONICLE OF THE 20TH CENTURY, by Clifton Daniel, Chronicle Publications, Mount Kisco, NY, p.510.

Chris, in previous sets of letters[80] I have mentioned the two laws that make civilization possible: 1) do all you have agreed to do and 2) do not encroach on other persons or their property. In the Hollywood version of history, we are taught that Central Europe was being carved up by Berlin. Clearly, this violated the second law, but what is seldom pointed out is that the second law was ripped to shreds in Central Europe by others governments, too, including Moscow, which was an ally.

President Roosevelt was an opponent of neutrality and fan of alliances. At a press conference on June 24, 1941, he announced that he was taking sides with Stalin.[81] (Chris, notice this was five months before America officially entered the war on December 7, 1941.)

In the Soviet-German Nonaggression Pact, Hitler and Stalin agreed not to attack each other. Don't laugh, they really did it, the two liars made a promise to each other that they would not stab each other in the back.

What is even more amazing, but nevertheless true, is that Stalin apparently believed it. He made no plans to defend against a German invasion.

Chris, a crucially important point to remember is that Moscow was part of the Allies, a "friend" of Paris, London, and eventually Washington D.C., but it was carving up Central Europe just like Berlin was. In fact, between 1919 and 1940, Moscow conquered much more territory than Berlin did.

---

[80] Uncle Eric is referring to several of Richard J. Maybury's books about these laws, principle among them WHATEVER HAPPENED TO JUSTICE? published by Bluestocking Press, web site: www.BluestockingPress.com.

[81] WORLD WAR II DAY BY DAY, by Donald Sommerville, Dorset Press, 1989, p.86.

Kazakhstan alone was larger than everything Hitler ever stole. This inconvenient fact is often left out of histories about World War II, it does not fit with the white hats versus black hats model.

Two days after the German invasion of Poland, the British and French declared war on Germany. (The British and French governments did nothing about the invasion of Poland by the Kremlin.) This meant all the British and French colonies around the world again found themselves at war with the Germans.

On June 10, 1940, Rome came into the war on the side of Berlin.

In September 1940, Rome, Berlin, and Tokyo signed the Tripartite Pact in which they agreed that if one of them went to war with someone, they all would. This completed the replay of the mistake that had led to the First World War, the creation of alliances. Now, all the Usual Suspects except the USG and China were linked — if one blundered into a war with someone, all would follow, exactly as in World War I. Some people never learn.

Uncle Eric

P.S. Chris, notice that Berlin did not declare war on London or Paris. London and Paris declared war on Berlin.

In other words, the British and French did not get into the war because they were attacked, they got into it because they promised Warsaw they would — because of alliances, one of the deadly ideas explained in my set of letters about World War I.[82]

---

[82] Uncle Eric is referring to Chapter 35 in Richard J. Maybury's book WORLD WAR I: THE REST OF THE STORY AND HOW IT AFFECTS YOU TODAY, published by Bluestocking Press, web site: www.BluestockingPress.com.

It was a repeat of World War I. In a domino effect, they all went to war simply because they promised they would, and the war spread around the world. A molehill grew into a mountain.

The Swiss were in the center of it all, but they were neutral and had no alliances, so they stayed out of the war.

Incidentally, Chris, if you are interested in studying the Swiss system, I suggest you get at it. Under a barrage of propaganda, and economic and political pressure from other governments, the Swiss system is slowly crumbling. In February 2002, the Swiss caved in and voted to join the United Nations. As I write this letter, this leaves the Vatican as the only nation voluntarily outside the UN. The Swiss model of heavily armed neutrality is fading away. Study it to learn all you can before it is gone.

Part Three

The U.S. Enters the War

14

The French versus the French

Dear Chris,

This group of letters may be the most important of this entire series. They will show you how America got into the war. Here is the story.

On October 3, 1939, the last significant units of the Polish army surrendered to the Germans. Hitler then turned his attention westward. On April 9, 1940, his forces invaded Norway, then on May 10th, France.

On June 10th, Italy's Mussolini declared war on France.

The British sent help to the French but it did little good. The armies of both countries were quickly pushed all the way back to the French coast at Dunkirk. Both had their backs to the sea, with the Germans closing in.

A massive rescue effort was launched from Britain. Every kind of vessel imaginable, including fishing boats and pleasure yachts, was sent to Dunkirk; 226,000 British soldiers were rescued, and 112,000 French. They reached England but were forced to leave all their heavy weapons behind. Even today, the word Dunkirk sends chills down the spines of the English.

Fascist ideas were already popular in much of France, due to France's long history of trying to copy the Roman Empire. Many French men and women sided with the Germans, and France split in two — "Occupied France" in the north, and "Vichy France" in the south. Vichy France sympathized with Fascist Germany.

On July 3rd, the British attacked the French fleet.

The attack enraged the French. Two days later, the French government based in the town of Vichy broke diplomatic relations with Britain and attacked the British base at Gibraltar.

For all practical purposes, the southern half of France — "Vichy France" — had now become part of the Axis, meaning an ally of Germany, Italy, and Japan.

And the northern half of France was directly under control of the Germans. The so-called Free French government and its army were in England.

On September 23rd – 25th, the Free French and Vichy French fought a naval battle against each other off French West Africa.

Please note, Chris, that the Hollywood version of history says that France was anti-German and pro-Ally, and the Americans helped "liberate" France. Actually, only some of the French were pro-Ally, others joined the Axis and fought against the Allies, including against other French.

This was repeated in Austria. Due to many centuries of trying to copy the Roman Empire, much of Austria was fascist, and Hitler may have been more popular there than in Germany. Some Austrians resisted Germany's takeover, but many also welcomed it.

The same in Czechoslovakia. When German troops entered the Sudetenland in September 1938, they were welcomed.

When American troops landed in North Africa in November 1942, they found themselves fighting not only the Germans, but the French, too. The French fought so hard that at one point part of the Western Task Force under General George H. Patton was in danger of being pushed into the sea.[83]

In May 1942, the British and French were fighting each other in Madagascar.

Incidentally, Chris, all of North Africa is Arab. When you read or see films about the North African front, notice that no one asks, why were Europeans fighting over ownership of Arab lands? How did the Europeans get those lands in the first place?

North Africa was a sample of the whole war. It was the Usual Suspects battling to decide the ownership of stolen loot.

Chris, the Hollywood version of history points out that Italy and Germany were fascist, and then allows us to assume the rest of Europe was anti-fascist and desirous of liberation. Not so. If you visit Europe you will see **fasces** in the art and architecture of Vienna, Paris, and many other cities and towns outside Germany and Italy. Fascism was *the* European political philosophy for thousands of years and was still popular all over Europe, especially in Austria and France, when World War II broke out.

The disagreement in World War II was not about conquest, it was about who should be the conquerors.

Uncle Eric

P.S. Chris, France was typical of Europe. Some people were fascist and others were not, it varied from house to house.

How much of Europe was fascist? There is no way to know. After 1945, few would admit to fascist beliefs, nor will many today.

---

[83] THE NEW DEALERS' WAR, by Thomas Fleming, Basic Books, NY, 2001, p.166-167.

After more than 30 years of studying World War II, my guess is that more than half of Western and Central Europe's populations were **true believers** in fascism, and most of the rest were true believers in socialism. In Eastern Europe, the reverse, mostly socialist, the rest fascist.

How many Europeans believed in the brand of liberty that Americans did at that time? Only a handful I'm sure. By 1940, the eastward-moving wave of liberty triggered by the American Revolution had died out, replaced by the hot new fashion of socialism.

As we shall see in future letters, World War II was mostly a battle between fascists and socialists, and with the USG's help, the socialists won.

15

Significance of the Higgins Boat

Dear Chris,

Very often, technology becomes so influential it stops being a tool of politics and becomes a shaper of politics. So it was with the Higgins boat — or rather the lack of the Higgins boat. The Germans had none.

In the U.S., the Higgins Boat Company developed this brilliant invention for landing troops and equipment on beaches. I am sure you have seen them in newsreels and movies. The Higgins boat is rectangular, with a ramp in the front. The boat hits the beach, the ramp drops, and the troops run out.

To invade England, the Germans had to capture a port so that their ships could unload on docks.

Ports are much more easily defended than hundreds of miles of beaches, so the lack of Higgins boats left the Germans with no reliable way to get ashore in Britain.

Without the ability to invade, the Germans resorted to bombing Britain in hopes of forcing a surrender from the air.

The British sent up fighter aircraft, and this part of the war came to be known as the Battle of Britain.

According to the U.S. Government's official history, as taught in the two film series WHY WE FIGHT and VICTORY AT SEA, the Battle of Britain was so serious that even if Japan had not attacked Pearl Harbor, America would still have needed to get into the war to save Britain.

Wrong.

The Germans had no Higgins boats, so the British won. Chris, this is crucially important. Look at the timing. The Battle of Britain ended on October 31, 1940, more than a year before the USG got into the war at Pearl Harbor.

After October 31, 1940, the Germans continued bombing Britain, but not in earnest, and they would never again pose a serious threat in the West. Why?

Look at a map or globe. After losing the Battle of Britain, Hitler turned his attention eastward, toward the Soviet Union.

On June 22, 1941, the Germans invaded the Soviet Union. As we shall see, this should have been the beginning of the end of the war.

Uncle Eric

16

Only Genghis Khan Did It

Dear Chris,

You might argue that between the end of the Battle of Britain and the German invasion of the U.S.S.R. eight months later, Britain was still in serious danger. Okay, maybe, but there can be no doubt that after the invasion of the U.S.S.R. began, in June 1941 — five months before the attack on Pearl Harbor — the British were out of the woods. In fact, almost the whole world was out of the woods.

The first lesson in military strategy learned by every new lieutenant is, never invade Russia. Anyone who invades Russia ends like Napoleon. They lose, and they lose horrifically. There is no such thing as a small defeat in Russia.

Napoleon, who called himself "the modern Caesar," may have been the most skilled general the world has ever seen. In mid-1812 he held territories from Gibraltar to Lithuania.

Then he invaded Russia.

He went into Russia with more than 450,000 troops, and he came back with 40,000.[84]

The reason?

Look at your map or globe again, Chris. Moscow is in the same latitude as Canada's Hudson Bay. St. Petersburg (Leningrad) is in the same latitude as Alaska.

Russia is too big, too flat, too wet, and too cold.

---

[84] GROLIER ENCYCLOPEDIA, CD-ROM, 1998, under the subject, Napoleonic Wars.

Hitler's generals knew what had happened to Napoleon. They fully understood that they could not fight a war on a 200,000 square mile mud flat, and so did everyone else. But the German generals could not talk Hitler out of it;[85] he was a fool.

In fact, his generals tried to talk him out of beginning the war in the first place. They knew Germany was too weak to take on the Allies and would eventually lose, but Hitler ignored them.[86]

Before the war began, the generals even threatened to go on strike if Hitler went to war, and the chief of the General Staff, Ludwig Beck, resigned.[87] It did no good, Hitler went to war and then greatly compounded his mistake by invading Russia.

Full-scale war is possible in Russia (or the former U.S.S.R.) only during the three months of summer.

During spring and fall, Russia is a vast mudflat nearly impassible for vehicles, and in winter the conditions are arctic.

Chris, to know what it is like in Russia during winter, imagine this: Hang a white bed sheet on the wall and put a chair in front of it. Before you sit down, don pants and a shirt with lots of pockets, and fill the pockets with ice. Then sit and stare at the sheet 24 hours per day for six months.

In other words, an invading army has only the three months of summer to carry out its intentions. After that it will be bogged down in the mud of autumn, then soon frozen

---

[85] HISTORY OF THE SECOND WORLD WAR, by B.H. Liddell Hart, Perigree Books, NY, 1982, p.147, 150.

[86] HISTORY OF THE SECOND WORLD WAR, by B.H. Liddell Hart, p.34-37.

[87] UNCONDITIONAL SURRENDER by Anne Armstrong, Rutgers University Press, New Brunswick, 1961, p.111,112.

in the whiteout conditions of winter. If you have seen the movie DOCTOR ZHIVAGO, you have seen a good picture of what a Russian winter is like.

Chris, as mentioned in an earlier letter, there have been more than 14,000 wars during the past 5,600 years.[88] I think we can safely assume there have been thousands of generals with skill and experience in the art of invasion. Yet the last person to mount a successful winter invasion of Russia was Genghis Khan in 1236 AD, and it took him four years.

Russians have always had the advantage of an extremely simple defensive strategy: keep retreating until winter comes. Winter is Russia's invincible ally. After the first snow falls, the invader finds himself deep in enemy territory, far from home, bogged down in freezing mud, snow and ice, and dependent on extremely long, fragile supply lines. After the snow falls, the Russians cut the supply lines, wait for the invader to weaken, then attack.

As expected, the Russians used this strategy against the Germans just as they did against Napoleon. On September 12, 1941, the first snow fell, and the Germans had not yet reached Moscow. That snowfall was the turning point of the war; it was the beginning of the end for the Germans.

In June 1941, the Germans had gone into Russia with a half-million vehicles. By November, only 75,000 were still working. By December, German transport was almost entirely by horse and sled.[89]

---

[88] DIRTY LITTLE SECRETS, by James F. Dunnigan and Albert A. Nofi, Quill/William Morrow, 1990, p.419.

[89] WHY THE ALLIES WON, by Richard Overy, W. W. Norton & Co., NY, 1995, p.216.

Remember that date, Chris — September 12, 1941, when the snow began falling in Russia.[90] It is probably the most important date in World War II. Here's why.

Americans have been taught that Hitler was the most evil and dangerous person in history. He was not, Stalin was, but Americans believe Hitler was the worst, so they believe it was necessary for America to get into the war to keep Hitler from conquering the world. They also believe America had to get into the war to keep Hitler from taking England, which was regarded as America's "special friend."

However, — crucially important — the USG did not get into the fight until December 7, 1941. By then, the Battle of Britain had ended, and the German invasion of England had been cancelled. The German war machine had been turned against the U.S.S.R., sealing its fate. As of September 12, 1941, when the first snow fell in Russia, Germany was no longer a world threat.

Not that it ever was. I will explain that in a future letter.

Through it all, the neutral Swiss, living peacefully in the center of the chaos, kept their rifles loaded, and sadly watched the massacres, shaking their heads as they had so many times before.

Uncle Eric

P.S. Chris, one of the most admired generals in Russian history was Field Marshal Mikhail Illarionovich Kutuzov, who was given the task of stopping Napoleon. The way Kutuzov did it was by sleeping. In his first confrontation with the

---

[90] WORLD WAR II DAY BY DAY, by Donald Sommerville, Dorset Press, 1989, p.94.

French, he was beaten, and he learned from that. Thereafter, as the French drove ever deeper into Russia, Kutuzov would order his troops to move out of the way, and then he would go back to bed. Week after week, the French marched east, and Kutuzov's advisors grew ever more worried as Kutuzov snored away. Then winter arrived.[91] Napoleon's army never recovered from the counterattack by the Russian winter, and almost a century and a half later, the German army never recovered from the counterattack by that same invincible force.

---

[91] CONDEMNED TO REPEAT IT, by Wick Allison, Jeremy Adams, Gavin Hambly, Penguin Group, NY, 1998, p.13-15.

17

The Solution

Dear Chris,

We are led to believe that because the Union of Soviet Socialist Republics was a member of the Allies, the German attack on the U.S.S.R. was a terrible blow.

On the contrary, Stalin's Soviet Socialist tyranny was the larger twin of Hitler's German Nazi tyranny.

If you are standing in front of a firing squad, you do not care whether the bullets are fascist or socialist.

Hitler's attack on Stalin was not a problem, it was the solution. What could have been better than having the two worst gangs of cutthroats on earth trying to demolish each other on the plains of Central Europe?

In launching his Operation Barbarossa against Russia, Hitler shot himself in the foot. Chris, I remember watching a filmed interview of a Russian officer who had fought in World War II. The officer said that soon after the first snowfall, he came upon the frozen body of a German officer. The German was wearing a summer uniform. Said the Russian, "I knew then that we would win."

For the next four years until the end of the war, a German soldier who received a transfer to the Eastern Front regarded it as a death sentence. The Germans might have been able to beat the Russian army but they did not have a chance against the Russian winter. Their engines froze, their rifles and cannons froze, their horses froze, and their hands and feet froze.

The Germans ran out of lubricants. On flat summer roads, their tanks used a pint of oil per 60 miles. In Russia's frozen bogs, they consumed four gallons of oil for that distance. Rubber seals became brittle and tank turrets would not traverse.[92]

The Russians had been born and raised in these conditions, and had developed equipment that would not freeze. They also had specially trained army and air force units that could operate in deep snow. These units would wait for the Germans to become immobile, and then they would pounce. The Germans never had a chance.

On November 19, 1941 — more than two weeks before the attack on Pearl Harbor — the temperature on the Russian battlefields dropped to fifty degrees below zero Fahrenheit.[93]

Even today, with the most modern equipment, no sane commander anywhere in the world would consider invading Russia.

Chris, knowing the events of World War II is important. Knowing the sequence is more important. America's entry into the war on December 7th was not needed because the German war machine was already in deep trouble on September 12th, when the first snow fell in Russia.

Okay, you say, that might make sense, but America had no choice about getting into the war, it was attacked by Japan at Pearl Harbor.

Are you sure about that?

Chris, this is another case where the Hollywood version of history is a long way from the truth. In my next letter I

---

[92] WHY THE ALLIES WON, by Richard Overy, W. W. Norton & Co., NY, 1995, p.216.

[93] STALIN, by Albert Marrin, Puffin Books, Penguin Group, NY, 1988, p.188.

will begin telling the shocking story of events leading to the attack on Pearl Harbor. As usual, this will be the rest of the story, the non-statist side that few Americans have ever heard. In my opinion, you cannot be well educated unless you know both sides.

Uncle Eric

P.S. Chris, often when I suggest that there was no need for America to get into World War II, listeners become angry and say that Hitler had to be stopped. My way of dealing with this is to agree. Yes, Hitler had to be stopped. Then I pause and say, snow fell in Russia on September 12th. This gets me a blank stare and the question, so what? I am then able to politely go into the explanation that three months before Pearl Harbor, the German army had already fallen into the **black hole** called Russia. This gave the USG three months to veer away from the oncoming collision with Japan. Why didn't the USG swerve? Stay tuned.

18

Events Leading to Pearl Harbor

Dear Chris,

In 1941, polls showed that more than 80 percent of the American people wanted to stay out of the war. Nevertheless, under the deadly idea of global protection[94] for U.S. merchant ships, FDR sent warships to escort cargo ships across the Atlantic to supply England with war goods.

On October 16, 1941, a German torpedo hit the U.S. destroyer *Kearny.*

On October 31st, the destroyer *Rueben James* was torpedoed, and 100 American sailors died. This was the first case of a U.S. warship being sunk in the war.

So FDR was clearly in the war before the attack on Pearl Harbor, which happened on December 7th.

Yet America's full entry into the war came in the Pacific, not the Atlantic. Why? Here's the story.

As I explained in an earlier letter, there was nothing new or special about the World Wars except the amount of the killing. These were just two more cases of the governments of the Old World doing what they have been doing for centuries: making war, building empires, and killing, killing, killing — trying to revive the glory of the Roman Empire.

---

[94] The deadly idea of Global Protection was explained in Chapter 15 of Richard J. Maybury's book WORLD WAR I: THE REST OF THE STORY AND HOW IT AFFECTS YOU TODAY, published by Bluestocking Press, web site: www.BluestockingPress.com.

Washington's Pacific Bases in 1940

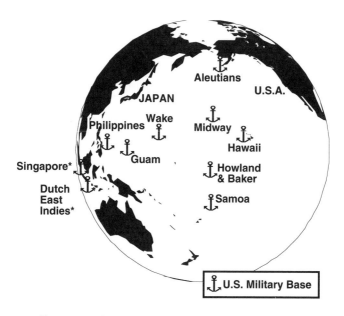

For more than 300 years, the British, Dutch, and other Europeans had been invading the Pacific and Orient, killing and conquering the people who lived there.

Tokyo planned to eject the Europeans and supplant the European Empires with a Japanese Empire in which the Japanese would do the killing and conquering.

Washington sided with the Europeans and for decades had been establishing bases challenging Tokyo's domination.

---

*The bases in Singapore and the Dutch East Indies (Indonesia) were British and Dutch. President Roosevelt had requested and received permission to station U.S. warships there.

In the Pacific and Orient, Tokyo and Washington D.C. were competitors. In 1741, Russians had "discovered" the Aleutian Islands and Alaska, which means they had begun taking them and killing the people who lived there. In 1867, the USG bought Alaska and the Aleutians from Moscow. This gave the USG a military foothold in the North Pacific.

In my previous set of letters about World War I[95] we saw how the USG got the Philippines.

The USG also took islands in Samoa and the Hawaiian Islands. By 1941, it had added the islands of Baker, Howland, Midway, Guam, and Wake.

Tokyo had been concentrating mostly on Manchuria and China.

For centuries, inhabitants of the Orient had been trying to fight off the Europeans who had come to conquer them, and there was strong feeling in the Orient that all Westerners should be thrown out. As the chief naval power in the Orient, the government in Tokyo came to see itself as the policeman who would do this and who would then take control of the Orient. Invasions of Manchuria and China were the beginning of this plan.

For decades, the governments of France, Italy, Germany, Austria-Hungary, Russia, the U.S., and Britain — the Usual Suspects — had all kept armed navy ships operating in and around China. The excellent movie SAND PEBBLES, starring Steve McQueen gives a picture of what these navy ships had been sent into. I recommend the movie and, as a follow-up, the History Channel's "History vs. Hollywood: Sand Pebbles."

---

[95] See Chapter 19 "The Splendid Little War" in Richard J. Maybury's book WORLD WAR I: THE REST OF THE STORY AND HOW IT AFFECTS YOU TODAY, published by Bluestocking Press, web site: www.BluestockingPress.com.

In 1937, a group of U.S. Navy ships led by the gunboat *Panay* was escorting merchant ships on the Yangtze River in China. This was a war zone. Chris, remember the two deadly ideas, global protection and interests?[96] They were why the *Panay* group was in China escorting these merchant ships.

On December 12, 1937, Japanese planes attacked the group, sinking the *Panay* and three oil supply vessels, and killing three people.[97] In August 1937, Japanese planes also attacked the British ambassador's car.[98]

Thus, by the end of 1937, Tokyo's intentions toward the West were clear: get out and stay out, the East is ours.

Again, not much new here, the governments of the Old World had been behaving this way, killing and conquering, for thousands of years.

What was new was the player that had recently entered the game of empire — the USG — and the USG controlled the mightiest industrial nation the world had ever seen. The Japanese already had their hands full to their west, in China; and now the USG was coming at them from the other direction. The Japanese were sandwiched and were about to be up to their necks in alligators.

Chris, although it was not recognized at the time, the *Panay* incident was America's entry into World War II. Notice that it happened two years after the Neutrality Act in which

---

[96] Global Protection and Interests are explained in Chapters 15 and 16 of Richard J. Maybury's book WORLD WAR I: THE REST OF THE STORY AND HOW IT AFFECTS YOU TODAY, published by Bluestocking Press, web site: www.BluestockingPress.com.

[97] DICTIONARY OF AMERICAN HISTORY by Michael Martin and Leonard Gelber, Dorset Press, NY 1978, p.477.

[98] WORLD WAR II DAY BY DAY, by Donald Sommerville, Dorset Press, 1989, p.13.

Congress had forbidden the President to use the U.S. armed forces to protect people who had taken the risk of entering a war zone.

The *Panay* incident would not be FDR's last incursion in the Orient. He had violated the Neutrality Act and gotten away with it. A precedent.

Uncle Eric

19

Hiding Facts about the Brawl

Dear Chris,

Thanks for your letter. You asked why I focus so sharply on the USG's role in the World Wars?

Suppose you came upon two or three-dozen adolescent boys brawling. Also suppose that in the center of this seething mass of bodies and flying fists you saw the heavyweight boxing champion of the world. The champion was throwing punches, crushing one opponent after another.

Where would your attention go? Who would you suspect as the most important player? Who would you see as the person least likely to have been hit by an unprovoked attack?

America has long been the undisputed industrial giant of the world, vastly more powerful in both economic and military terms than any other nation. To my mind, the only sane people who would attack the United States are those who feel they have no other choice.

Even a rabbit will fight if cornered.

Chris, in documentaries about World War II, we are usually shown a map of the Axis spreading across Europe. The picture is focused tightly on Europe, showing little of the rest of the world.

Europe is small, only 6.6% of earth's land surface. The maps usually show the Axis controlling about half, which would be 3.3%.

The British, an Ally, had already conquered 22% of the earth's land surface, and the Russians, another Ally, 16%.

In India alone, areas conquered by the British had a population of 257 million, which was more than all the lands conquered by Hitler when the Third Reich was at its peak.[99] Russia's Kazakhstan had less population than Hitler's Empire, but was much larger territory.

The British had been so powerful for so long, and well protected by the moat called the English Channel, that their island had not been invaded since the Norman Conquest almost nine centuries earlier.

And, in both World Wars, mighty London and Moscow were backed by the even mightier USG.

This should give you a taste of how distorted our view of the World Wars has been. The Axis was a pip-squeak compared to the Allies, and Axis rulers knew it. They could look at a globe as easily as you or I can. Why did they get into the war?

Our view has also been distorted by the hiding of facts. Much about America's entry into World War II was known in the 1940s, but was suppressed by the desire to see the war in terms of a Hollywood movie — good guys against bad guys. Anything that did not fit neatly into this good guy versus bad guy model was forgotten.

Not until formerly secret documents were revealed under the 1966 Freedom of Information Act did the evidence become so overwhelming that it began to pry open the eyes of those who had previously chosen not to see. I was one of those and was shocked and embarrassed when I began to understand how much I had swallowed.

Soon you and I will begin to look at these little-known facts.

Uncle Eric

---

[99] ECONOMIC GEOGRAPHY, by Whitbeck and Finch, McGraw-Hill, New York, 1941, p.619-621.

20

The Great World War II Myth

Dear Chris,

Here is a summary of the story generally accepted by Americans for how the USG got into World War II.

- Bad men rose to power in Germany, Italy, and Japan (the chief Axis powers) with the intention of taking over the world by force.

- The rulers of Britain, France, the Soviet Union, and America (the chief Allied powers) had no such intention. They believed in liberty and justice for all.

- The most evil, dangerous person in history was Adolph Hitler.

- The Allies delayed intervention until it was too late to nip the problem in the bud.

- The Allies were outgunned by the Axis, and by the fall of 1941, they were losing.

- The U.S. entered the war on December 7, 1941, with the Japanese attack on Pearl Harbor. This was a tragedy, but in the long run it was for the best because the U.S. saved the world.

- Victory was a near thing. The good rulers in Britain, France, and the Soviet Union had little chance of beating the bad rulers in Germany, Italy, and Japan without the help of America.

- If the U.S. had not saved the day, our world would now be in the grip of fascism and we would all be slaves. Everyone in the U.S. would be forced to speak German, Italian, or Japanese.

- The lesson of World War II is that America must intervene, early and often, in disputes in every corner of the world to keep these conflicts from becoming a global bloodbath like that of the 1940s. Also, America must intervene to keep another Hitler from coming to power.

Summarizing the view taught to most Americans, World War II was a battle of good versus evil, and good triumphed only by the skin of its teeth. To prevent another such catastrophe in which we might not be so lucky, the U.S. must have military forces that are global police officers, ready to go to any corner of the globe to fight evil.

Chris, now that you know some of the rest of the story, I think you can already see that most of this official story is, to say it politely, not supported by the facts.

In my next letter, we will get into one of the least known parts of the real story.

Uncle Eric

President Franklin D. Roosevelt's Pearl Harbor Speech December 8, 1941

To the Congress of the United States:

Yesterday, Dec. 7, 1941 — a date which will live in infamy — the United States of America was suddenly and deliberately attacked by naval and air forces of the Empire of Japan.

The United States was at peace with that nation and, at the solicitation of Japan, was still in conversation with the government and its emperor looking toward the maintenance of peace in the Pacific.

Indeed, one hour after Japanese air squadrons had commenced bombing in Oahu, the Japanese ambassador to the United States and his colleagues delivered to the Secretary of State a formal reply to a recent American message. While this reply stated that it seemed useless to continue the existing diplomatic negotiations, it contained no threat or hint of war or armed attack.

It will be recorded that the distance of Hawaii from Japan makes it obvious that the attack was deliberately planned many days or even weeks ago. During the intervening time, the Japanese government has deliberately sought to deceive the United States by false statements and expressions of hope for continued peace.

The attack yesterday on the Hawaiian Islands has caused severe damage to American naval and military forces. Very many American lives have been lost. In addition, American ships have been reported torpedoed on the high seas between San Francisco and Honolulu.

Yesterday, the Japanese government also launched an attack against Malaya.

Last night, Japanese forces attacked Hong Kong.

Last night, Japanese forces attacked Guam.

Last night, Japanese forces attacked the Philippine Islands.

Last night, the Japanese attacked Wake Island.

This morning, the Japanese attacked Midway Island.

Japan has, therefore, undertaken a surprise offensive extending throughout the Pacific area. The facts of yesterday speak for themselves. The people of the United States have already formed their opinions and well understand the implications to the very life and safety of our nation.

As Commander in Chief of the Army and Navy, I have directed that all measures be taken for our defense.

Always will we remember the character of the onslaught against us.

No matter how long it may take us to overcome this premeditated invasion, the American people in their righteous might, will win through to absolute victory.

I believe I interpret the will of the Congress and of the people when I assert that we will not only defend ourselves to the uttermost, but will make very certain that this form of treachery shall never endanger us again.

Hostilities exist. There is no blinking at the fact that our people, our territory and our interests are in grave danger.

With confidence in our armed forces — with the unbounding determination of our people — we will gain the inevitable triumph — so help us God.

I ask that the Congress declare that since the unprovoked and dastardly attack by Japan on Sunday, Dec. 7, a state of war has existed between the United States and the Japanese Empire.

End

21

A Secret Agreement

Dear Chris,

At 7:55 am on December 7, 1941, the Japanese navy attacked U.S. forces in the Pacific. The main thrust of the attack was at Pearl Harbor in Hawaii, and secondary attacks occurred in the Philippines, Wake Island, Midway Island, and elsewhere.

At Pearl Harbor, five battleships, three cruisers, and three destroyers were sunk, and other ships damaged; 188 aircraft were destroyed on the ground; 2,403 American soldiers, sailors and civilians were killed, and 1,178 wounded.

Today in Hawaii you can visit the Battleship *Arizona* Memorial and see the *Arizona* just beneath the surface. Inside the ship are the bodies of hundreds of sailors. Nearly 90% of the *Arizona's* crew were killed when the ship exploded.

In the final paragraph of his December 8th speech asking for a declaration of war, President Roosevelt said this attack was unprovoked.

Was it? In this and my next few letters we will look at the evidence.

We begin with the fact that four months before the attack, on August 9, 1941, British Prime Minister Winston Churchill on the battleship *Prince of Wales,* and President Roosevelt on the cruiser *Augusta,* met in the Atlantic off the coast of Newfoundland. This was the so-called Atlantic Charter Conference.

The Atlantic Charter was a loosely worded agreement for the governments of Britain and the U.S. to work together toward peace, economic advancement, freedom of travel, and "general security." It sounded good.

Chris, evidence is strong that at this meeting there was another agreement between Churchill and Roosevelt that was secret, and this agreement was not so harmless.

The chief intelligence officer at Pearl Harbor was Commander Edwin T. Layton. In Layton's 1985 book AND I WAS THERE, he gives the evidence of this secret agreement.

One item Layton points to is the minutes of the Joint Army-Navy Board meetings after the Atlantic Charter Conference. These show how FDR "put a de facto Anglo-American alliance against Japan into effect by making preparations to commit our forces to a war even if it was British rather than our territory that the Japanese struck," says Layton. "The records now available confirm that the board members were making their plans on the assumption that America would be at war if Japan attacked British, but not United States, territory."[100]

Highly important is the fact that in making this secret agreement to go to war on the side of Britain, President Roosevelt was violating the Constitution. Congress did not approve the agreement, as the Constitution requires; it was hidden.

Also, of course, it violated the Neutrality Act.

Layton reports that on November 24, 1941, a letter from the Chief of Naval Operations to Admiral Kimmel contained a copy of a memo from Admiral Stark and General Marshall to President Roosevelt. The memo referred to an agreement

---

[100] AND I WAS THERE, by Edwin T. Layton, published by William Morrow, NY, 1985, First Quill Edition, p.131-137.

that the U.S. would not only go to war if Japan attacked British forces, but would also go to war if Japan attacked Siam (Thailand), Dutch territories, or the Malay Peninsula.[101] This, too, violated the Constitution; Congress had not voted on it.

On December 5, 1941, Admiral Hart in the Philippines was shocked to see a message sent from London to the British commander in Malaya. This message referred to guarantees of American support if Japan attacked the Dutch East Indies or Isthmus of Kra on the Malay Peninsula or any other part of Siam.[102]

The astounded Hart fired off a message to the Navy Department: "Learn from Singapore we have assured British armed support under three or four eventualities. Have received no corresponding instructions from you."[103]

In other words, the evidence is overwhelming that President Roosevelt had made an illegal secret agreement to go to war and did not even tell the commanders who were supposed to prepare their troops and equipment to fight the war, much less Congress.

Presidents have been impeached for less.

Chris, in the election campaign of 1940, Roosevelt had promised the American people, "Your boys are not going to be sent into any foreign wars."[104] This was not the first time a president had lied — and certainly not the last.

The lie is especially interesting because the year before, on September 11, 1939, Roosevelt had written to Britain's Winston Churchill suggesting they should work together

---

[101] AND I WAS THERE, by Edwin T. Layton, p.186.

[102] AND I WAS THERE, by Edwin T. Layton, p.259.

[103] AND I WAS THERE, by Edwin T. Layton, p.259.

[104] DAY OF DECEIT, by Robert B. Stinnett, The Free Press (Simon & Schuster), NY, 2000, p.17.

through a secret system of communication. Churchill wrote back saying, "I am half American and the natural person to work with you. It is evident that we see eye to eye. Were I to become Prime Minister of Britain we could control the world."[105]

Fascinating, Chris, be sure to remember that phrase, "we could control the world." I will come back to it later. It should not be a surprising phrase, controlling the world is what the rulers of Britain had been after for centuries. They had already conquered and controlled 22% of it.

What did Churchill mean by "the natural person to work with you?" We are not mind readers, but we do know Churchill and Roosevelt were distant cousins and good friends.[106] In fact, Churchill and Roosevelt had the closest personal and official relationship that has ever existed between a U.S. President and the head of another government; they met often and were in contact via mail and telegram almost daily.[107]

Uncle Eric

---

[105] THE FINAL STORY OF PEARL HARBOR, by Harry Elmer Barnes, published by Left and Right, NY, 1968, p.15.

[106] Seventh cousins once removed.

[107] FRANKLIN D. ROOSEVELT AND THE WORLD CRISIS, 1937-1945, edited by Warren F. Kimball of Rutgers University, D.C. Heath & Co., Lexington, Mass. 1973, p.177.

World War II Warship Types

In case you are not familiar with World War II warship types, they are listed here in order of size. A fully loaded Iowa class battleship weighed 52,000 tons. A fully loaded PT boat weighed 58 tons.

Battleship

Aircraft carrier

Battle cruiser

Heavy cruiser

Light cruiser

Destroyer

Frigate

Corvette/Cutter

PT boat

22

Why Did The Japanese Attack?

Dear Chris,

For years I have asked members of the World War II generation (people who were adults in 1941), *why* did the Japanese attack Pearl Harbor?

Rarely do I meet anyone who has thought about it. They just seem to assume that the Japanese were evil, and this is what evil people do.

Chris, the real story is more complicated, but not widely known. Much of the information was kept secret for decades and was not revealed until historians began digging it out, one small scrap at a time, with the help of the Freedom of Information Act passed in 1966.

The reason the Japanese attacked has always been fascinating to me because of the mind-boggling difference between the two countries. Here are some of the details.

There is an old saying about war: Amateurs talk about strategy while professionals talk about logistics. Logistics is the ability to supply bullets and beans to the troops.

Modern war is mostly about production — the ability to produce more and better weapons and equipment than the enemy — and transport it to the battlefield. Even the best warriors can be wiped out if good factories do not supply them.

Like today, America in 1941 was an industrial giant with a huge population and vast natural resources. But unlike today,

Japan in 1941 was an island nation of farmers and fishermen with no large supplies of natural resources except fish, water, and timber.

Japan had less than 4% of the world's manufacturing capacity; America had 29%.[108]

All this was known in 1941, any economist could verify it. Whitbeck and Finch published it in the 1941 McGraw-Hill reference book ECONOMIC GEOGRAPHY.

In 1941, America produced more steel, aluminum, oil, and motor vehicles than all other major nations combined.[109] This meant America could make more weapons than all the others together, and the Japanese knew this. Their strategists had calculated that America's war potential was at least seven hundred percent greater than that of Japan.[110]

Incidentally, Chris, Germany, too, was a small country poor in natural resources. A 1945 LIFE magazine article showed Germany's dependence on imported materials. At the beginning of the war in 1939, reports the magazine, Germany had to import annually 100% (17,000 tons) of its nickel ore, 89% (18,469,000 tons) of its of iron ore, 55% (229,000 tons) of its manganese, 94% (981,000 tons) of its bauxite, 59% (99,000 tons) of its lead ore, 77% (195,000 tons) of its copper, 100% (9,000 tons) of its tin, 100% (123,000 tons) of its chrome ore, 100% (688 tons) of its mercury, and 43% (120,000 tons) of its zinc ore, plus nearly all its oil.[111]

---

[108] A REPUBLIC NOT AN EMPIRE by Patrick Buchanan, Regnery Publishing, Washington, 1999, p.291.

[109] WHY THE ALLIES WON, by Richard Overy, W. W. Norton & Co., NY, 1995, p.190.

[110] NO CLEAR AND PRESENT DANGER, by Bruce M. Russett, Westview Press, Boulder, CO 1977, p.54.

[111] "The Control of Germany," by James Bryant Conant (President of Harvard University), LIFE magazine, April 2, 1945, p.65.

Once the Germans began attacking other countries, these supplies were reduced or cut off entirely.

If I had to make a list of the major countries that were not suited to wage war, Germany and Japan would have been tied neck-and-neck for first place.

Granted, Chris, Japan's navy was larger than America's Pacific fleet, and the Japanese had 11 aircraft carriers to America's total of 7. But, because of Japan's limited amount of industry, its fleet had taken 20 years to create.[112] Japan's ships could not be mass-produced, and sunken ships could not be easily replaced.[113]

Within four years America would have 100 aircraft carriers.[114] Total carriers produced by America during the 44 months of the war were an astounding 146, or three per month.[115] Henry J. Kaiser's shipyards turned out 50 of them in 365 days.[116, 117] (As I write this today, the U.S. has twelve

---

[112] JANE'S FIGHTING SHIPS OF WORLD WAR II, Crescent, NY, 1989, p.179-204.

[113] A REPUBLIC NOT AN EMPIRE by Patrick Buchanan, Regnery Publishing, Washington, 1999, p.292.

[114] DAY OF DECEIT, by Robert B. Stinnett, The Free Press (Simon & Schuster), NY, 2000, p.122.

[115] MOBILIZING U.S. INDUSTRY DURING WORLD WAR II, by Alan Gropman, Institute for National Strategic Studies, National Defense University, Washington, DC, 1996, p.96.

[116] "Modern Marvels — Liberty Ships," History Channel documentary.

[117] These were not the supercarriers of today. Kaiser's fifty were "escort" carriers of about 10,000 tons each. The largest of the World War II carriers, the Midway class, was 55,000 tons fully loaded, a bit more than half the size of today's Nimitz class. It carried 137 planes, which was a lot more than today's carriers because planes now are larger. But for their time, the World War II carriers were the masters of the sea. The Essex class carriers were the main "fleet" carriers, the backbone of the navy. At 33,000 tons fully loaded, an Essex carrier had a crew of 2,900 and 82 aircraft; 24 Essex carriers were built.

carriers and is considered the world's most powerful naval force.)

Again, the Japanese knew America had this much industry, but they attacked anyhow. Why?

Read on.

Perhaps the two statistics that most clearly show the difference between Japan and America are those for motorized vehicles — cars and trucks — produced for civilians before the war. In America there were 200 motorized vehicles per thousand people. In Japan there was less than one vehicle per thousand.[118]

This was in an age in which war had become mechanized. The side with the ability to move quickly and transport the most supplies to the battlefield would be the winner. Americans could drive. Japanese had to walk and carry their supplies on their backs.

Try it yourself. In one hour, how much can you transport on your back and how far? How much and how far can you transport in your parents' car?

I am sure it is a difference of at least 100 to 1.

Chris, are you beginning to see what I meant in an earlier letter when I said that if you look at the war the way an economist would, you see a lot that others miss?

At any given moment in the Pacific Theater of the war, for every American soldier, there were four tons of supplies. For every Japanese there were two pounds.[119]

At the height of the war, Americans were producing a Jeep every 90 seconds.[120]

---

[118] WHY THE ALLIES WON, by Richard Overy, W. W. Norton & Co., NY, 1995, p.224.

[119] WHY THE ALLIES WON, by Richard Overy, p.210.

[120] "Does Anyone Care...," by Bob Green, CHICAGO TRIBUNE, January 14, 2001, p.2.

They produced a 10,000-ton cargo ship every 12 hours.[121] I previously wrote about the Higgins boat, the landing craft built by the Higgins Boat Company. At the beginning of the war, the Higgins Company had 50 employees. After, it had 20,000, and they built 21,000 Higgins boats.[122]

Again, any economist, American or Japanese, could have seen this coming. America was a land of giant industrial cities while Japan was a land of farms and fishing villages.

In short, Japan was a prizefighter with one solid punch and a glass jaw.

And the Japanese knew it.

The commander of the Pearl Harbor attack force, Admiral Yamamoto, was right when he said, "I fear we have awakened a sleeping giant and filled him with a terrible resolve." Yamamoto had visited America and was in awe of America's industry. He knew that the American way of fighting a war was (still is) to hit the enemy with a deluge of ships, planes, tanks, and artillery — to overwhelm them with machinery. Yamamoto thought he could hold the U.S. off for only about six months, and he tried desperately to persuade Japan's rulers not to attack.[123]

His six-month prediction was perfectly on target. In six months, at the Battle of the Coral Sea on May 8, 1942, the Japanese advance would be stopped. Less than a month after that, at the Battle of Midway, the Japanese would be decimated and would never recover.

---

[121] LIBERTY SHIPS, by John Gorley Bunker, Ayer Company, Salem, New Hampshire, 1991, p.3 to 17. During the course of the war, 2,751 Liberty ships were built.

[122] Story about the Higgins boat on CBS Sunday Morning, June 4, 2000.

[123] AND I WAS THERE by Rear Admiral Edwin T. Layton, William Morrow, NY, 1985, p.72.

The loss rate for Japanese aircraft in the first 18 months of the war was 96%.[124]

The Japanese might handle the Chinese, who were also very primitive, but handling the U.S. was a whole different matter. Your high school football team looks tough when they go up against another high school team, but how would they do against the Green Bay Packers?

Again, in 1941, America produced more steel, aluminum, oil, and motor vehicles than all other major nations combined,[125] and the Japanese knew it.

The size of Montana, Japan is a land of volcanic islands; it has almost no oil, iron, or other resources necessary for a modern industrial economy except a small amount of coal. For these necessities the Japanese must rely on imports from other nations.

In 1941 their chief supplier was America.[126]

Chris, it is very important to remember that the Japanese economy and military forces were heavily dependent on imported oil.

The American assumption seems to be that these farmers and fishermen woke up one morning and said, here's a good idea, let's attack the most powerful nation the world has ever seen, the nation we most rely on for the resources and products we must have.

Does this sound reasonable? Were the Japanese really this stupid?

Not likely.

---

[124] WHY THE ALLIES WON, by Richard Overy, W. W. Norton & Co., NY, 1995, p.223.

[125] WHY THE ALLIES WON, by Richard Overy, p.190.

[126] ECONOMIC GEOGRAPHY by R.H. Whitbeck & V.C. Finch, McGraw-Hill, NY, 1941, p.545-558.

So why did they do it?

Because they had little choice.

Chris, in my next letter I will begin explaining why the Japanese attacked.

By the way, nothing I write is meant to imply that Japanese rulers were innocent or that they were nice people; they certainly were not. They were brutal. All the major governments of the Old World were brutal and always had been. The rulers of Japan were quite typical of that breed.

But none of the others would have dreamed of attacking the U.S. Why did the Japanese?

Even a rabbit will fight if cornered.

More in my next letter.

Uncle Eric

23

Pearl Harbor
FDR's Deceit

Dear Chris,

One of the U.S. Government's top experts on Japan was Lieutenant Commander Arthur H. McCollum. In early 1940, McCollum was placed in charge of all intelligence information about Japan that was routed to President Roosevelt.

McCollum believed the U.S. should get into the war to help Britain defeat Germany.[127] But a Gallup Poll showed 88% of Americans opposed U.S. involvement in the war.[128]

McCollum, a navy officer, believed something should be done to change the minds of the American people, and the way to do this was to goad the Japanese into attacking U.S. Navy ships.[129]

We have no way of knowing how much McCollum talked with Roosevelt or how early they began planning to provoke a Japanese attack. We do know that in October 1940, McCollum circulated a memo containing this eight-point plan:[130]

---

[127] DAY OF DECEIT, by Robert B. Stinnett, The Free Press (Simon & Schuster), NY, 2000, p.261-267.

[128] DAY OF DECEIT, by Robert B. Stinnett, p.17.

[129] DAY OF DECEIT, by Robert B. Stinnett, p.8.

[130] DAY OF DECEIT, by Robert B. Stinnett, p.8.

1. Get permission from the British to put U.S. ships in Britain's Pacific bases, especially Singapore (near the oil fields of the Dutch East Indies, which are now called Indonesia).

2. Get permission from the Dutch to put U.S. ships in the Dutch East Indies.

3. Give all possible aid to the Chinese government, led by Chiang Kai-Shek, against Japan.

4. Send heavy cruisers to the Orient.

5. Send submarines to the Orient.

6. Move the U.S. fleet from San Diego to Hawaii (a location difficult to defend due to being closer to Japan and surrounded 360 degrees by ocean).

7. Ask the Dutch to cut off supplies of oil to Japan.

8. Cut off U.S. and British supplies of oil and all other supplies to Japan.

McCollum's 1940 memo ends with his hope that by these eight steps "Japan could be led to commit an overt act of war."[131]

In short, McCollum's plan was to poke the Japanese with sharp sticks while at the same time starving them so that they

---

[131] DAY OF DECEIT, by Robert B. Stinnett, The Free Press (Simon & Schuster), NY, 2000, p.8.

would feel forced to go out and steal the oil and other resources they needed. To steal these supplies, they would first need to chase the U.S. Navy from the Pacific because the U.S. Navy was between them and the oil of the Dutch East Indies.

The USG still keeps secret much of its archive relating to World War II, so no one has been able to find ironclad evidence that President Roosevelt was intentionally following McCollum's 8-step plan. In his office, Roosevelt had a recording machine wired to automatically record all conversations, but the machine was disconnected a few weeks after McCollum's memo was circulated.[132]

We do know that Secretary of War Stimson wrote in his diary that he favored the plan.[133] And we know the steps President Roosevelt took between the time McCollum came to work for him and December 7, 1941. On the pages that follow, Chris, I've listed the steps for you, along with other relevant events. Except as footnoted, these were taken from WORLD WAR II DAY BY DAY, by Donald Sommerville,[134] an excellent reference. I recommend it.

Chris, these are in chronological order. I have asterisked each event that fulfills a step in McCollum's plan and included the number of the step to which it corresponds. (The steps were not taken in the same order as listed in the plan, and some were taken before the memo was circulated.)

The chronological order is very important. Many of these events have been written about extensively, but as far as I know, no one has ever before listed them in sequence so that the reader can clearly see the development.

---

[132] DAY OF DECEIT, by Robert B. Stinnett, p.26.

[133] DAY OF DECEIT, by Robert B. Stinnett, p.9.

[134] WORLD WAR II DAY BY DAY, by Donald Sommerville, Dorset Press, 1989, ISBN 0-88029-333-0

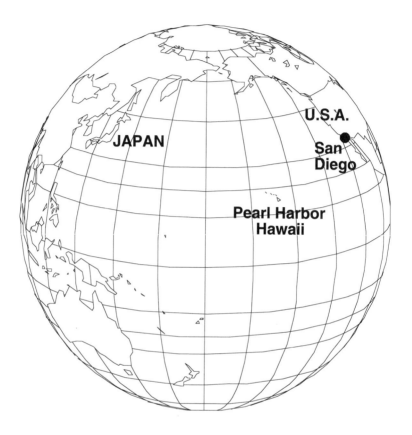

In April 1940, President Roosevelt began moving the U.S. Pacific Fleet from the safety of San Diego to Pearl Harbor.

The fleet's commander, Admiral Richardson, protested to Roosevelt and was fired.

San Diego was 1,200 miles farther from Japan than Pearl Harbor was and could be attacked only from the west.

Pearl Harbor could be attacked from any direction, and the new commander, Admiral Kimmel, was not given enough long-range search planes to cover the whole area.

* **Apr 1940 (Step 6)**. President Roosevelt (FDR) begins moving the Pacific fleet from San Diego to Pearl Harbor. The fleet's commander, Admiral Richardson, protests that Pearl Harbor is too exposed and vulnerable to attack; he begins a nine-month campaign to get the fleet moved back to the safety of San Diego.[135]

* **25 Jul 1940 (Step 8)**. FDR reduces the supply of oil and metals to Japan.

Sept 1940. FDR gives 50 destroyers to Britain for use against Germany.

* **26 Sept 1940 (Step 8)**. FDR cuts off the supply of iron to Japan.

Oct 1940. Admiral Richardson flies to Washington D.C. to protest to FDR again. He wants the fleet back in San Diego where it is safe. Richardson tells FDR he strongly disagrees with sacrificing navy ships to get into a war with Japan.[136]

* **4 Oct 1940 (Step 1)**. Churchill gives permission to put U.S. warships in Singapore,[137] which is near the oil fields of the Dutch East Indies (Indonesia).

[135] AND I WAS THERE by Rear Admiral Edwin T. Layton, William Morrow, NY, 1985, p.52-55 and DAY OF DECEIT, by Robert B. Stinnett, The Free Press (Simon & Schuster), NY, 2000, p.10-17.

[136] DAY OF DECEIT, by Robert B. Stinnett, The Free Press (Simon & Schuster), NY, 2000, p.10-11.

[137] DAY OF DECEIT, by Robert B. Stinnett, p.10.

31 Oct 1940. Battle of Britain has ended, British have won; threat of German invasion evaporates.

* 13 Nov 1940 (Steps 2 & 7). Under pressure from FDR, the Dutch reduce their supply of oil to Japan. They also give permission to base U.S. warships in the Dutch East Indies (Indonesia).[138]

17 Dec 1940. FDR announces his intended new policy of Lend-Lease in which he will side with Britain against Germany. This is the final nail in the coffin of America's neutrality. FDR is not stopped, so the Neutrality Act is now dead. The U.S. is allied with Britain.

31 Dec 1940. A succession of trade restrictions has halted U.S. shipments of aviation fuel, metals, machinery, and machine tools to Japan.[139]

* 1 Jan 41 (Step 5). Twenty-four U.S submarines have been sent to the Orient.[140]

24 Jan 1941. Navy Secretary Frank Knox declares he is in agreement with Admiral Richardson; Pearl Harbor is dangerous. Knox cites Pearl Harbor's vulnerability to air bombing attack, air torpedo attack, sabotage, submarine attack, and bombardment by naval gunfire.[141]

---

[138] DAY OF DECEIT, by Robert B. Stinnett, p.39,40.

[139] THE FINAL SECRET OF PEARL HARBOR, by Admiral Robert A. Theobald, Devin-Adair, NY 1954, p.12.

[140] DAY OF DECEIT, by Robert B. Stinnett, p.28,29.

[141] DAY OF DECEIT, by Robert B. Stinnett, p.30.

Chris, here I should interrupt to point out that Navy Secretary Frank Knox was right, as was Admiral Richardson, which you can see for yourself if you ever visit Honolulu. Your plane will probably fly over Pearl Harbor before it lands. Take a close look. The harbor is small and easily approached by carrier-based planes from any direction. Imagine being a Japanese pilot; it was like shooting fish in a barrel. In protesting FDR's order to move the fleet to Hawaii, Admiral Richardson called Pearl Harbor "a damned mouse trap" for the American Navy.[142]

27 Jan to 29 Mar 1941. In secret talks between British and American officials in Washington D.C., the two governments agree that if the U.S. goes to war with Japan, the top U.S. priority will be to help Britain defeat Germany first.[143]

1 Feb 1941. FDR will no longer tolerate Admiral Richardson's protests. He fires Richardson, ending Richardson's career, and replaces him with Admiral Kimmel.[144]

1 Mar 1941. Harry Hopkins, FDR's special envoy to Winston Churchill, tells Churchill, "The President is determined that we shall win the war together. Make no mistake about it. He has sent me here to tell you

---

[142] THE FINAL STORY OF PEARL HARBOR, Harry Elmer Barnes, Left and Right, Vol. IV, 1968, p.23.

[143] ALMANAC OF AMERICA'S WARS, edited by John S. Bowman, Mallard Press, NY no copyright, p.116.

[144] DAY OF DECEIT, by Robert B. Stinnett, The Free Press (Simon & Schuster), NY, 2000, p.11.

that at all costs and by all means he will carry you
through, no matter what happens to him — there is
nothing he will not do so far as he has human
power."[145]

* 11 Mar 1941 (Step 3). Congress passes FDR's
"Lend-Lease Act," which gives money and other
resources to the governments of Britain and China to
fight the Japanese. (Three months later, U.S. aid will
go to Stalin and anyone else who will fight Japan or
Germany.)

* 15 Mar 1941 (Step 4). FDR begins sending cruisers
and destroyers into Japanese home waters. His orders
to do this are secret, so the American public does not
know. But the Japanese are fully aware that U.S.
warships are in their territory. One location is the
Bungo Strait between two Japanese home islands.
This would be equivalent to Japan sending warships
into Chesapeake Bay or Puget Sound.[146]

26 May 1941. The Japanese economy is shaken by
FDR's embargoes. Admiral Kimmel warns FDR that
U.S. Pacific forces are under-gunned, vulnerable to
Japanese attack, and spread too thin to protect troops
at widely scattered bases.[147]

---

[145] THE NEW DEALERS' WAR, by Thomas Fleming, Basic Books, NY,
2001, p.83.

[146] DAY OF DECEIT, by Robert B. Stinnett, The Free Press (Simon &
Schuster), NY, 2000, p.10.

[147] AND I WAS THERE by Rear Admiral Edwin T. Layton, William
Morrow, NY, 1985, p 112.

Bungo Strait

March 1941, President Roosevelt secretly ordered U.S. warships to begin sailing 6,000 miles across the Pacific to encroach on Japanese home waters, including the Bungo Strait. He called these invasions "Pop Up Cruises" because the Japanese never knew where the U.S. warships would appear. This would be equivalent to Japan sending warships into Chesapeake Bay in Virginia or Puget Sound in Washington State.

31 May 1941. Against enraged protests from Kimmel, FDR has removed from Pearl Harbor and sent to the Atlantic: one aircraft carrier, three battleships, four cruisers, and 18 destroyers. The fighter aircraft and anti-aircraft guns on these ships will be sorely missed. America's Pacific forces are now even weaker and more vulnerable than when Richardson was protesting about the move to Pearl Harbor.

22 Jun 1941. Hitler turns east, invades Russia. This is the beginning of the end for Germany. And if Stalin cannot get help from FDR, the Eastern Front maelstrom[148] promises to demolish Soviet Socialism as well as German Nazism. The Eastern Front is three-quarters of the war.

24 Jun 1941. FDR announces that he has taken sides with Stalin against Hitler and will send aid to Stalin. Churchill made a similar announcement two days earlier.

19 Jul 1941. Admiral Turner, who is the Director of War Plans, warns FDR that the Japanese are bellicose, antagonizing them further will trigger an attack.[149]

* 26 Jul 1941 (Step 8). FDR **freezes**[150] all Japanese assets and reduces Japanese oil supply by 90%.

---

[148] Maelstrom. A violent and dangerous whirlpool. The term can be applied to a dangerous or turbulent state of affairs.

[149] AND I WAS THERE by Rear Admiral Edwin T. Layton, William Morrow, NY, 1985, p.121.

[150] Freeze: to hold assets and prevent the owner from having access to them.

* Aug 1941 (Step 3). FDR has illegally[151] given permission for creation of the Flying Tigers to help Chiang Kai-Shek fight the Japanese in China.[152]

9-12 Aug 1941. Atlantic Conference. FDR tells Churchill he plans to get into the war.[153] No one tells Admiral Kimmel at Pearl Harbor.

11 Sept 1941. FDR tells the nation that the destroyer *Greer* has been attacked by a German submarine, and henceforth U.S. warships have the standing order to "shoot on sight" at any German vessel west of Iceland. He does not reveal that the *Greer* had stalked the submarine for three hours in cooperation with a British patrol plane before the German turned and fired.[154]

9 Oct 1941. The USG intercepts Japanese "bomb plot" message indicating Pearl Harbor is a target for attack by carrier-based planes. No one tells Kimmel.[155]

25 Nov 1941. FDR meets with his war council. Secretary of War Stimson notes in his diary the group's belief that U.S. forces are "likely to be attacked perhaps as soon as next Monday." The President is

[151] This violated the Neutrality Act.

[152] "One Last Combat Victory," by Ralph Vartabedian, LOS ANGELES TIMES, July 6, 1991, p.1.

[153] THE FINAL SECRET OF PEARL HARBOR, by Admiral Robert A. Theobald, Devin-Adair, NY 1954, p.188.

[154] THE NEW DEALERS' WAR, by Thomas Fleming, Basic Books, 2001, p.89.

[155] AND I WAS THERE by Rear Admiral Edwin T. Layton, William Morrow, NY, 1985, p.158-163.

concerned about the problem of "how we should maneuver them into the position of firing the first shot." No one tells Kimmel.[156]

26 Nov 1941. After meeting with Roosevelt in the White House, Admiral Stark and General Marshall radio Kimmel ordering him to send his two remaining carriers and their planes out to sea away from Pearl Harbor. Minutes of the meeting say they intend to reduce fighter strength at Pearl Harbor by half knowing full well that "there will be nothing left at Hawaii until replacements arrive." "Nothing left" is an exaggeration, but not much; Pearl Harbor's defenses against air attack now are greatly weakened. In this same meeting with Roosevelt, Stark and Marshall draft a message telling Kimmel that hostilities may be near, but do not tell him what kind of hostilities or in what part of the Pacific.[157]

1 Dec 1941. In Hong Kong and Singapore, the British declare a state of emergency in preparation for Japanese attack.[158]

4 Dec 1941. The CHICAGO TRIBUNE newspaper reveals "Rainbow Five," the top-secret war plan drawn up at FDR's order. Rainbow Five calls for the creation of a 10-million-man army, including an **expeditionary** [159]

---

[156] AND I WAS THERE by Rear Admiral Edwin T. Layton, William Morrow, NY, 1985, p.195.

[157] AND I WAS THERE by Rear Admiral Edwin T. Layton, p. 195-211.

[158] DAYS OF INFAMY, by Michael Coffey, Hyperion, NY, 1999, p.135.

[159] Expeditionary force: a military force whose job is not defensive but offensive, to leave the country and fight abroad.

force of five million to invade Europe in 1943 on the side of Moscow and London.[160]

6 Dec 1941. General Hap Arnold lands in Sacramento, California, to warn the air base that war with Japan is imminent.[161] President Roosevelt reads an intercepted Japanese message and tells his assistant Harry Hopkins, "This means war."[162] No one tells Kimmel.

7 Dec 1941. The Japanese attack. They begin their campaign against Americans in Hawaii, Wake, Midway, Guam, Corregidor, and in June 1942, the Aleutians. Terrible U.S. losses. The main Japanese objective is to steal the oil and other natural resources in the Dutch East Indies. To do this they must chase the U.S. armed forces from the Pacific.

13 Dec 1941. Aircraft carrier Saratoga is racing full speed from West Coast. It will be too little too late. All Far East bases will be overrun. Thousands killed. Tens of thousands taken prisoner. FDR is never officially accused of anything. A hero to the socialist left, he will go down in history as a great President who won World War II.

17 Dec 1941. Admiral Kimmel and General Short relieved of command and blamed for the disaster.

---

[160] THE NEW DEALERS' WAR, by Thomas Fleming, Basic Books, 2001, p.1.

[161] Exhibit at McClellan AFB Air Museum, Sacramento, California.

[162] THE FINAL SECRET OF PEARL HARBOR, by Admiral Robert A. Theobald, Devin-Adair, NY 1954, p.28.

Chris, most of this information has been available for years but, as I said, I have never before seen the events listed in chronological order so that the reader could clearly see what was unfolding.

This is why I said in an earlier letter that knowing the events is important but knowing the sequence is even more important. I think that if you will ask 100 Americans when FDR cut off Japan's supplies of oil and other raw materials, 99 would say sometime *after* the attack on Pearl Harbor. They think the attack was unprovoked because FDR said so.

Was it? Here is the opinion of Captain Russel Grenfell of the British navy in his 1952 book MAIN FLEET TO SINGAPORE:

> No reasonably informed person can now believe that Japan made a villainous, unexpected attack on the United States. An attack was not only fully expected but was actually desired. It is beyond doubt that President Roosevelt wanted to get his country into the war, but for political reasons was most anxious to insure that the first act of hostility came from the other side; for which reason he caused increasing pressure to be put on the Japanese, to a point that no self-respecting nation could endure without resort to arms. Japan was meant by the American President to attack the United States. As Mr. Oliver Lyttelton, then British Minister of Production, said in 1944, "Japan was provoked into attacking America at Pearl Harbor. It is a travesty of history to say that America was forced into war."

Even a rabbit will fight if cornered.

Chris, it is impossible to exaggerate the importance of the fact that snow had fallen in Russia on September 12, 1941.

As of that moment, there could be no reason for America to get into the war. The German army was in deep trouble. In a replay of what had happened to Napoleon's army, the three months of summer had passed and the Germans had failed to take Russia. Now Russia's invincible ally, winter, had pounced.

Even if goading the Japanese into an attack had been necessary before that, it was no longer necessary. FDR's pressure on the Japanese should have been stopped immediately when the first snowflake hit the ground in Russia.

Joseph Rochefort, the highly respected commander of an intelligence office that had been reading Japanese messages and passing them along to the USG prior to the Pearl Harbor attack, said of the Japanese, "We cut off their money, their fuel and trade. We were just tightening the screws on the Japanese. They could see no way of getting out except going to war."[163]

Again, none of this is meant to imply that Japanese rulers were nice guys or innocent victims. They were cutthroats, murderers, whatever you want to call them. But in the Old World they were nothing unusual. Old World rulers have typically been brutal gangsters who regularly commit mass murder. This is the way it has been for thousands of years and still is.

There was no reason to single out the Japanese except for the fact that in 1941 they happened to be the bullies most easy to provoke. They were highly dependent on oil, and Roosevelt had the ability to cut off their oil.

Then he rubbed salt in the wound. After the Japanese oil supply was severed, American oil was sent to Japan's enemy,

---

[163] DAY OF DECEIT, by Robert B. Stinnett, The Free Press (Simon & Schuster), NY, 2000, p.121.

Russia, via Vladivostok. The American tankers passed near the shores of oil-starved Japan.[164]

Why did Roosevelt do it? We will never know for sure. No scrap of evidence linking him directly to the setup of Pearl Harbor Commanders Kimmel and Short has ever been uncovered.

But my guess is that he knew the Germans were in trouble and he wanted into the war before it ended.

After all, Chris, what is the point of spending your life trying to acquire power if, once you have it, you cannot use it on someone?

Military force is the most satisfying use of this power.

Uncle Eric

P.S. Chris, I know it is hard to believe a President would deliberately sacrifice American lives. How do we know Roosevelt was really willing to do this? Journalist and navy World War II veteran Robert B. Stinnett is an expert on the Pearl Harbor attack. Stinnett points out that on September 7, 1940, President Roosevelt "called for sending cruisers into Japanese territory to antagonize the Japanese militarists so they would take over the civilian government. President Roosevelt called them pop-up cruisers. 'I want them popping up here and there, but I don't want to lose five or six cruisers. I don't mind losing one or two.' Well, if you lose one or two cruisers, you're losing 900 men each," writes Stinnett. "That was about 1,800 men he was prepared to lose to put this provocative action in place."[165]

---

[164] FRANKLIN D. ROOSEVELT AND THE WORLD CRISIS, 1937-1945, edited by Warren F. Kimball of Rutgers University, D.C. Heath & Co., Lexington, Mass. 1973, p.87.

[165] Stinnett speech at The Independent Institute Conference Center, May 24, 2000.

May 28, 1941

My dear President:

I, the father of six sons of military age, have been an ardent New Deal Democrat, proud of my party's social interest, proud indeed of my great President . . . In your campaign speeches, I heard you promise several times that you would never send our boys to fight on foreign soil. But last night, I listened attentively to your speech, and I now fear that you have changed your mind. I fear that we are near, very, very near to actual war. But, my dear President, for you to say that you intend to destroy Hitler and all for which he stands; for you to say that we are out to assure all people everywhere freedom of speech, freedom of religious worship, freedom from want, and freedom from fear—that is a big order. If that is what you mean to do, taking the law of averages, I shall have sons buried in the sands of Africa, in the wastes of Siberia, in the blood soaked soils of Europe . . .

—Fred Langenkamp
Tulsa, Oklahoma[166]
from THE PEOPLE AND THE PRESIDENT: AMERICA'S
CONVERSATION WITH FDR
by Lawrence W. Levine and Cornelia R. Levine
Beacon Press

[166] THE PEOPLE AND THE PRESIDENT: AMERICA'S CONVERSATION WITH FDR by Lawrence W. Levine and Cornelia R. Levine, Beacon Press, 2002.

24

The Flying Tigers and B-17 Bombers

Dear Chris,

You may have seen movies about the Flying Tigers in World War II. Created months before the attack on Pearl Harbor to fight the Japanese, their official name was the American Volunteers Group.

Officially these men and their planes were not working for the USG, they were independent volunteers hired and financed by the Chinese government.

Historians have long suspected that Roosevelt secretly created this group.

In other words, historians have long suspected that Roosevelt planned to send U.S. military forces against the Japanese prior to the attack on Pearl Harbor.

In 1991, survivors of the Flying Tigers went to court to get U.S. veteran's benefits. The truth came out. The Flying Tigers were not independent volunteers; they were secretly created and financed by the USG for the purpose of fighting the Japanese.[167]

At least three months before the attack on Pearl Harbor, 112 Flying Tiger pilots arrived at an air base near Toungoo, China, and began preparations to shoot down Japanese aircraft.[168]

---

[167] "One Last Combat Victory," by Ralph Vartabedian, LOS ANGELES TIMES, July 6, 1991, p.1.

[168] "Lt. General Claire Lee Chennault," by Amy Alexander, INVESTORS BUSINESS DAILY, August 27, 2001.

On May 3, 1991, the Pentagon confirmed that the Flying Tigers were working for Roosevelt and granted veterans benefits to them.[169]

Most importantly, in 1941, Japanese rulers knew all about it. Japanese spies had found out about the Flying Tigers and had been watching them train.[170] Also, Japan's rulers knew that in March 1941, Congress had granted FDR permission to send money and equipment to the Chinese under the Lend-Lease Act.

In short, by launching the Flying Tigers, President Roosevelt declared war on the Japanese before the Japanese attacked the U.S. He gave the Japanese the legal right to bomb Pearl Harbor and did not tell either the American people or the commanders at Pearl Harbor.

Another little-known provocation was B-17 bombers in the Pacific. At that time the B-17 Flying Fortress was the toughest, most deadly long-range bomber in the world. It was greatly feared by anyone who had to fight it.

By November 1941, the entire factory production of B-17s was going to the Philippines[171] where their only conceivable targets could be Japanese.

The Japanese knew about this B-17 force in the Philippines and were greatly alarmed, as you can imagine.

And the USG knew they were alarmed. Japan's secret messages about the B-17s were being intercepted and decrypted.[172]

---

[169] "One Last Combat Victory," by Ralph Vartabedian, LOS ANGELES TIMES, July 6, 1991, p.1.

[170] "One Last Combat Victory," by Ralph Vartabedian, p.1.

[171] AND I WAS THERE by Rear Admiral Edwin T. Layton, William Morrow, NY, 1985, p.503.

[172] AND I WAS THERE by Rear Admiral Edwin T. Layton, p.177.

General MacArthur in the Philippines had requested 250 maps of targets in and around Tokyo.[173]

Did the Japanese find out about these maps? We don't know, but we do know they told their attaché in Berlin to ask the Germans for data about the effect of British B-17s on German cities.[174]

On November 21st, General Marshall's staff completed a study in which they estimated the ability of incendiary bombs dropped by B-17s to "burn up the wood-and-paper structures of the densely populated Japanese cities."[175] This was two weeks before the attack on Pearl Harbor.

Again, we do not know if the Japanese found out that the USG was making preparations to bomb their cities. We know only that (1) they knew the Flying Tigers were working for the USG, (2) they could see B-17s arriving in the Philippines, (3) they knew what B-17s could do, and (4) they knew Japan was the only conceivable B-17 target in that region.

Chris, if you were them, what would you have done?

Uncle Eric

---

[173] AND I WAS THERE by Rear Admiral Edwin T. Layton, p.504.

[174] AND I WAS THERE by Rear Admiral Edwin T. Layton, William Morrow, NY, 1985, p.117.

[175] AND I WAS THERE by Rear Admiral Edwin T. Layton, p.177.

Was the Attack Unprovoked?

President Roosevelt's military
moves against the Japanese prior
to December 7, 1941

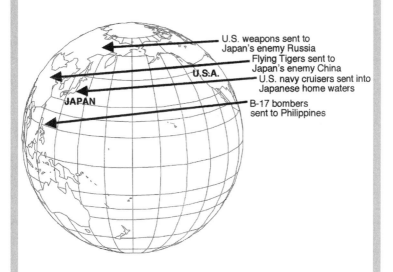

U.S. weapons sent to
Japan's enemy Russia

Flying Tigers sent to
Japan's enemy China

U.S. navy cruisers sent into
Japanese home waters

B-17 bombers
sent to Philippines

President Roosevelt also cut off
nearly all Japan's supplies of natural
resources including oil.

25

"Caught With Their Pants Down"

Dear Chris,

One of the worst accusations against Admiral Kimmel and Hawaii's Army Commander General Short is that they were warned on November 27th that a Japanese attack was coming but did nothing.

Americans have been given the impression that these men totally ignored the danger and failed to prepare their forces for the attack.

Hundreds of movies, books, and articles depict military personnel in Hawaii sunning on the beach and dancing the hula when they should have been preparing to fight.

One of the most popular books is titled AT DAWN WE SLEPT.

The often-repeated (and rather crude) comment is that U.S. forces at Pearl Harbor were "caught with their pants down."

The evidence says otherwise.

Kimmel and Short knew that Roosevelt was squeezing the Japanese — the embargo of oil and other raw materials was reported in the newspapers — so they knew an attack was likely. Instead of Roosevelt warning them, Kimmel warned Roosevelt.

Meeting personally with FDR on June 9, 1941, Admiral Kimmel told Roosevelt that he was afraid a Japanese attack was coming and he had too few planes and antiaircraft guns to protect the fleet.[176]

Roosevelt ignored the request for more planes and guns and refused to give back the ships, planes, and guns he had taken away in May. And, as noted in my chronology a couple letters ago, on November 26th Roosevelt took away even more planes.

Kimmel did his best to cope with the shortage. To understand his actions it helps to know a bit about military operations.

It is impossible to keep all weapons manned and ready at all times. Humans must eat, sleep, and take care of their families.

If you know anyone in the military, ask him (or her) how long it would take to put his base on alert, fully manned and ready for battle. He will say at least several days, maybe weeks. Weapons and ammunition are kept under lock and key, and at any given time many of the people trained to operate them are at home, on vacation, or deployed to distant areas.

At the time of the attack on Pearl Harbor, Kimmel's standing orders required that ammunition for all antiaircraft guns be stored near the guns and that at least a fourth of the guns be manned and ready to fire at all times. Also, Kimmel required that enough gunners be on the ships at all times to man all the guns. [177]

---

[176] AND I WAS THERE by Rear Admiral Edwin T. Layton, William Morrow, NY, 1985, p.115.

[177] ADMIRAL KIMMEL'S STORY, by Husband E. Kimmel, Henry Regnery Co., Chicago, 1955, p.18.

After the attack, investigators learned that all the anti-aircraft guns in the fleet were firing within seven minutes of the beginning of the attack.[178]

Let me emphasize, *all* the guns that Kimmel had were firing within seven minutes. Anyone with military experience will tell you this is possible only on a base in an extremely high state of readiness.

The only reason all the guns were not firing instantly is that troops cannot be kept at their weapons 24 hours per day, seven days per week.

The reason the Japanese were able to inflict so much damage is that Roosevelt had left Kimmel with too few planes and guns to protect the fleet.

Nevertheless, the Americans were able to shoot down 29 Japanese planes.[179] This would be an impressive performance for a base on full alert. For a base on modified alert, as Pearl Harbor was, it is awesome, a testimony to the preparations Kimmel and Short were able to make despite the President taking away so many of their weapons.

As for the famous November 27th "War Warning," it is undeniable that this message was delivered to Kimmel.

In fact, it was not the only one. Kimmel and Short began receiving war warnings on June 17, 1940, while Roosevelt was moving the fleet from the safety of San Diego to the shooting gallery of Pearl Harbor. More war warnings were received in 1941: January 21st, February 1st, February 3rd, April 3rd, May 14th, July 3rd, July 24th, July 25th, July 31st,

---

[178] ADMIRAL KIMMEL'S STORY, by Husband E. Kimmel, Henry Regnery Co., Chicago, 1955, p.18.

[179] WORLD WAR II DAY BY DAY, by Donald Sommerville, Dorset Press, Greenwich, CT 1989, p.106.

August 21st, August 28th, September 23rd, October 16th and November 24th.[180]

There was nothing in the November 27th message to indicate it was more important than the others, so how was Kimmel to know that the November 27th warning was the real thing?

In other words, someone in the USG was playing the boy who cried wolf. They warned Kimmel repeatedly month after month, so when the real warning finally arrived, Kimmel had no way to recognize it.

In my opinion, this "cry wolf" trick was the key to pinning the blame on Kimmel. Few Americans know about the steady stream of war warnings that came before the famous November 27th warning.

Chris, now are you beginning to understand why, in 1999, Congress declared that Kimmel was not responsible for what happened at Pearl Harbor?

Notice that the first war warning came on June 17, 1940, a full 17 months before the attack. Did someone in the USG decide this far ahead to frame the commanders at Pearl Harbor?

When Kimmel died in 1968, he was probably the most hated man in America. Millions would have listed him beside Benedict Arnold and John Wilkes Booth.

How did Kimmel feel? I don't know, Chris; how would you have felt?

Uncle Eric

---

[180] ADMIRAL KIMMEL'S STORY, by Husband E. Kimmel, Henry Regnery Co., Chicago, 1955, chapter 3.

26

Planes Parked Too Close Together

Dear Chris,

Thanks for your letter asking why Kimmel and Short had their planes parked in the open, close together, enabling the Japanese to hit them easily.

The messages sent to Kimmel throughout 1941 spoke not only of possible air attack but also of sabotage and espionage.

To guard against air attack, a commander scatters his parked airplanes widely around the base in camouflaged spots so that the enemy cannot easily see them and can hit only one at a time.

To guard against sabotage and espionage, he parks them close together in lighted areas so that guards can watch them.

Even after the USG knew the Japanese carrier fleet was headed for Pearl Harbor — meaning an air attack — Kimmel was not told.

He had to flip a coin — was he to guard against air attack, or sabotage and espionage?

Pearl Harbor was thousands of miles from Japan, and 40 percent of the population of Hawaii was of Japanese descent, so Kimmel reasoned that the greater threat was sabotage and espionage; he parked his planes close together. This enabled the Japanese to destroy 188 American planes, most before they could get off the ground.

Kimmel is often accused of dereliction of duty for parking his planes close together. General Douglas MacArthur did the same thing in the Philippines and had his planes destroyed,[181] but no one says anything about it.

Speaking of messages, the time and place of the Japanese attack was fully known in the USG because American code breakers had cracked the Japanese codes and were reading their messages for more than a year.[182]

No one told Kimmel.

Another source of information confirmed the Japanese plan to attack. Max W. Bishop at the U.S. Embassy in Tokyo had a friend in Tokyo who was a diplomat from Peru. The friend had learned of the attack. On January 27, 1941, Secretary of State Cordell Hull received a message from Bishop warning that the Japanese would "attempt a surprise attack on Pearl Harbor."[183]

Note that this was ten months before the event, yet no one told Kimmel. He was forced to operate on his own in Hawaii, at the center of the bull's-eye, without benefit of the information that was freely available to President Roosevelt who lived safely in Washington D.C.

Uncle Eric

---

[181] "Remember Pearl Harbor," by Stephen Ambrose, WALL STREET JOURNAL, May 27, 1999, p.A26.

[182] DAY OF DECEIT, by Robert B. Stinnett, The Free Press (Simon & Schuster), NY, 2000, p.23.

[183] DAY OF DECEIT, by Robert B. Stinnett, p.31.

27

The Prokofiev Seamount

Dear Chris,

Here is another crucially important fact never publicized, until the book DAY OF DECEIT by Robert B. Stinnett appeared 59 years after the Pearl Harbor attack.

The Navy keeps warehouses full of records including log books of ships' captains. Stinnett spent years digging through these records to find out what really happened at Pearl Harbor.

Stinnett learned that Kimmel was so convinced Roosevelt was goading the Japanese into some kind of attack that Kimmel made an attempt to ambush the Japanese before the Japanese could get to Pearl Harbor.

Studying all that was known about Pearl Harbor's vulnerability and Japanese firepower, Kimmel guessed that if he were the Japanese commander he would move an aircraft carrier fleet to the area of the Prokofiev Seamount (an extinct underwater volcano 200 miles from Hawaii) and launch his planes from there.

In November 1941, Kimmel sent his own fleet to the Prokofiev Seamount. Stinnett found that the fleet arrived on November 23rd and began searching for the Japanese.[184]

Think about it. Kimmel had 46 warships and 126 aircraft ready to ambush the Japanese.

---

[184] DAY OF DECEIT, by Robert B. Stinnett, The Free Press (Simon & Schuster), NY, 2000, p.145-152.

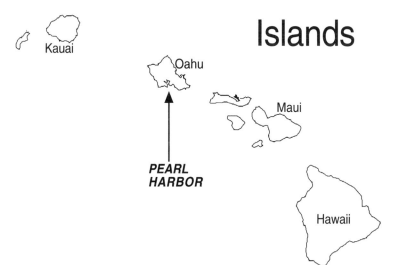

The Japanese aircraft carriers launched their planes from the Prokofiev Seamount, about 200 miles from Oahu. In November, Admiral Kimmel had sent his fleet to this spot to ambush the Japanese, but was ordered to put the fleet back in Pearl Harbor.

White House military officers heard about this and immediately ordered Kimmel to put the fleet back in Pearl Harbor.[185]

Not having detected the oncoming Japanese fleet, Kimmel and Short kept their planes parked close together to protect against sabotage and espionage.

Later, Kimmel was ordered to send his 21 modern ships, including his aircraft carriers, to the west — away from Hawaii — but to keep his older ships at anchor in Pearl Harbor.[186]

When the Japanese arrived, they found Pearl Harbor containing only a few small ships and a lot of large, undergunned relics from World War I.[187] The battleship *Arizona* was launched in 1915. The *Oklahoma* in 1914. The *Utah* in 1909.

The *Arizona* had eight antiaircraft guns. By way of contrast, the up-to-date battleship *Washington*, which was commissioned May 15, 1941, had 87 antiaircraft guns, but it was not in Pearl Harbor, nor was any other modern large ship. Their guns were sorely missed.

Again, Chris, someday when you fly to Hawaii, be sure to look out the window as you pass over Pearl Harbor. It is nothing more than a small lake with one narrow exit, a bottle. Kimmel had been ordered to keep his poorly protected older ships — and their crews — in this bottle. They were sitting ducks.

Incidentally, the Japanese safely launched their planes from the Prokofiev Seamount.

Uncle Eric

---

[185] DAY OF DECEIT, by Robert B. Stinnett, The Free Press (Simon & Schuster), NY, 2000, p.145-149.

[186] DAY OF DECEIT, by Robert B. Stinnett, p.152-154.

[187] DAY OF DECEIT, by Robert B. Stinnett, p.154.

P.S. Chris, why did so much information about Pearl Harbor remain hidden for decades? Because in World War II it was classified "secret" and then buried in the Pentagon's warehouses. Scholars, like Stinnett, have spent decades sifting through these warehouses, digging out and assembling bits and pieces of the story one at a time. It is a safe bet that much is still hidden.

28

The Necessary Sacrifice?

Dear Chris,

Setting up the attack, then framing Kimmel and Short for it was bad enough, but perhaps the most outrageous act of the whole Pearl Harbor story was the one committed by the press, who were not members of the military and not subject to military orders. Let's see what you think.

In a November 25th meeting with his Cabinet, President Roosevelt quoted a comment by General Marshall: "The United States is on the brink of war with the Japanese." Marshall had made this comment in a briefing for the news media on November 15th. At the briefing Marshall had told journalists the war would break out in the "first ten days of December."[188]

Why didn't Kimmel hear about this?

Because the press briefing was secret. Reporters from the NEW YORK TIMES, NEW YORK HERALD TRIBUNE, TIME, NEWSWEEK, THE ASSOCIATED PRESS, UNITED PRESS, and INTERNATIONAL NEWS SERVICE were told about the coming attack, but Kimmel was not.

The reporters had been asked to keep the story quiet until after the attack.

---

[188] DAY OF DECEIT, by Robert B. Stinnett, The Free Press (Simon & Schuster), NY, 2000, p.157.

And they did.[189] They were not legally required to do so; they did it as a favor to the government. They trusted the government's judgment.

If Kimmel had been allowed to do his job, and if he had been told what every high ranking official and news reporter in Washington D.C. knew, it would have been the Japanese, not the Americans, who would have been ambushed on December 7th.

Very likely, that would have been the end of America's involvement in World War II. Kimmel would have gone down in history alongside John Paul Jones as one of America's greatest naval heroes. He would have been called the American naval counterpart of Germany's "Desert Fox," General Erwin Rommel.

And all those American soldiers, sailors, and airmen who died in the next three and a half years would not have died.

In 1953, Fleet Admiral William F. Halsey wrote:

> I have always considered Admiral Kimmel and General Short to be splendid officers who were thrown to the wolves as scapegoats for something over which they had no control. They had to work with what they were given, both in equipment and information. They are our outstanding military martyrs.[190]

Chris, any book you read about Pearl Harbor will contain many of the facts I have given you in these letters. However, in nearly every case the writers will come to the conclusion that the whole sorry event was the result of foul-ups and

---

[189] DAY OF DECEIT, by Robert B. Stinnett, p.158.

[190] THE FINAL SECRET OF PEARL HARBOR, by Admiral Robert A. Theobald, Devin-Adair, NY 1954, p.ix.

incompetence, not deliberate intent, and Franklin Roosevelt did not know what was happening.

I think you can see that if he did not know, he was the only high official who didn't; even the press knew.

Few are willing to face the possibility that the President and his cronies planned it all.

However, each year, under the Freedom of Information Act, more facts are dug out of the Pentagon's files, and the idea is wearing thin that there was no plan to use the soldiers and sailors at Pearl Harbor as bait for an attack.

So another theory is gaining popularity. Among those who do have the courage to accept that there was a plan to use the Americans at Pearl Harbor as bait, most will nevertheless come to the conclusion that it was necessary. American opinion had to be changed to get into the war to stop Germany, we are told.

We can call this the "Necessary Sacrifice" explanation.

But, as we have seen, by invading Russia, Hitler had made his fatal mistake. As of September 12th, when the first snow fell on German troops struggling through the mud in Russia, the Necessary Sacrifice clearly was not necessary.

In 1955, looking back at the Pearl Harbor disaster, Kimmel made an interesting comment. He said that in 1941 he and General Short were, frankly, confused. They suspected what Roosevelt was doing but found it so outrageous and hard to believe that their doubts prevented them grasping the complete picture until it was too late.[191] They fumbled the ball because they could not believe a quarterback would call such an insane play.

---

[191] ADMIRAL KIMMEL'S STORY, by Husband E. Kimmel, Henry Regnery Co., Chicago, 1955, page 2.

The Pearl Harbor disaster was not quite the "unprovoked surprise attack" story we were all taught, was it?

Chris, we hear little of the real facts, I suppose, because, like Kimmel and Short, so few can bring themselves to believe a President would do it.

Roosevelt is generally regarded as one of America's greatest Presidents. In a balanced survey of liberal and conservative historians during the year 2000, the WALL STREET JOURNAL found that Franklin D. Roosevelt was rated third behind George Washington and Abraham Lincoln.[192]

If we face the truth about what FDR did, how can we ever again have confidence in any President?

For non-statists this is no big deal.

For statists it is a thought they would find hard to live with. They want to believe that political power does not corrupt. If they face what really happened at Pearl Harbor, how can they ever again trust Our Father Who Art In Washington?

Chris, now that you have more of the rest of the story about the World Wars, here is an interesting question: if you had been one of the reporters at the November 15th press briefing, would you have stayed quiet about the coming attack?

Uncle Eric

P.S. The attack on Pearl Harbor caused near panic. On February 19, 1942, President Roosevelt signed Executive Order No. 9066 requiring U.S. Army troops to round up persons of Japanese ancestry.

The move was widely popular at the time, and, among some people, still is. As Americans of Japanese descent were

---

[192] "Ranking the Presidents," WALL STREET JOURNAL, November 16, 2000, p.A26.

rounded up, the LOS ANGELES TIMES editorialized, "A viper is nonetheless a viper wherever the egg is born — so a Japanese-American, born of Japanese parents, grows up to be a Japanese, not an American."[193]

About 113,000 people were forced to abandon their homes, farms, and businesses; many became impoverished.

They were taken to "relocation centers" in remote places such as Manzanar in the desert of eastern California, near Lone Pine. These centers were prison camps surrounded by barbed wire and guard towers manned by soldiers with machine-guns.

In these camps, called "concentration camps" by President Roosevelt,[194] the Japanese-Americans were often brutally beaten by their guards.[195]

Not one of these Japanese-Americans was ever convicted of spying, sabotage, or anything else that might have helped Japan. These innocent people, about 70 percent of whom were citizens like you and me,[196] were imprisoned in complete violation of the Constitution, and no government official was ever prosecuted for it.

The Supreme Court upheld it, citing "pressing public necessity."[197]

---

[193] "Yellow Peril Reinfects America," by David Boaz, WALL STREET JOURNAL, April 7, 1989, p.A10.

[194] "Consequences of Terror," THE ECONOMIST, September 22, 2001, p.67.

[195] "Consequences of Terror," THE ECONOMIST, p.67.

[196] "U.S. Internment Camps Revisited," Associated Press story in SACRAMENTO BEE, December 25, 1994, p.B7.

[197] "Net Cast To Snare Terrorists Catches Some Who Aren't," by Michael Orey, WALL STREET JOURNAL, November 2, 2001, p.B1.

The "pressing" nature of locking up innocent people can be seen from the fact that in early 1942, Congress was considering also locking up all Italian-Americans — because Italy was part of the Axis — but dropped the plan when an attorney pointed out that this would require imprisoning the father of baseball star Joe DiMaggio.[198]

Two questions, Chris. First, none of these camps was anywhere near as awful as Russian or German concentration camps, but what if the U.S. had been losing the war? What do you think would have happened in those camps then?

Second, was this a precedent? The government got away with it cleanly, so might this happen again if America gets into another war that frightens us as much as the attack on Pearl Harbor did?

---

[198] "America Saw Itself In DiMaggio," WALL STREET JOURNAL, May 9, 1999, p.1.

29

You've Seen The Photos

Dear Chris,

Here is an interesting fact to ponder. We have all seen hundreds of photos and newsreels of the attack on Pearl Harbor. One of the most famous pieces of motion picture film is of the battleship *Arizona* exploding. Shot in color (although usually shown in black and white) this film of the explosion is shocking. At the time I write this you can see photos of the Battleship *Arizona* at the web site: http://www.history.navy.mil/photos/events/wwii-pac/pearlhbr/ph-az.htm

The photos and films of Pearl Harbor were immediately shown around the country. Young men saw them and went straight to the nearest recruiting centers. Your grandfather tells of lines of men stretching hundreds of yards around the block at the recruiting center near his home.

These photos and films completely erased any serious opposition to the USG getting into the war. In every city and town, Americans were outraged and looking for revenge.

The strange thing is that in 1941, portable motion picture cameras were rare, and portable motion picture cameras shooting color film were almost unknown. The convenient videotape cameras did not come into wide use until the 1980s.

I have never heard anyone ask the question, how long after the attack began did the *Arizona* blow up?

I checked into it.

Logs of other ships in the harbor report that the explosion

was 12 minutes after the attack began. The *Arizona* was one of the first ships hit.

So when the attack began, there on the scene within sight of battleship row, at 8:00 a.m. on a Sunday morning, was a photographer with a movie camera loaded with color film.

What a strange coincidence.

Or maybe it wasn't coincidence.

Chris, what do you think?

Uncle Eric

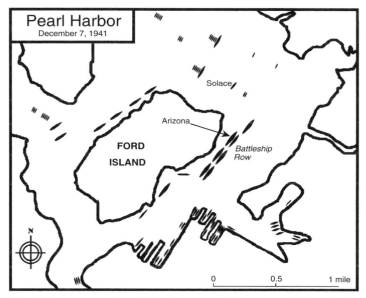

The *Solace* was a hospital ship moored in a central location in Pearl Harbor with a view of battleship row. This was the safest spot in the harbor. Hospital ships are not considered legitimate military targets; the *Solace* was not hit and was not damaged in any way. At 8:00 a.m. on a Sunday morning, a photographer with a movie camera shooting color film was standing on the deck of the *Solace*. The photographer got clear pictures of the attack, including the destruction of the battleship *Arizona*. Was his presence there a coincidence, or did someone know the attack was coming and tell the photographer to be there?

Part Four

The Economics of the War

30

The Myth of German Might

Dear Chris,

Now we will spend some time looking at the war the way an economist would (or should). You will see the war in a way few ever have.

We will begin by returning to the idea of Necessary Sacrifice. In the past half-century, so much evidence about what really happened in 1941 has come to light that some will concede that FDR planned it. He used the Pacific fleet as a lure for a Japanese attack and deliberately provoked Japan into striking.

Many take refuge in the Necessary Sacrifice belief. They say the neutrality of the American people had to be erased in order to get into the war to keep Hitler from conquering the world.

Germany was the key player, the anchorman of the Axis. Japan and Italy were lightweights compared to Germany, and other members of the Axis even more so. Italy switched sides, joining the Allies in 1943.

The German threat is the one that drew the most attention in the 1940s and still does today, and rightfully so; without Germany there would have been no Axis and no war.

The official Hollywood version of history says Hitler could have taken over the world if the U.S. had not stopped him.

Chris, in earlier letters I explained that the Germans never had the ability or the desire to conquer much territory, if we define "much" as the amounts the British and Russians (Allies) had conquered. It is important to appreciate that Europe is a tiny part of the world. Hitler overran a few small countries. All of them together were smaller than Kazakhstan, which was conquered by the Russians — or India, which was conquered by the British. And, he did not control much of what he overran; guerrillas fought his troops almost everywhere. At the height of German power in 1942, I doubt he controlled five percent of the world population.

Natural resources are difficult to calculate, but I am sure that at the height of his power Hitler did not control one percent.

Since 1941, we have been bombarded by frightening images of superb German technology — fighter planes, tanks, machine guns, artillery, and on and on. The official story is that the Germans were way ahead of anyone else and were easily mowing down their opposition.

Chris, in earlier letters you learned that the German technology was no match for the Russian winter, so you already have some skepticism about German superiority. Now let's look a bit closer at German technology.

This is where we begin to get more deeply into the economics of the war. But don't be intimidated. Economics is just the study of the production and distribution of goods and services; in this case, the goods and services of war. It tells a much different story about the war than the one commonly believed.

I will start by describing an incident that will give you a taste of where I am headed.

One of the most famous German tank units was the fearsome Panzer Lehr Division. On the morning of July 25, 1944, Panzer Lehr was in the path of Allied forces moving eastward across France near St. Lo. If you have seen many war movies you will instantly recognize this as an ominous situation for the Allies, one guaranteed to have the audience shaking in their boots. What will the Allies do?

Panzer Lehr had 2,200 men and 45 operational tanks.

The Allied attack on Panzer Lehr began with waves of P-47 Thunderbolt fighters, fifty at a time. Every two minutes a wave would sweep across Panzer Lehr dropping **napalm**.

When hundreds of P-47s had dropped all their napalm, they departed and were replaced by waves of medium bombers dropping 500-pound bombs.

After the medium bombers departed, the surviving Germans heard a sound that would raise the hair on the back of anyone's neck: 1,500 heavy four-engine B-17 and B-24 bombers. Chris, in your mind try to picture 1,500 bombers. Imagine the sound of 6,000 engines passing overhead.

The B-17s and B-24s laid a carpet of bombs across Panzer Lehr, churning the earth into a landscape of craters and wreckage. Tanks were thrown into the air, landing in pieces upside down.

But that was not the end of it. After the heavy bombers departed, another 300 P-38 Lightning fighters swept across the remnants of Panzer Lehr dropping incendiaries and antipersonnel fragmentation bombs.

Then hundreds of artillery pieces opened up.

The next day, Allied tanks and infantry came in to "mop up" what was left.

More than 2,000 Allied planes had attacked the 45 tanks of Panzer Lehr.[199]

Were the German tanks well made?

Yes, they were much superior to the American Sherman tank.

Did their quality make any difference?

No.

Perhaps the most important question is: A tank division normally has between 400 and 700 tanks; why did Panzer Lehr have only 45 and no aircraft to protect them?

Because the tanks and aircraft had been used up in Russia years earlier, and German factories could produce few replacements.

Uncle Eric

P-47M of the USAAF 66th Fighter Group in Europe.

---

[199] WHY THE ALLIES WON, by Richard Overy, W. W. Norton & Co., NY, 1995, p.208.

31

Focus On The Eastern Front

Dear Chris,

Before I go further into the myth of German technology, I need to give you some perspective about the "theaters" in which the technology was used.

The Pacific Theater of the war was mostly the U.S. versus Japan.

The European Theater had two "fronts." The Western Front was mainly Britain, parts of France, and later the U.S., against Germany.

The Eastern Front was Germany versus the U.S.S.R., or Hitler versus Stalin.

In the European Theater there was also the "Italian Campaign" in Italy, plus other less important conflicts, such as the ones in the Balkans.

The Eastern Front — the battle between Hitler and Stalin — was the main battlefield of the war. This is crucially important but not generally understood in America. The Eastern Front was where Germany's technology had to shine if the Germans were to win.

Other battles, such as those at Midway, Iwo Jima, Normandy, and El Alamein, were certainly horrific for the people who were in them, but in terms of scale and importance, nothing comes close to the Eastern Front.

As an example, one battle on the Eastern Front — at Stalingrad (now Volgograd) — was the worst in all of human history. That single clash lasted five months and killed 1,110,000.[200]

This is almost exactly equal to the number of lives America has lost in all the wars it has ever fought.[201]

By way of contrast, the biggest battle on the Western Front was the D-Day landings on the Normandy beaches. Except for small pockets of resistance, that battle was over in 72 hours. Deaths of Allied troops numbered less than 2,500. German and civilian deaths are unknown but were probably not more than 10,000.

So, 12,500 deaths versus 1,110,000. By this measure, the Eastern Front was 89 times as bad as the Western Front.

Another way to say it is that the biggest battle on the Western Front lasted three days and killed a bit more than one percent of the number killed at the Battle of Stalingrad, which lasted five months.

Three-quarters of all deaths in the war happened on the Eastern Front. Most were Soviet.

Chris, the scale and horror of other battles should never be overlooked, but when studying World War II, the Eastern Front should be the center of your attention. If battles were mountain ranges, the collision between Hitler and Stalin would be the Himalaya of world history, and everything else in World War II would be foothills.

Hitler's attack on Stalin in June 1941 was the single largest military operation in all of human history. Of the

---

[200] GUINNESS BOOK OF WORLD RECORDS, Guinness Publishing, NY, 1999, p.329.

[201] WORLD ALMANAC, World Almanac Books, 2000, p.217.

Wehrmacht's 209 **divisions**,[202] Hitler used 144 to attack the Soviet Union.[203]

On June 6, 1944, when the invasion of Normandy began on the Western Front, British and American forces in France and Italy faced no more than 90 Axis divisions. The Red army on the Eastern Front faced more than 250.[204]

To put that in perspective, since 1945, there has probably been no case in which any government has used more than 20 divisions in any single campaign.[205]

Eight out of ten Wehrmacht soldiers killed in World War II were killed on the Eastern Front.[206]

The Red army suffered more casualties than all the rest of the Allies together.[207]

In 1942, to General Douglas MacArthur, FDR wrote, "the Russian armies are killing more Axis personnel and destroying

---

[202] Division: Generally, six brigades. An infantry division is about 10,000 troops. An armored division, about 600 tanks. Typically, but not always, there are nine troops in a squad, three squads to a platoon, four platoons to a company, six companies to a battalion, two battalions to a brigade, and six brigades to a division.

[203] THE RISE AND DECLINE OF THE STATE, by Martin van Creveld, Cambridge University Press, 1999, p.345.

[204] FRANKLIN D. ROOSEVELT AND THE WORLD CRISIS, 1937-1945, edited by Warren F. Kimball of Rutgers University, D.C. Heath & Co., Lexington, Mass. 1973, p.165.

[205] THE RISE AND DECLINE OF THE STATE, by Martin van Creveld, Cambridge University Press, 1999, p.345.

[206] Stephen Ambrose, interviewed in History Channel TV documentary "The Last Days of World War II."

[207] Stephen Ambrose, interviewed in History Channel TV documentary "The Last Days of World War II."

more Axis materiel than all other twenty-five United Nations [Allies] combined."[208]

Newspaper editor and World War II veteran Max Norris once wrote an article about the four-year war on the Eastern Front. He described it as "a thousand Iwo Jimas back to back."[209]

Norris was not exaggerating, Chris. Iwo Jima was one of the most horrific battles in American history, 28,000 Americans and Japanese were killed; the Marines will never forget it. No one knows how many people were killed on the Eastern Front, but judging from the table of casualty estimates in the ENCYCLOPEDIA BRITANNICA[210] it was probably in the neighborhood of a thousand times as many, 28 million.

Why do Americans so often ignore the overwhelming importance of the Eastern Front? My guess is the movies. More in my next letter.

Uncle Eric

---

[208] FRANKLIN D. ROOSEVELT AND THE WORLD CRISIS, 1937-1945, edited by Warren F. Kimball of Rutgers University, D.C. Heath & Co., Lexington, Mass. 1973, p.160.

[209] "The Greatest Generation...," by Max Norris, SACRAMENTO BEE FORUM, August 29, 1999, p.F1.

[210] ENCYCLOPEDIA BRITANNICA, Internet.

32

Of Photographs and Weather

Dear Chris,

In answer to your question: Yes, there might be a kind of Hollywood conspiracy to ignore the Eastern Front, but not a conspiracy in the sense you might think.

Americans want to see movies about Americans. I doubt many would pay to see movies about Germans fighting Russians.

A producer who makes a movie that is not popular runs the risk of going broke.

In fact, in one of the best World War II movies ever made, THE GREAT ESCAPE, Americans played little part in the real escape, but they were starred in the movie so that the movie would have a better chance of making money.

I think a more interesting reason the Eastern Front is little known to Americans is due to an accident of geography and climate.

Our interest and memory of the World Wars are mostly from newsreel images. The images from the Eastern Front are sparse and of low quality. Try taking pictures in a snowstorm and you will know why.

At the other extreme, Americans have the impression that the battles in the Pacific were enormous. These battles were quite small. Again, this is not to say they were small for the people who were in them, but in terms of the Big Picture, the Pacific battles were fringe events.

The Pacific battles seem so huge and more important to us than the Eastern Front for two reasons. The first is that a combat cameraman in the South Pacific was working in clear, sunny weather most of the year. He could shoot plenty of high quality footage.

The other is that combat on a coral atoll is a far different thing than combat on the plains of Russia. The size of the island of Tarawa, for instance, was nine square miles. Iwo Jima was eight square miles. Wake Island, three square miles.

In such a confined space, a hundred yards is a long way.

On the Eastern Front, artillery duels at ten miles were common, while on a coral atoll in the Pacific it was hand grenades at fifty feet.

Some of the Pacific film footage shows troops from both sides in the same frame. This is a lot more dramatic and more likely to appear in movies than a hazy shot of a howitzer in a snowdrift.

On Iwo Jima, there were almost 100,000 people fighting on just eight square miles of land.

Also, we tend to remember scenes that are shocking. In many cases, dead bodies in the Pacific and on the Western Front were easily filmed because the cameramen found them in groups on open ground. Bodies on the enormous Eastern Front were more widely scattered and buried in mud and snow.

In the whole Pacific Campaign, America suffered less than 50,000 dead.[211] This was less than a sixth of all U.S. dead and far less than one percent of all the people killed in the war.[212]

---

[211] CONDEMNED TO REPEAT IT, by Wick Allison, Jeremy Adams, Gavin Hambly, Penguin Group, NY, 1998, p.8.

[212] It was 0.13%.

So, Chris, do not be misled by what you see on the screen. If you want to understand the Second World War, you must focus most of your attention on the Eastern Front, the main battlefield. Everything else was **ancillary** to the fight between Hitler and Stalin.

And, on September 12, 1941, the first snow fell in Russia. That was the day the Germans began to lose, and that was the day the "Necessary Sacrifice" at Pearl Harbor could no longer be necessary.

But Roosevelt apparently wanted into the war, so he went ahead and continued provoking the Japanese.

Why did he want into the war? We can only guess. There was Anglo-Saxonism. And remember Churchill's offer to Roosevelt: "I am half American and the natural person to work with you. It is evident that we see eye to eye. Were I to become Prime Minister of Britain we could control the world."[213]

More about that in a future letter about Unconditional Surrender. For now we need to look more closely at the myth of German might and what happened to the Germans on the all-important Eastern Front.

Uncle Eric

P.S. Chris, if you want to know what the Eastern Front was like, see the 2001 movie ENEMY AT THE GATES about the Battle of Stalingrad. I am sure the movie's story about the hero is mostly fiction but the depiction of the battle itself is quite accurate, almost a documentary.

---

[213] THE FINAL STORY OF PEARL HARBOR, by Harry Elmer Barnes, published by Left and Right, NY, 1968, p.15.

33

German Production of Weapons

Dear Chris,

Now back to the myth of German might.

The Germans, Japanese, and Italians were latecomers to the game of empire; they were the younger members of the Usual Suspects. The British already had a fourth of the world to draw on for raw materials, talent, and manpower. The Russians had a sixth. Compared to these vast empires, the German, Italian, and Japanese "Empires" were Lilliputian.[214]

The Axis powers came on strong early in the war simply because they moved first. The British and Russians had not yet fully geared up. Also, the British, French, and Russian generals made a lot of mistakes, while German generals were brilliant.

Chris, if a high school football team playing the Green Bay Packers starts running plays early, when the Packers have only two or three players on the field, they will look invincible for a few minutes. But how will they look after the rest of the Packers arrive?

Of the three Axis leaders, the Germans were by far the most powerful, but this power remained intact only until it was devoured by the Russian winter.

Here are some statistics to show what happened after the British and Russians did gear up for the war. These are the

---

[214] Tiny.

Production of the Three Main Old World Combatants

Production of Aircraft[215]

	1939	1940	1941	1942	1943	1944	1945	totals
Britain	7,940	15,049	20,094	23,672	26,263	26,461	12,070	131,549
USSR	10,382	10,565	15,735	25,436	34,900	40,300	20,900	158,218
Germany	8,295	10,247	11,776	15,409	24,807	39,807	7,540	117,881

Production of Tanks[216]

	1939	1940	1941	1942	1943	1944	1945	totals
Britain	969	1399	4841	8611	7476	5000	2100	30,396
USSR	2950	2794	6590	24446	24089	28963	15400	105,232
Germany	1300	2200	5200	9200	17300	22100	4400	61,700

Production of Artillery Pieces[217]

	1939	1940	1941	1942	1943	1944	1945	totals
Britain	1400	1900	5300	6600	12200	12400	0	39,800
USSR	17348	15300	42300	127000	130300	122400	31,000	485,648[218]
Germany	2000	5000	7000	12000	27000	41000	0	94,000

[215] WHY THE ALLIES WON, by Richard Overy, W. W. Norton & Co., NY, 1995, p.331.

[216] WHY THE ALLIES WON, by Richard Overy, p.332.

[217] WHY THE ALLIES WON, by Richard Overy, p.332.

[218] Includes light, medium and heavy artillery. Figures for the Allies are medium and heavy only. Breakouts of Soviet categories were not available.

numbers for each country's own production, they do not include weapons contributed by the USG. Compare the production of the Allies (Britain and the U.S.S.R.) to that of the Germans. Chris, look at the first year of the war, 1939. Already the two Allied powers were outproducing the Germans. The Allies' weapons were not yet fully deployed for maximum effective use, but already in 1939 it was obvious what would happen to the Germans when Britain and Russia were fully in the war. This is why the German generals tried to talk Hitler out of starting the war in the first place.

And, as mentioned in an earlier letter, the economic potential of the three powers was well understood. None of these statistics would have been surprising to an economist in 1939.

Chris, now look at the totals. Add the Allied (Britain and U.S.S.R.) totals together; then compare them to that of Germany.

Now that you have more of the rest of the story about World War II, what do you think about the assumption that Britain and Russia needed America's help to beat the Germans?

Certainly they *wanted* help — if you are in a fight you want all the help you can get — but did they *need* it?

Some have the impression that the British and Russians could not gear up because German bombers were destroying their factories. Actually, in 1940 it was already known that German bombers were pathetic, and they never improved much. They were small, slow, short-range, poorly armed, and no match for the swift fighters put up against them.

Look at the statistics for 1940. A year before the U.S. got into the war, the British and Russians were already gearing up, and they were already outproducing the Germans by a wide margin. On the Western Front, the most important weapon was the airplane, and the British were already superior to the Germans in aircraft. On the Eastern Front, because of frequent bad flying weather, tanks were most important, and the Soviets were already superior in tanks.

Remember, the British and Russians were allied against the Germans, and the Germans were sandwiched between them.

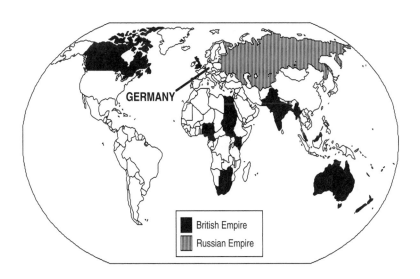

The Germans had some help from the Italians and other minor players, but these countries produced little and did not amount to much.

In fact, the Italians gave up and switched sides in 1943, tilting the odds even more against the Germans.

Also, consider that Germany's population was 66 million while Britain had 46 million and the Soviet Union 166 million. The Germans were outnumbered three to one, and this does not take into account the more than 500 million people in Britain's colonies.[219]

In short, by the end of 1941, when the "Necessary Sacrifice" at Pearl Harbor happened, the British and Russians were already swamping the Germans in both production and population.

Do you see what I mean about viewing the war through the eyes of an economist? It makes a big difference.

The Germans still had the **strategic**[220] advantage, but their tremendous handicap in the production of weapons was clearly destined to erase this.

Chris, why would anyone be surprised at this? Look at a globe. London's empire was more than a fifth of the world, and Moscow's was a sixth. Compared to them, Germany was a pip-squeak; its fate was sealed on June 22, 1941, when Hitler attacked Stalin. Remember that date, it is one of the most important of the war.

Once Stalin got his factories moved eastward to the Urals, to the Volga region and to Kazakhstan — far beyond the reach of the puny German bombers — he could produce all the weapons he needed without interference. This while German industrial cities were bombed continually by the huge four-engine British Lancasters.

To get a feel for what the Germans were up against in Russia, look at the statistics on production of tanks and

---

[219] ECONOMIC GEOGRAPHY by R.H. Whitbeck & V.C. Finch, McGraw-Hill, NY, 1941, p.620.

[220] Strategy refers to planning, maneuver and placement of forces; not *what* the forces are, but *where* they are and *how* they are used.

artillery. (The Russian artillery numbers are inflated by the addition of light pieces, but there can be no doubt that the Russians outproduced the Germans by a wide margin.)

And the Russians had the most powerful weapon of them all, their winters.

Chris, Russia's extensive use of artillery reflects the Russian savvy about their winters. Artillery can be highly accurate, it can penetrate the enemy's bunkers, and it works fine in any weather, night or day. Planes and most other weapons were slowed or stopped by bad weather or darkness, but not artillery. Also, unlike planes, artillery gives the ability to stand off at a great distance and pound the enemy without risking the life of an expensively trained pilot.

The British had the advantage of a 21-mile-wide moat between them and the Germans, and they had a big navy that had sunk most of the small German navy. The German monster could crawl east, but he could not swim west.

In short, Hitler was crazy. This is not a mere accusation, it is a profoundly important strategic fact of the war, and it became abundantly obvious on June 22, 1941. There was simply no way the Germans could beat both the British and the Russians. Perhaps they could have beaten one, but certainly not both.

Again, the Necessary Sacrifice was not necessary.

In fact, the need for the U.S. to get into the war was already suspect in November of 1937. That is when Hitler tipped his hand, announcing that he planned to acquire *lebensraum* (living space) for Germans in East Europe. Four years before the attack on Pearl Harbor, the USG was aware that Hitler was likely to become entangled in a war in the vast Soviet Union.

Chris, an interesting sidelight here is that the first woman elected to Congress was Jeannette Rankin, a Republican from Ohio. When President Roosevelt asked Congress to declare war on December 8, 1941, which was the day after the attack on Pearl Harbor, the only member of Congress who refused to follow Roosevelt was Rankin — she voted no.[221]

When I was your age, I had been taught this was because Rankin was a woman, and we cannot expect women to have the courage of men. In fact, I was told several times that this proves women cannot be trusted to make important decisions.

It turns out that Rankin was the only one with any sense.

She also voted against U.S. participation in World War I and led protest marches against the Vietnam War.

Chris, you said you are looking for a 20th century political leader on whom to do a research paper. Rankin would be my suggestion. This does not mean I think she was right about everything, but about getting into World War II, she was more right than anyone else at the time.

Uncle Eric

P.S. In case you are wondering, here are the totals for U.S. production from 1939 to 1945: aircraft: 324,840; tanks: 88,479; artillery pieces: 224,874.[222]

In warfare, the sky is the ultimate "high ground" that gives greatest advantage. If you will compare the American aircraft production to that of the other powers, I think you will see

---

[221] "American Foreign Policy, The Turning Point," by Ralph Raico, THE FAILURE OF AMERICA'S FOREIGN WARS, edited by Richard Ebeling & Jacob Hornberger, The Future of Freedom Foundation, Fairfax, VA 1996, p.71.

[222] WHY THE ALLIES WON, by Richard Overy, W. W. Norton & Co., NY, 1995, p.331.

why no one wanted to fight the U.S. (then or now — the U.S. still has the ability to outproduce any other nation by a wide margin).

Also, Chris, as I write this letter, I know of no case of an unprovoked attack on the U.S.

Chris, now what do you think about the claim that the Germans nearly won the war?

Incidentally, after the attack on Pearl Harbor, President Roosevelt said the attack was unprovoked, meaning the USG had done nothing to cause it. After the September 11th attack, Americans were told this again. Chris, you've read my original set of letters about the Mideast[223] which were written two years before September 11, 2001, so you know the truth of the old saying that history repeats.

---

[223] Uncle Eric is referring to Richard J. Maybury's book THE THOUSAND YEAR WAR IN THE MIDEAST: HOW IT AFFECTS YOU TODAY, published by Bluestocking Press, web site: www.BluestockingPress.com.

34

Germany's Unknown Second Army

Dear Chris,

The strategic importance of Hitler's insanity was already apparent in 1941. The man was so convinced he could beat the Soviet Union that he decided Germany had sufficient weapons and supplies, and he ordered cutbacks in war production.[224]

The "victory" over the U.S.S.R. became a German rout after the snow began to fall on September 12, 1941; great amounts of equipment and supplies were lost. By early 1942, the desperate German army was running low on nearly everything it needed, and the factories were unable to resupply it.

What about Germany's invincible technology — all those vastly superior planes, tanks, and guns?

A little known fact is that the Germans actually had two armies. One was the high tech mechanized force you have seen so often in movies. The aircraft, tanks, and artillery are impressive, no doubt about it.

But this force was small. It was only the tip of the spear. The rest of the spear, the main body of the army, was foot soldiers and horses.

---

[224] SECRET WEAPONS OF THE THIRD REICH by Leslie E. Simon, We, Inc. Publishers, Old Greenwich, CT, 1971, p.97.

Yes, horses. When Hitler's massive invasion force was poised on the Soviet frontier in June 1941, it was at its peak. Lined up ready to strike at Stalin were 3,350 tanks.

And 650,000 horses.[225]

Hollywood devotes a lot of film to the tanks, but how often have you seen the thousands of horses?

Most of the horses were used as substitutes for trucks, but the Germans even had a horse cavalry division that was thrown against the Russians.[226]

Let's be very clear about this. Most of the high tech German menace that Americans were taught to fear was actually foot soldiers and horses.

When the British and Americans invaded Normandy in June 1944, they were fully mechanized while the German army was still dependent on 1,250,000 horses.[227]

When Hitler launched his mad invasion of Russia, he had 3,350 tanks to throw at Stalin. Stalin had 15,000[228] to throw at him.

The Russian generals were incompetent, so the Germans did great damage early on, and this looked horrific in the newsreels in American movie theaters. But the Russians soon learned how to fight more effectively, and the winter arrived; that was the beginning of the end for Germany — September 12, 1941.

Chris, in my next letter I will get into specific details about German technology. Until then, here is an example of

---

[225] WHY THE ALLIES WON, by Richard Overy, W. W. Norton & Co., NY, 1995, p.5.

[226] HISTORY OF THE SECOND WORLD WAR, by B.H. Liddell Hart, Perigee Books, NY, 1982, p.243.

[227] WHY THE ALLIES WON, by Richard Overy, p.5.

[228] WHY THE ALLIES WON, by Richard Overy, p.211.

the German dependence on horses and how small was the mechanized tip of their spear.

To turn his army against Russia, Hitler had to withdraw units from France. Left facing Britain were forty-six and a half divisions.

Of these, a half-division was armored, meaning tanks, and one other division was mechanized infantry, meaning soldiers transported by trucks.

The remaining 45 divisions were foot soldiers with horses.[229]

In one of my earliest letters, Chris, I mentioned that when you understood the economics of the war you would see what others do not. Now do you know what I meant?

Uncle Eric

---

[229] HISTORY OF THE SECOND WORLD WAR, by B.H. Liddell Hart, Perigee Books, NY, 1982, p.153.

35

Tank Treads, Trucks, and Submarines

Dear Chris,

We have all seen films, books, and articles about the superiority of German technology. Some of this technology was superior, no doubt about it, but overall, it was not remarkable. The Germans made a lot of mistakes.

The Russian T-34 tanks decimated German tanks. One reason is that German tanks were designed to operate in Western Europe where the weather was not arctic and roads were paved. Their treads were narrow for greater speed.

In Russia, few roads were paved. With narrow treads, German tanks sank into the mud and snow and became immobile. This made them easy targets for enemy tanks and infantry who could approach at leisure from well-covered positions.

Chris, it is important to be aware of cultural differences. The German culture emphasizes quality over quantity, so Germany is not and never has been big on mass production.

In the civilian world, this is fine. If people want to pay extra for goods that are finely made in small quantities, there is nothing wrong with that. But in war it is fatal.

Industries always face a choice. You can have a lot of the item, or you can have the items made perfectly, but you cannot have both. The Germans characteristically opt for highest quality with less production, and they did this in the Second World War.

They also opted for change whenever they found a better design.

The result would have been laughable had it not cost lives.

In the assault on the Soviet Union, the German army had two thousand different types of vehicles and had to carry with it over a million spare parts.[230]

One tank division went into battle with 96 types of personnel carrier, 111 types of truck, and 37 kinds of motorcycle.[231]

I am sure most of these vehicles were of excellent German quality, but imagine how many trained mechanics it took to keep them running. Imagine the nightmare of trying to find the right oil pump for the truck you are trying to repair.

By November 1941 — which was before the U.S. got into the war — that tank division reported only 12 percent of its vehicles still running.[232]

Chris, Germany's perfectly designed and manufactured weapons look impressive on film, but when I hear someone comment about the superiority of German weapons, I say, yes, they were excellent, but how many could the Germans make? How many could they keep in operation?

Now you know why they needed horses. With horses there is no problem with spare parts.

The German weakness in mass production was obvious at the start of the war. Those invincible German tank divisions that Americans were taught to fear in 1940 were equipped mostly with Panzer I and Panzer II tanks. These were training tanks never intended for combat.

---

[230] WHY THE ALLIES WON, by Richard Overy, W. W. Norton & Co., NY, 1995, p.217.

[231] WHY THE ALLIES WON, by Richard Overy, p.217.

[232] WHY THE ALLIES WON, by Richard Overy, p.217.

The heaviest gun on a Panzer II was a 20mm cannon, which in terms of tank weapons was a popgun. The heaviest armor on a Panzer II was only 1.4 inches thick, and most of the armor was less than 1 inch. This was a very light tank.

As you might expect, the Panzer I was a joke. Its heaviest gun was a machine gun, and its thickest armor was a half-inch. In other words, in movies it looked like a tank, but it was really an armored car. Real tanks have armor that is several inches thick, often a half-foot or more.

Every army officer in the U.S. tank corps understood all this and knew what he was looking at in newsreels about the German army, but the public was not told.

The Germans were so slow in producing real tanks that as late as April 1942, a total of 860 of the flimsy Panzer IIs were still in use.[233]

The Germans' first serious tank, meaning one that was a match for the Russian T-34s, was the Panzer IVF2, which did not begin coming off the assembly line until March 1942.[234] The Germans were able to make only 1,724 of them.[235]

Let me emphasize, Chris, the mighty German tank divisions that Americans were taught to fear when the war began were equipped with thin-skinned training tanks, many of which were really armored cars.

The later medium tanks — the Panzer III, IV and V — were better, but the Germans were unable to produce a genuine heavy tank until the first Tiger rolled off the assembly line in August 1942. This was three years after the start of the war.

---

[233] GERMAN TANKS OF WORLD WAR II, by DR S. Hart & DR R. Hart, Barnes & Noble Books, 1999, p.17.

[234] GERMAN TANKS OF WORLD WAR II, by Hart & Hart, p.75.

[235] GERMAN TANKS OF WORLD WAR II, by Hart & Hart, p.76.

The Tiger looks frightening on film, and I certainly would not want to meet one in a dark alley. But the Tiger was so complicated and needed so many spare parts that it could only be repaired by putting it on a train and shipping it back to repair factories in Germany, a distance of up to 2,000 miles.[236] One reason it was so complex is that Hitler, a politician by trade, was endlessly telling his engineers how to do their jobs. He interfered in the design of tanks and most other principal weapons, endlessly making "improvements" so that nothing was ever really finished, and assembly lines were often halted to retool for his changes.

Hitler required tanks to be so large and complicated that they not only broke down a lot, they were impossible to make in large quantities. They also could not maneuver well and were easily trapped and destroyed.

The Tiger was a good example of German excellence getting in the way of victory. The Tiger was one of the first tanks to have interleaved wheels, which gave better weight distribution and a more stable ride. But the deep snow and mud in Russia would become packed between the wheels, and during the night it would freeze, preventing the wheels from turning. The Russians discovered this and timed their attacks for dawn when the Tigers could not move.[237]

The most feared German tank was the King Tiger, or Royal Tiger. This amazing machine weighed almost 70 tons — as much as a modern American M-1 tank — and its turret frontal armor was 7.3 inches thick; there is no surviving evidence that any Allied round ever penetrated this armor. The King

---

[236] WHY THE ALLIES WON, by Richard Overy, W. W. Norton & Co., NY, 1995, p.218.

[237] "Tiger MK1 and MK2," by Chris Ellis and Peter Chamberlain, WAR MONTHLY, April 1974, p.12.

Tiger's 88mm gun was extremely accurate and very power-ful.

The King Tiger looks absolutely fearsome in the movies, but its awesome firepower and armor were matched by its awesome complexity. The first five broke down so completely they had to be destroyed before they could see combat, and the Germans were able to field a total of only 489 King Tigers. These tanks were so unreliable that most were used only as stationary artillery.[238]

The Germans' inability to produce good tanks in large quantities showed up in the invasion of Normandy. The Allies landed on June 6, 1944, and within 44 days had destroyed 2,117 German tanks. To replace these losses the Germans were able to send only 17 tanks.[239]

In short, Hitler the politician was brilliant, but Hitler the engineer and general was a disaster. Coupled with the German cultural tendency to build for quality rather than quantity, he made victory impossible.

Tanks were one of the most important weapons of the war. The Soviet T-34 was excellent, heavily armored and high powered, with a 76mm gun. The T-34 came out at a time when German tank guns were 37mm and 50mm, so the T-34 made short work of German tanks.

When the first T-34 appeared — only 17 days after Hitler invaded the U.S.S.R., and long before the Germans had heavy tanks (also long before the U.S. entered the war) — the T-34 attacked a German armored column, cutting a nine-mile wide swath of destruction, blowing up 40 tanks and armored

---

[238] GERMAN TANKS OF WORLD WAR II, by DR S. Hart & DR R. Hart, Barnes & Nobel Books, 1999, p.133-143.

[239] WHY THE ALLIES WON, by Richard Overy, W. W. Norton & Co., NY, 1995, p.169-170.

vehicles. The Germans managed to stop this T-34 only by moving up a 100mm cannon to hit it from behind.[240]

One T-34 absorbed 24 hits from German tanks and continued firing.[241]

Chris, the movie image of the typical German soldier is a spit-and-polish superman riding atop a huge tank or flying a high performance aircraft. But these advanced weapons were few, and many did not work well.

The typical German soldier was an average Joe, no more remarkable than an American, and he was carrying a World War I bolt-action rifle and leading a horse-drawn wagon. After the Battle of Stalingrad ended in early 1943, he was, as likely as not, dragging the rifle and pulling the wagon himself. When you think of the German army, this is the true picture you should have. The idea that the mighty British and Russian Empires needed America's help to beat little Germany is quite absurd.

Chris, at the Museum of Science and Industry in Chicago you can see an example of German World War II perfection, a captured German submarine.

In World War II, German submarines were sunk at a horrific rate, most did not last more than a few months. The movie DAS BOOT is an excellent depiction of this awful story.

Look closely at the quality of the workmanship on that submarine in Chicago. The vessel must have been built to sail for a hundred years. It was like making a handcrafted sterling silver soda can that would be thrown away after the first use.

Again, if you make them perfectly, how many can you make?

---

[240] "Decisive Weapons," History Channel Documentary.

[241] GERMAN TANKS OF WORLD WAR II, by DR S. Hart & DR R. Hart, Barnes & Nobel Books, 1999, p.58.

What really caught my eye at the museum was the submarine's flare pistol. A flare pistol is rarely used and has no need for accuracy. In fact, on a submarine that would likely be sunk in a few months, it might not ever be used at all. The flare pistols I handled in the U.S. Air Force were what you would expect, crude and cheap.

This German flare pistol looks like it was hand crafted by Smith & Wesson for use in Olympic target matches.

I repeat, if you make your weapons perfectly, how many can you make?

The German desire for perfection shows up in the production statistics. Using the U.S.S.R. as a comparison, in 1943, the U.S.S.R. turned 8 million tons of steel and 90 million tons of coal into 48,000 heavy artillery pieces and 24,000 tanks.

Germany that same year turned 30 million tons of steel and 340 million tons of coal into only 27,000 heavy guns and only 17,000 tanks.[242]

In other words, using more than three times as much steel and coal, the Germans made only two-thirds as many weapons.

Uncle Eric

P.S. Chris, if you ever visit the German part of Switzerland or parts of Germany that have never been bombed, you will see the German penchant for perfection. The towns and villages are so neat, clean, and well preserved they look like model railroad layouts; they are works of art. This kind of attention to detail is wonderful for civilian life, but in war it is a great handicap. War is a sloppy business.

---

[242] WHY THE ALLIES WON, by Richard Overy, W. W. Norton & Co., NY, 1995, p.182.

36

Germany's Wonder Weapons

Dear Chris,

Much of the reason the Germans got so little production from such heavy use of raw materials is that they were constantly trying to build new and better weapons, so their factories were endlessly shutting down to retool for the next upgrades. The Germans tried dozens of types of planes, tanks, and guns, so they were only able to produce small numbers of each.

The Soviet Union stuck to just two main types of tank, three main types of fighter aircraft, one main type of bomber, and one main type of fighter-bomber. Once a Soviet factory was up and running, it didn't stop.

Much is made of Germany's so-called wonder weapons. The Hollywood version of history says that Germany's scientists and engineers were fast developing advanced technologies that would soon have obliterated the Allies if the USG had not come to the rescue.

The rest of the story is that these advancements were not a strength, they were a weakness. I will use the famous V-2 rocket as an example.

The V-2 was years ahead of anything the Allies had. In fact, it was so far ahead that it would eventually sire the American space program.

Hitler wanted the V-2 for the purpose of bombing Britain, to frighten the British into submission. The V-2 would be launched to the edge of space and then it would drop back to the target at such great speed that it was hardly visible.

About 6,000 V-2 rockets were built, and 1,403 were fired at Britain.

Another 30,000 of the "flying bomb" V-1 ramjet missiles were built, too; 5,800 were launched and 2,420 reached Britain.[243] The V-1 was an early cruise missile.

The missiles were certainly terrifying, and they killed thousands, but this only stiffened British resolve. The missiles did almost no damage to military targets because they were impossible to aim accurately.

Also, each missile carried only one bomb. This means only 3,823 of these bombs reached Britain. This was roughly equal to the number dropped in one large raid by aircraft, and with much less accuracy.

The cost to the Germans?

The two programs consumed billions of marks and absorbed the labor of tens of thousands of workers. After the war, an American Bombing Survey estimated that if these resources had been devoted instead to producing conventional aircraft, the Germans could have built another 24,000 planes.[244]

In other words, the V-1s and V-2s that are so often cited as proof that Germany was about to take over the world actually achieved no military gains at all, and they were equivalent to the Germans shooting down 24,000 of their own planes.

Chris, the German scientists and engineers were brilliant, but the ability to invent is a different thing than the ability to mass produce.

---

[243] WHY THE ALLIES WON, by Richard Overy, W. W. Norton & Co., NY, 1995, p.240.

[244] WHY THE ALLIES WON, by Richard Overy, p.240.

Isn't it revealing how much you understand when you look at the economics?

This difference between the ability to invent and the ability to mass produce was repeated in the U.S.S.R. after World War II. Soviet scientists and engineers developed many **prototype** aircraft that looked great at air shows, but the production versions were terrible. The MiG-25 jet fighter was an example. Capable of flying at three times the speed of sound, this plane, first flown in 1965, threw such a scare into the Pentagon that the USG launched a crash program to build the excellent F-15.

After the F-15 was in the air, the Pentagon discovered that when a mass production version of a MiG-25 flew at three times the speed of sound, its engines burned up.

The Germans had the same kind of problem. They could build amazing prototypes, but making large numbers of equally good production versions escaped them.

As early as summer of 1940, the British were already producing 500 planes per month against Germany's 140.[245]

Well, how about the atomic bomb?

Germans were working on the bomb, but so were others. None had the resources of the U.S. and all were many years behind the U.S. The Russians got the bomb in 1949 and the British in 1952, which was 14 years after nuclear fission was discovered in 1938.

Germans were the discoverers of fission but never got close to a usable bomb. Again, there is a big difference between invention and production.

The U.S. Manhattan Project that was developed to build an atomic bomb went from concept to a combat-ready weapon in just four years, 1941 to 1945.

---

[245] DAYS OF INFAMY, by Michael Coffey, Hyperion, NY, 1999, p.66.

Chris, to be fair to the people who think Hitler's advanced technology could have won the war, I should say a few words about Germany's ME-262 jet fighter. The ME-262 gets my vote as the finest weapon of the war, and the Germans managed to make 1,430 of them. This is not a lot, but it is significant. With a top speed of 540 mph — a hundred mph faster than the superb American P-51— the ME-262 deserves all the praise anyone might heap upon it. The American P-59 Aracomet jet and the British Meteor jet could not touch it.

In my opinion, the ME-262 was the only German wonder weapon that really was as advertised by the USG.

The ME-262 points us to the crucial strategic importance of the fact that Hitler was crazy. He loved dive bombers. He was so impressed at the success of his Stuka dive bomber early in the war that he decreed that all his bombers, even big ones with four engines, must have dive-bombing capability.[246] This prevented development of a large German bomber.

He also required the ME-262 — a fighter — be used for bombing as well as other roles.

Hitler's meddling in the design and production of the ME-262 resulted in more than three-quarters of them never being used against the enemy.[247]

If Hitler had not meddled with the ME-262, the outcome of the war might have been different. In one battlefield test, six ME-262s, armed with the new R4M air-to-air rockets, shot down fourteen B-17 Flying Fortresses, with no losses to

[246] WHY THE ALLIES WON, by Richard Overy, W. W. Norton & Co., NY, 1995, p.219.

[247] ENCYCLOPEDIA OF MILITARY AIRCRAFT, by Enzo Angelucci, Rand McNally, NY, 1980, p.239.

themselves.[248] Amazing. But Hitler's meddling prevented these awesome weapons from being widely used.

Far from a military genius who was about to take over the world, Hitler was the best weapon the Allies had. If I were the Allies, I'd have been trying to clone Hitler. Each clone would have been worth 50 aircraft carriers.

Hitler was so far out of touch with reality that in planning strategies against the Soviets he would try to order armies into existence, as if he were a god who could create men and equipment out of thin air.[249]

One of the greatest follies of the war, often cited in histories, was the Maginot Line built by the French to repulse the Germans. Look at a map, Chris, the Maginot Line ran along the French-German border from Belgium to Switzerland.

The Germans smoothly beat the Maginot Line. Then, having proved how easily this kind of defense could be defeated, Hitler began building a giant copy of it called the Atlantic Wall.

Consuming vast amounts of labor and millions of tons of cement, steel, and other materials that were in short supply, Hitler's Atlantic Wall ran along the coast from the Arctic Circle to the Pyrenees Mountains at the French-Spanish border.

On June 6, 1944, the Allies punched through the Atlantic Wall in one day.

Hitler's lunacy was known early on. In his 1940 book, FAILURE OF A MISSION, Britain's ambassador to Germany, Sir Nevile Henderson, described baffling conversations with

---

[248] SECRET WEAPONS OF THE THIRD REICH by Leslie E. Simon, We Inc. Publishers, Old Greenwich, CT, 1971, p.128.

[249] Historian Norman Polmar, co-author of AMERICA AT WAR, interviewed in History Channel TV documentary "The Last Days of World War II."

Hitler starting in 1937. Henderson explained that Hitler had "a phenomenal capacity for self-deception and was able to forget everything which he had ever said or done in the past, if it no longer suited his present or future purpose to remember it."[250]

Summarizing, Chris, German technology was, on balance, the most advanced in the war, but this was a weakness, not a strength. In their 1940s factories, the Germans could produce only small numbers of 1950s weapons, while the allies stuck to producing unimaginable amounts of 1940s weapons.

And, of course, there was the madman Hitler, always finding creative new ways to sabotage the work of his technicians.

Chris, you may have heard of the super cannon called the Hochdruckpumpe (HDP). The HDP had the ability to fire an 8-foot long, 150-pound projectile 75 miles, enabling the Germans to shell England. The HDP sometimes gets publicity as an example of the super weapons Germans would have used to take over the world. What you have not been told is that German factories could not make the gun strong enough. Once in every three shots the barrel exploded.[251]

The idea that advanced German weapons were about to take over the world would be laughable — if it were not for so many people believing it — it still guides U.S. foreign policy today. Americans have a fear that "another Hitler" will take over the world if we do not meddle everywhere to prevent it.

---

[250] FAILURE OF A MISSION, by Sir Nevile Henderson, G.P. Putnam's Sons, NY, 1940, p.56.

[251] SECRET WEAPONS OF THE THIRD REICH by Leslie E. Simon, We Inc. Publishers, Old Greenwich, CT, 1971, p.191.

In trying to fight Britain and Russia at the same time, Germany was a wolf who had attacked two lions. The wolf caught the lions asleep, so he looked tough in the opening round, but then the lions had him for lunch.

Any economist could have seen it coming.

Chris, the Japanese experience against America was the same as the German experience against Britain and Russia. Wolves versus lions. The lions had been caught asleep, but once they woke up, it was no contest. In my next letter I will write about Japan.

Uncle Eric

P.S. Earlier I mentioned the German cultural tendency to choose quality over quantity. Their desire for perfection crippled their ability to produce weapons in large numbers.

Looking at photos of American planes in the final years of the war, you may have noticed that they were no longer painted except for their insignia. Americans realized that the average plane flew only a few weeks or months before it was shot up, so it would not last long enough to corrode. Painting costs a lot of money, time and labor, so Americans stopped doing it, and devoted these resources to other efforts.

The German V-1 and V-2 missiles were able to fly only a single one-way mission.

They were painted.

Chris, the war of Germany versus the Allies was a war of craftsmen versus industrialists. Anyone who looked at the economics could have predicted the outcome.

Why didn't they? I have wondered about that. All I can come up with is the fact that in those days people trusted the government and they kept their mouths shut. Saying something that contradicted what the government was saying could invite charges of disloyalty.

As I remember, Chris, it was not until President Ronald Reagan came along in 1981, saying, "Government is not the solution, it is the problem," that Americans became comfortable exposing harsh truths about the government.

I can tell you this. Were it not for Reagan, you would not be reading these letters because I would be afraid to write them.

37

Oil and Rifles

Dear Chris,

Thanks for your letter asking about the weapons of the other two main Axis powers — Italy and Japan.

I will not write much about them because there is not much to write about. Early in the war the Japanese fighter plane, called the Zero, was superior to those of the U.S., but beyond that, I cannot think of anything the Japanese or Italians had that was comparable to the weapons of the Allies. And the Zero was soon greatly outclassed by several U.S. fighters including the superb F4U Corsair.

Roy Grumman of Grumman Aircraft Corporation (a U.S. company) received a letter from a navy squadron commander who reported the loss rate of Japanese planes against Grumman F6F Hellcats was 200 to 1.[252]

The Italian equipment was, well, Italian. As builders of giant bridges, skyscrapers, and other architectural wonders, the Italians have long been among the world's top experts. Maybe it's the Roman heritage.

But, as builders of weapons, the Italians have not excelled, and you don't win wars with skyscrapers, you win them with weapons.

As an example of Italian weapons, the Model 38 Carcano infantry rifle had a reputation for blowing up in the face of

---

[252] History Channel, "Modern Marvels," aired in Sacramento, California, November 4, 2000.

its owner. Italian soldiers called it "the rifle that never killed anyone on purpose."

Incidentally, this piece of junk is claimed to be the rifle that was used to kill President John Kennedy.

I once saw a Model 38 in a military museum. It looks like something a high school student might cobble together in metal shop.

The Italians were good against the spear-throwing tribesmen of Ethiopia in 1935, but they really did not have the weapons or, more importantly, the heart for a fight with a modern, heavily industrialized opponent. In 1943, they switched sides, arrested Mussolini, and later killed him.

As for Japanese weapons, in films showing Japanese rifles, you have probably noticed the length of the Japanese bayonets. American bayonets were about the length of kitchen knives. Japanese bayonets were short swords 15.5 inches long.

Japanese bayonets were long because the Japanese expected to need them. The Japanese bolt-action rifle was awful. Slow firing, it dated from 1905 and was accurate only at short range.[253] Also, supplies of ammunition from this minor industrial power were usually meager.

Japanese soldiers were encouraged to use their bayonets whenever possible,[254] and their officers carried swords. I am sure most Americans think the Japanese officers' swords were ceremonial, but these weapons were carried into battle, as in wars hundreds of years earlier. It is something to think about, Chris. In films we see the Japanese Zero, and we see Japanese officers carrying swords. We are impressed by the Zero,

---

[253] WHY THE ALLIES WON, by Richard Overy, W. W. Norton & Co., NY, 1995, p.222.

[254] WHY THE ALLIES WON, by Richard Overy, p.222.

and fail to recognize the importance of the fact that the officer was armed with a weapon from the Middle Ages.

When the war began in 1939, the only major country with a semiautomatic[255] infantry rifle as standard issue was the U.S; 50,000 were already in the hands of the troops.[256] This rifle was the M-1 Garand, which even today is regarded as one of the finest rifles ever invented. Highly reliable and accurate at long range, the M-1 fired eight shots as fast as the soldier could pull the trigger.

The M-1 Garand was also better than the German rifle, which was bolt-action. A single American could lay down as much fire as three or four Germans or Japanese, and more accurately.

The German rifle was similar to the American Springfield rifle from World War I. Invented before the turn of the century, the German weapon was very good quality for its time, but for World War II it was outdated, far outclassed by the M-1. The M-1 had the effect of doubling the size of an American platoon without risking any more American lives.

Tanks? Japanese and Italian tanks were tin cans. If you ever get a chance to visit a military museum that has tanks from the Second World War, compare the Japanese and Italian tanks to the Russian T-34. But don't laugh; it's not polite.

Trucks? Chris, like the Germans, the Japanese were dependent mostly on horses, each division had about 3,000.[257] How many Japanese horses have you seen in films?

All this reflects the fact that the Axis powers were the younger members of the Usual Suspects and were only

---

[255] Semiautomatic: no need for the soldier to operate the mechanism, the gun fires automatically with each pull of the trigger.

[256] THE FIGHTING GARAND, edited by Nolan Wilson, Desert Publications, El Dorado, AR, 1984, p.3.

[257] WHY THE ALLIES WON, by Richard Overy, W. W. Norton & Co., NY, 1995, p.221.

beginning to develop their empires and their mass-production economies. In the world of the 1940s, they were children rebelling against adults. They caught the adults by surprise, so they looked fierce early on, but after the adults were fully awake, the young rebels were smashed.

Perhaps the single greatest weakness of the Axis was its lack of oil. After the Spanish Civil War, it was obvious that offensive war (as opposed to defensive guerrilla war) would now be highly mechanized and, therefore, almost totally dependent on oil.

Chris, the Axis had very little oil. Any economist in 1940 could show that the Allies controlled 90 percent of the world oil supply and the Axis 3 percent.[258]

Worse, most of Germany's (and Japan's) oil came from the New World on the other side of the Atlantic. After the British sank the small German navy, the German war machine was doomed to remain a horse.

To me, Chris, if you are trying to show the difference between the firepower of the Axis and the Allies, you don't need to say much more than that the Allies had 90 percent of the oil and the Axis had 3 percent. Without oil, tanks don't run, planes don't fly, and ships don't sail.

It is not much of an exaggeration to say World War II was really an oil war. After FDR cut off the Japanese oil supply, the Japanese began moving south to capture the oil of Southeast Asia and Indonesia. They attacked the U.S. Navy in order to clear the way to the oil fields.

Germany could not win without the oil of Romania and of the Southern U.S.S.R. The Allies continually bombed the oil fields in Romania. In their attempt to take the Soviet fields,

---

[258] WHY THE ALLIES WON, by Richard Overy, W. W. Norton & Co., NY, 1995, p.228.

1,500 miles from home, the Germans were stopped at Stalingrad (Volgograd). As early as summer of 1941, the German advance against the U.S.S.R. was being slowed by shortages of gasoline.[259]

Chris, please let that fact sink in. The Germans were running out of gasoline *before* the U.S. was in the war.

So, Chris, now you have the rest of the story about the supposedly awesome Axis war capability. As I said, the Japanese and Italian weapons were so inferior they deserve little comment. As for the Germans, here is my summary:

The Allies controlled almost all the oil. No oil means no engines, which means no tanks, planes or ships. The Axis had to fall back on using horses.

Germany had two armies. The small point of the spear was the high-tech blitzkrieg (lightning war) force depicted in so many films. The rest of the spear was almost indistinguishable from an army of the 1800s. When we think of German soldiers we think of men driving tanks or flying Stuka dive bombers, but the typical German soldier was really a foot soldier carrying a bolt-action rifle and leading a pack horse. (The same can be said for the Japanese.)

The wonder weapons such as the V-2 rocket were so advanced they were a handicap. They absorbed vast amounts of money and manpower that could have been used to make weapons proven to yield real results.

---

[259] WHY THE ALLIES WON, by Richard Overy, W. W. Norton & Co., NY, 1995, p.231.

Germany's navy was small compared to that of the British and was sunk early. The famous battleship *Graf Spee* went down in December 1939; the *Bismark* in May 1941. Except for its submarines, Germany was a land power only, and most of its submarines eventually went to the bottom, too.

The Germans had nothing remotely like the thousands of well-defended B-17, B-24 and B-29 heavy long-range bombers thrown at them. Germany never developed a fleet of heavy long-range bombers, so it could not do great damage to British or Russian industry.

Like many armies before them, German troops and machinery were helpless in the face of Russia's most powerful weapon, its winters.

Most importantly, Germany had Adolph Hitler, a madman who never missed a chance to sabotage the work of his generals and engineers. The catastrophic effects of his madness became clear for all to see on June 22, 1941, when he attacked the Soviet Union. It may not be an exaggeration to say that with Hitler on their side, the Allies could not lose.

Chris, whenever I hear someone say that Germany could have conquered the world, my reply is, where is the evidence?
The idea that Hitler almost conquered the whole earth, so America must be a global cop meddling in every nation to prevent the rise of a new Hitler is, to put it politely, a bit out of touch with reality.

Uncle Eric

38

Americans Were Less Intelligent?

Dear Chris,

Americans have been taught to have such great awe of Germany's superweapons that I am sure some think the Americans of that era were not as bright as the Germans. This is part of the myth that World War II was a close call and the Germans nearly won. Chris, I will give you three examples of why this myth is wrong. The close call never happened.

You can see my first example with your own eyes if you ever attend the annual Reno Air Races in Reno, Nevada. You will notice that many of the racing planes are P-51 Mustangs, and many of the winners will be P-51s.

These P-51s were built more than a half-century ago.

The P-51 is generally regarded as the finest propeller-driven aircraft to come out of World War II. Even today, if you ask pilots what aircraft they would most want to own, or even just fly for a few hours, I am sure nearly all would be quick to say a P-51.

The P-51 was faster than the early British and American jets (the Gloster Meteor and P-59 Airacomet). With a maximum altitude of 41,900 feet, it could fly almost as high as a jet, and it had enough range to escort bombers all the way to their targets in Germany and back.[260] The P-51 was also highly maneuverable.

---

[260] ENCYCLOPEDIA OF MILITARY AIRCRAFT, by Enzo Angelucci, Rand McNally, NY, 1980, p.200,208.

The P-51 was truly a breathtaking invention, and beautiful, too, both in sight and sound. The roar of the Rolls Royce Merlin engine is so smooth it is almost musical. Even people who know nothing about aircraft can tell by the sound that this machine is something special.

When the war began, America's front-line fighter was the P-40. The USG and London were planning big orders for P-40s, but no one was happy about it. The Japanese Zero and the German Me-109 were better.

Engineers at North American Aviation thought they could build a better plane than the P-40, and they decided to give it a try.

From the moment they went to work on the P-51, to the first one in the air, was 121 days.[261] Equally amazing, 15,686 of these superb machines were built.[262]

Chris, no other country could possibly have done that, and, as I write this letter, no country could today. The production capacity does not exist. But it did then, in America, and only in America.

My second example is the B-24 Liberator bomber. Early in 1941, the Ford Company was invited to make parts for the B-24. Henry Ford replied that he wanted to build the whole plane, and if he could not do the whole job he would not do it at all. The government gave in, and in March 1941, Ford began building the B-24 plant at Willow Run, Michigan.

When the Willow Run plant was finished, the assembly line was more than a mile long. The main assembly building covered 67 acres, and the total site was 900 acres.[263]

---

[261] ENCYCLOPEDIA OF MILITARY AIRCRAFT, by Enzo Angelucci, Rand McNally, NY, 1980, p.234.

[262] ENCYCLOPEDIA OF MILITARY AIRCRAFT, by Enzo Angelucci, p.234.

[263] WHY THE ALLIES WON, by Richard Overy, W. W. Norton & Co., NY, 1995, p.196.

A four-engine B-24 contained 1.5 million parts.[264]

Henry Ford's Willow Run plant turned out one B-24 every 63 minutes.[265]

No other country could possibly have matched that performance and, as I write this letter, no country could today. The production capacity does not exist. But it did then, in America, and only in America.

A total of 18,188 B-24 Liberators were built at all aircraft plants, [266] in addition to 12,729 B-17 Flying Fortresses[267] and 3,970 B-29 Superfortresses.[268] (Plus about 290,000 other U.S. aircraft.[269])

These numbers are staggering, especially in light of the fact that the Germans never developed any heavy bombers at all. The closest thing they had to a heavy bomber was the two-engine Heinkel He-177, which was a complete failure.[270] About 1,000 of these excessively complex planes were built, and only 200 ever left the ground.[271]

In short, Chris, the Germans were able to put up 200 heavy bombers, compared to America's 34,887 heavy bombers, plus 13,512 four-engine British Halifax and Lancaster heavy bombers.[272]

That was 48,399 against 200, or 242 to one.

---

[264] WHY THE ALLIES WON, by Richard Overy, W. W. Norton & Co., NY, 1995, p.196.

[265] WHY THE ALLIES WON, by Richard Overy, p.197.

[266] ENCYCLOPEDIA OF MILITARY AIRCRAFT, by Enzo Angelucci, Rand McNally, NY, 1980, p.291.

[267] ENCYCLOPEDIA OF MILITARY AIRCRAFT, by Enzo Angelucci, p.288.

[268] ENCYCLOPEDIA OF MILITARY AIRCRAFT, by Enzo Angelucci, p.296.

[269] WHY THE ALLIES WON, by Richard Overy, p.331.

[270] ENCYCLOPEDIA OF MILITARY AIRCRAFT, by Enzo Angelucci, p.293.

[271] ENCYCLOPEDIA OF MILITARY AIRCRAFT, by Enzo Angelucci, p.293.

[272] ENCYCLOPEDIA OF MILITARY AIRCRAFT, by Enzo Angelucci, p.290.

In early 1941, when Gallup polled Londoners to ask what made them most depressed, the weather came out ahead of the German bombers.[273]

How could anyone believe the Axis almost won?

They believe it because they have never looked at the economics.

The Japanese had only one type of heavy bomber, the four-engine Nakajima G8N Renzan. Total production was four. No, not four hundred or four thousand, just four.[274] The main Japanese bomber was a two-engine Mitsubishi G4M Betty, which was about the size of the B-25 Mitchell medium bomber. Japanese air crews referred to the Betty as the "flying cigar" or the "flying lighter" because it burned so easily; only 2,446 were built.

The effect of the 48,399 American and British heavy bombers on German industry can be seen by the fact that by 1944, Germany was so short of aluminum and other metals that the new Heinkel 162 jet fighter had to be made mostly of wood, like an aircraft from the First World War.[275] The shortage of brass and steel even forced German arms makers to try to invent a rifle cartridge in which the "brass" contained no metal.[276]

During World War II, American factories were so huge and well tooled that each American aircraft worker produced more than twice as much as his German counterpart, and four times as much as his Japanese counterpart.[277] And there were

---

[273] WHY THE ALLIES WON, by Richard Overy, W. W. Norton & Co., NY, 1995, p.109.

[274] ENCYCLOPEDIA OF MILITARY AIRCRAFT, by Enzo Angelucci, p.295.

[275] SECRET WEAPONS OF THE THIRD REICH by Leslie E. Simon, We Inc. Publishers, Old Greenwich, CT, 1971, p.23.

[276] SECRET WEAPONS OF THE THIRD REICH by Leslie E. Simon, p.30.

[277] WHY THE ALLIES WON, by Richard Overy, p.197.

a lot more Americans than there were Japanese or Germans. The American population was nearly equal to that of Germany and Japan combined.[278]

Remember, this does not include the awesome production of Britain and Russia, either.

By the end of 1942 — only 13 months after the attack on Pearl Harbor — America was already outproducing the Japanese, Germans, and Italians combined. America's factories had cranked out 47,000 aircraft to 27,000; 24,000 tanks to 11,000; and six times as much artillery.[279]

And, again, this does not include the production of the British and Russians.

My third example is the Liberty ship. At 420 feet in length, and capable of carrying 9,000 tons of cargo, the Liberty ship was the main cargo ship of World War II. It could carry as much as 300 railroad freight cars. That was 2,840 jeeps, or 440 light tanks, or 230 million rounds of rifle ammunition.[280]

Henry J. Kaiser ran the Kaiser Motor Car Company and had built Hoover Dam and the San Francisco Bay Bridge. Dubbed "Hurry-up Henry," Kaiser had a reputation for doing the impossible.

When the war began, Kaiser knew nothing about ships, but he thought he could work out a way to build them on an assembly line as if they were cars. At his shipyards in Richmond, California, he set out to do it.

At the beginning of the war, the rule of thumb for the time required to build a cargo ship the size of a Liberty was

---

[278] ECONOMIC GEOGRAPHY by R.H. Whitbeck & V.C. Finch, McGraw-Hill, NY, 1941, p.619.

[279] WHY THE ALLIES WON, by Richard Overy, W. W. Norton & Co., NY, 1995, p.192.

[280] LIBERTY SHIPS, by John Gorley Bunker, Ayer Company, Salem, New Hampshire, 1991, p.7.

one year. By 1943, Kaiser had it down to eight days.[281] One Liberty ship, the *Robert E. Peary*, was built in four days.[282] Try to imagine it, Chris, an entire oceangoing cargo ship capable of carrying 2,840 jeeps, built in four days. The total number of Liberty ships produced (1941-1945) was 2,751,[283] which works out to nearly two per day, in addition to the thousands of other ships built.

Chris, the idea that the Germans were technical geniuses and Americans were not is quite absurd. Some Germans were brilliant, no doubt about it, but neither they nor anyone else except Americans would have tried to produce a four-engine bomber every hour, or a 9,000-ton cargo ship in four days. Americans took on the challenge and did it.

Yet, despite this and all the other evidence that has been uncovered in the past half-century, many Americans still think Germany almost won World War II.

The aircraft carrier was (still is) the undisputed super weapon. The nation that had the most carriers in World War II was well on its way to victory.

In a previous letter I mentioned that America built 146 aircraft carriers in 44 months. Hard to believe, but true.

An aircraft carrier is the most complex device humans make. It is a floating city with its own international airport. Aircraft carriers contain electrical power plants, restaurants, barber shops, movie theaters, dental offices, libraries, laundries, warehouses, hotels, hospitals, and everything else you would find in a small city.

---

[281] WHY THE ALLIES WON, by Richard Overy, W. W. Norton & Co., NY, 1995, p.194.

[282] LIBERTY SHIPS, by John Gorley Bunker, Ayer Company, Salem, New Hampshire, 1991, p.12.

[283] LIBERTY SHIPS, by John Gorley Bunker, p.17.

Americans built 146. How many did the "superior" Germans build?

One. Or I should say, almost one. The Germans had a lot of technical problems and gave up before the ship was finished.

German troops were highly experienced and led by generals who were brilliant, but the battlefield effect of America's technical ability and production capacity can be seen in this remark by a German general in Normandy:

> I cannot understand these Americans. Each night we know that we have cut them to pieces, inflicted heavy casualties, mowed down their transport. But — in the morning, we are suddenly faced with fresh battalions, with complete replacements of men, machines, food, tools and weapons. This happens day after day.[284]

The assumption that little Germany nearly won the war is a hallucination, propaganda, another example of the Holly-wood version of history. This assumption can be a great plot device to make the audience root for the American movie heroes, but the economic fact of the matter is that the Germans never had a prayer, nor did the Japanese.

The evidence shows clearly that the supreme technical geniuses of the war, by far, were the Americans, but you would never know it if you did not study the economics.

Uncle Eric

---

[284] WHY THE ALLIES WON, by Richard Overy, W. W. Norton & Co., NY, 1995, p.319.

P.S. Chris, for the rest of your life you will meet people who have strong opinions about World War II. You will rarely meet anyone who has looked at the economics, as you now have. I suggest you keep in your wallet a 3"x5" card listing important data. Read through my most recent dozen or so letters and pull out statistics you consider most revealing. Note the page numbers on which you found them so that you can refer back as needed.

For example, most Americans believe the war was a close call, the Japanese and Germans nearly won. On your 3"x5" card you might list the fact, from one of my previous letters, that the Allies controlled 90% of the world oil supply, versus the Axis 3%. And, from today's letter, you might note that the Germans and Japanese were able to put 204 heavy bombers into the air versus the American and British total of 48,399.

Speaking of the British, the World War II myth says the British would have lost to the Germans if they had not been rescued by the U.S.

Chris, ever since the Battle of Taranto in November 1940, the most important military weapon has been the aircraft carrier. Even one or two small carriers are a mighty advantage against an opponent who has none.

As we have seen, the Germans failed to build even one carrier; they could not solve the technical problems. The British had 65 carriers that could each launch more than 20 planes, and a total of 185 carriers. Ten of the large British fleet carriers were launched before the war began, five of them more than two decades earlier. This is one indication of how much technical lead the British had over the Germans.

Chris, did the Germans make good weapons? In most cases, yes. But, how many could they make? And, did the British really need U.S. help? What do you think?

39

The Brookings Revelation

Dear Chris,

The inability of little Germany to produce the weapons and supplies it needed to win World War II was fully understood before the U.S. got into the war. The Institute of Economics at the prestigious Brookings Institution in Washington, D.C. anticipated the question and in June 1941 published a 194-page study called NAZI EUROPE AND WORLD TRADE.

I have a copy in my library. The study was available to anyone who cared to look at the facts; the cover price was $2.00. I think we can fairly assume President Roosevelt had the $2.00 and so did his economic advisors.

The Brookings Institution found that Germany, Italy, and their allies were not only woefully short of lead, copper, cobalt, and most other industrial raw materials needed to make and operate weapons, they were also short of food.

Remember, this was five months *before* the U.S. was in the war, and weeks before FDR cut off the Japanese oil supply. It was a published fact that Nazi Europe was already in deep trouble, unable to produce what it needed to beat England and Russia.

In regard to Nazi Europe's supplies of fuel and lubricants, page 97 of the Brookings study describes Germany's and Italy's condition as "poverty." This alone was the death knell for the Third Reich.

It was also a highly accurate prediction. A key reason the Third Reich lost the war was that it ran out of fuel. Any soldier who was in Europe at the end of the war will tell you he often saw German tanks and trucks in good condition, except that their fuel tanks were dry, abandoned by the side of the road.

The Brookings' pages 176 and 177 offer a list of German industries described as "severely handicapped" due to cut-offs of raw materials: manufacturing, mining, transportation, agriculture, communication, and food production, among others. This was pretty much the whole German economy.

Page 178 reports that, "Germany's supply problem has not been solved by her seizure of neighboring territories. On the contrary, it has been made more difficult." Like Germany, these neighboring areas had been dependent on imports, and when Germany captured them, supplies to these areas, too, were cut off.

Chris, in my opinion, this Brookings study is the long-sought smoking gun,[285] proof that little Germany did not have a prayer of beating the mighty British and Soviet Empires, and there could be no ethical reason for President Roosevelt to provoke the Japanese into attacking. The "necessary sacrifice" at Pearl Harbor was not necessary, and this was clear to any informed person *before* President Roosevelt cut off the Japanese oil supply.

That was the production side of Germany's war effort. In my next letter, logistics.

Uncle Eric

---

[285] Smoking gun: proof of guilt. In a murder, if a suspect is found standing over the body and holding a smoking gun, the police will take this as proof that the suspect committed the homicide.

P.S. Chris, on balance, German technical ability was no better than that of the British, Russians or Americans. In most cases it was far worse, due to shortages of raw materials and difficulties with mass production. As I have said, if you look at the war the way an economist would (or should), you will be continually saying, yes, that's a fine weapon, but how many could they make?

However, there was one field in which the Germans far surpassed all others: haberdashery.[286] The German army's tailors, especially those of the SS,[287] were awesome, and it would be hard to exaggerate their importance.

I kid you not. The Germans were no more a master race than the Americans or anyone else, but they certainly *looked* like a master race. And they were far superior at marching.

Allied propagandists and movie makers have been wonderfully creative in using the dazzling uniforms and precise marching to give the impression that only by the skin of its teeth did the world escape conquest by Germany.

---

[286] Haberdashery: men's clothing and accessories.

[287] SS: the elite military unit of the Nazi party. Noted for ruthlessness and lack of ethics, the SS served as Hitler's personal guard and as a security force in Germany and occupied areas.

40

Russia Invaded by Keystone Kops

Dear Chris,

In an earlier letter I mentioned that when it comes to war, amateurs talk strategy and professionals talk logistics.

Logistics is the ability to transport bullets and beans to the troops. The outcomes of nearly all wars are determined by logistics; the first side to run out of bullets and beans loses.

Military historian Martin van Creveld estimates that "logistics make up as much as nine-tenths of the business of war."[288]

Hitler's attack on Stalin was the largest military operation in history, which means, among other things, that it was probably more dependent on good logistics than any other military operation in history.

The Germans not only botched their production, they botched their logistics.

Chris, you can read all about it in van Creveld's fine book about logistics, SUPPLYING WAR.[289]

Van Creveld points out that little Germany was dependent on the mighty U.S.S.R. for a great many products including oil and rubber, so when Hitler attacked, these crucial

---

[288] SUPPLYING WAR, by Martin van Creveld, Cambridge University Press, 1977, p.231.

[289] SUPPLYING WAR, by Martin van Creveld, Cambridge University Press, 1977.

supplies were immediately stopped. Even in cases where Germans could capture Russian gasoline, they were still handicapped because their engines needed a higher octane than the Russians were making.

Also, most roads in the Soviet Union were unpaved, so transportation by truck became almost impossible when the heavy rains began and the roads turned to mud.

The Germans had to resort to using railroads.

But the Soviets had long feared invasion by rail, and they had made their railroad tracks a different gauge — wider — than those used in Western Europe.

The Soviets had moved most of their rail equipment east, beyond the reach of the Germans, so the Germans were forced to use their own equipment.

Every yard of rail the Germans used had to be pulled up and reset to the gauge needed by their own trains.

As the shortage of gasoline and tires became critical and more roads turned to mud, more of the German invasion was restricted to rail routes.

Normally in an invasion, the advance force is the best of the tanks, planes, and infantry, with the logistics troops following behind.

The German need to move the rails caused their invasion to turn into a scene from a Keystone Kops[290] movie. The advance units were the logistics troops who were moving the rails, followed by the tanks, planes, and infantry. The point of the German spear was gandy dancers.[291]

---

[290] Keystone Kops: in early movies, a mob of policemen who could do nothing right. They were often shown rushing hither and yon with no plan.

[291] Gandy dancers: railroad track workers. They commonly used tools made by the Gandy Manufacturing Co. in Chicago.

With all their men, vehicles, and supplies crammed into a limited number of rail routes, the disorganization became so extreme that whole trains were lost and never found. What happened to them, no one knows. My guess is that they were stuck on sidings where they were discovered and hit by Soviet guerrillas.

Short of food, ammunition, and nearly everything else, German units began stealing from each other. Their air force was so desperate to protect its meager supplies that it stationed German air force officers with submachine guns on its trains to protect them from the German army.

Chris, when you hear an account of the swift, efficient German advances, remember the way they botched their logistics in the U.S.S.R. The first side to run out of bullets and beans loses, and the Germans were the first to run out.

The Eastern Front was three-quarters of the war, so when the Germans botched the Eastern Front logistics in the summer of 1941, they botched the war.

The idea that the Germans were so skilled and efficient that they could have taken over the world is quite ridiculous. Many German generals were brilliant, but Hitler and his Nazi cronies in Berlin were fools, they made decisions that no amount of brilliance in the field could overcome. As I said, Keystone Kops.

German generals saw this unwinnable war coming and began plotting to get rid of Hitler and his Nazis in the 1930s. More about this in a future letter.

Uncle Eric

P.S. Chris, after examining the economics and logistics of the war, I have come to the conclusion that little Germany could have been beaten by either the British or Soviet Empires alone. It would have been very tough, but either could have done it eventually if for no other reason than that Germany was a small nation with limited natural resources, and the other two were vast empires with resources galore.

The two together, with Germany sandwiched between them, made it a slam dunk.

After the U.S. with its 29%[292] of all the industry in the world, got into the war, Germany was a mouse fighting an elephant.

Again, the movie image of the German soldier is a spit-and-polish super warrior riding atop a huge tank or flying a high-performance aircraft. Some were that, but only a few, the ones at the point of the spear in the early stages of the war. The rest of the spear, meaning the *typical* German soldier, was an average Joe carrying a World War I bolt-action rifle and leading a horse-drawn wagon.

---

[292] A REPUBLIC NOT AN EMPIRE by Patrick Buchanan, Regnery Publishing, Washington, 1999, p.291.

41

Omaha Beach
Bravery versus Heroism

Dear Chris,

If a person plays chicken with a train, risking his life to beat it to the railroad crossing, is he brave?

Certainly.

Is he a hero?

Not hardly. Bravery does not become heroism unless it is for a good cause.

I have heard people say I am a hero for risking my life when I was in the Air Force. They are wrong. I may have been brave, but I was not a hero; I was a fool because I risked my life for a cause that was absurd. If I had died, it would have been no different than if I had lost a race with a train.

If you have not seen the movie SAVING PRIVATE RYAN, I hope you will. Colonel David Hackworth has told me the first 20 minutes of that movie are the most realistic depiction of infantry warfare that he has ever seen. An infantryman and veteran of three wars, Hackworth should know. At the time I write this letter, Hackworth is the most decorated living veteran, including eight purple hearts. Purple Hearts are awarded for being wounded in combat.

SAVING PRIVATE RYAN shows the Allied invasion of Normandy, including the worst part of that invasion, Omaha Beach. Remember the date, it's important, June 6, 1944.

That movie and every other I have seen about the invasion allows the audience to assume the purpose of the invasion was to liberate France and the rest of Western Europe. Any military historian can tell you this assumption is wrong. The invasion did free these areas of German control, but this was only a fringe benefit. The real purpose was to open a second front to help Stalin.[293]

As soon as the USG was in the war, Stalin began demanding that the British and Americans invade Western Europe to draw German troops away from the Eastern Front. In early 1942, Churchill and FDR began planning the invasion of Normandy to appease Stalin.[294]

At a lengthy meeting of American, British, and Soviet officials in Moscow in October 1943, the Soviets again complained that they were bearing most of the burden of fighting the Germans (true) and they demanded help. The American and British delegates promised that a landing on the French coast would take place in the spring of 1944.[295]

The American people did not question the need for this invasion. They had been taught that Hitler was the most evil person on earth and they should do whatever it might take to help Stalin beat him. The fact that Stalin's murder rate was twice Hitler's was rarely discussed.

Chris, if you point out that Hitler's German Nazis and Stalin's Soviet Socialists pounding each other to dust in Eastern Europe was a dream come true for any who believe in liberty, I cannot disagree. The battle between these two cutthroats was not a problem; it was the solution. Why side with Stalin?

---

[293] UNCONDITIONAL SURRENDER by Anne Armstrong, Rutgers University Press, New Brunswick, 1961, p.64.

[294] HISTORY OF THE SECOND WORLD WAR, by B.H. Liddell Hart, Perigee Books, NY, 1982, p.310.

[295] UNCONDITIONAL SURRENDER by Anne Armstrong, Rutgers University Press, New Brunswick, 1961, p.64.

We cannot know what was in FDR's mind but we do know he leaned heavily socialist, and Stalin was leader of the Union of Soviet Socialist Republics.

Why Washington D.C. and London backed Stalin, we can only guess. I think it may also have had something to do with the fact that it is nearly impossible to fight a war without being racist against the other side.

A soldier usually cannot kill someone if he is conscious that the person is just like him — that the person has the same feelings, the same importance to his wife and children, mother and father. The enemy must be dehumanized, seen as a vicious beast deserving of death, so the enemy is tagged with insulting names such as Japs, Chinks, Krauts, Gooks or Ragheads.

In World War I, the Germans were dehumanized. This is why it was so easy for the British and French to punish them with the Treaty of Versailles.

When the next world war broke out, the Germans were already dehumanized. The Russians were not, they had been part of the Allies in World War I, so Americans did not question siding with Stalin. In their minds, I believe, the Germans were worse because the propaganda of the First World War had taught them so.

By D-Day, on June 6, 1944, the USG had already been sending convoys of planes, trucks, ammunition, and food to Stalin for years. The invasion of Normandy was simply the logical next step. Stalin had been clamoring for it for two and a half years, and Washington D.C. and London just went ahead and did it as if rescuing the Kremlin's Empire was a fine and noble thing.

And, through it all, the neutral Swiss, living in the center of the chaos, kept their rifles loaded and watched the massacres, shaking their heads.

I am as certain as it is possible to be about such things that if aid had not been sent to Stalin and if the invasion of Normandy had not been executed, the outcome of the war would have been much better. The German Nazis and Soviet Socialists would have demolished each other in Eastern Europe, and the Kremlin's Empire would have disintegrated in 1945 instead of enduring almost another half-century. (The **Berlin Wall**[296] did not fall until 1989.)

Chris, in my opinion, if you compare the military power of the German Nazis with that of the Soviet Socialists, they were about evenly matched. The Soviets had more production capacity, but the paranoid Stalin had killed off his best generals before the war began. The Germans had less production capacity, but brilliant generals.

If the USG and London had simply remained on the sidelines and let Stalin and Hitler fight it out, the two groups of gangsters probably would have beaten each other to a pulp, and both would have ceased being a threat to the rest of the world. But, fighting Britain and Russia together, Germany had little chance of doing that much damage to Russia.

In the unlikely event that Hitler and Stalin had both survived, they would have counterbalanced each other after the war. After all, this is what Europe and Asia have been for thousands of years — a vast region ruled by tyrants in a balance of power. Lacking any understanding of liberty, peace was never an option, nor is it today. As I write this, at least two dozen wars rage in East Europe and Asia.

---

[296] Berlin Wall: The wall between West Berlin and East Berlin erected in 1961 by the Kremlin. The wall was designed to keep Germans in Soviet-controlled East Germany from escaping to the West. The Berlin Wall became a symbol of Soviet tyranny, and when it was torn down in 1989, this triggered a domino effect that led to the collapse of the entire Soviet Empire.

As it turned out, the USG got involved in World War II on the side of Stalin, and this gave Stalin's forces such a great advantage that they nearly obliterated the Germans.

The Union of Soviet Socialist Republics emerged from the war intact and proceeded to terrorize the world for another 45 years. Two generations of American children grew up waiting to be suddenly vaporized by a hail of nuclear missiles fired by the U.S.S.R.

The world did not end in nuclear war between the U.S. and the U.S.S.R., but there were some close calls. One of the worst was the Cuban Missile Crisis in 1962. America was very lucky. (A good research project. You might start by watching the movie THIRTEEN DAYS to learn the story.)

In short, the invasion of Normandy depicted so well in SAVING PRIVATE RYAN did not help, it made things vastly worse; it saved the Kremlin and made the U.S.S.R. into a superpower.

Chris, in the battle between two of the most brutal tyrants the world has ever seen, the USG sided with the worst of them. Stalin was referred to in the U.S. as "Uncle Joe."

In my opinion, the invasion of Normandy, as depicted in SAVING PRIVATE RYAN, was really about saving Joseph Stalin. Saving Stalin is really what Omaha Beach and the rest of the Normandy invasion were intended to do, and this is what they did.

However, I am not saying the Americans who stormed the beaches in Normandy and defeated Hitler understood what they were doing. The first casualty of war is truth.

Were these men brave?

Certainly.

Were they heroes?

Chris, I am often asked how I got started in this business. It was in the Air Force during the 1960s.

After nearly getting killed several times in the 605th Air Commando Squadron, I started wondering what I was really willing to die for.

I made two lists. One was the things I thought I should be willing to die for, and the other was things the government thought I should be willing to die for. My list was short, I could have written it on a postage stamp. The government's was about nine feet long.

On June 6, 1944, Joseph Stalin and his Soviet Socialists were on the government's list.

Uncle Eric

P.S. Speaking of racism and propaganda, as a youngster during World War I, Theodor Geisel, better known as Dr. Seuss, sold U.S. war bonds. As an adult, Geisel held strong political views. He was opposed to fascism and American neutrality and used the medium of editorial cartoons to voice his position. Many of these are reprinted in the book DR. SEUSS GOES TO WAR: THE WORLD WAR II EDITORIAL CARTOONS OF THEODOR SEUSS GEISEL.[297] Cartoons like these helped form Americans' opinions. The book gives a good overview of ideas held by those who wanted into the war and their attitude toward the people of the Axis, as well as Japanese-Americans suspected of helping the Axis. The cartoons on pages 65, 89, 146, 163, and 169 are especially revealing.

In the cartoon on page 31, Stalin is recognized as a brute as evil as Hitler. This was published May 15, 1941. The next month, President Roosevelt announced he was siding with Stalin.

---

[297] DR. SEUSS GOES TO WAR: THE WORLD WAR II EDITORIAL CARTOONS OF THEODOR SEUSS GEISEL by Richard H. Minear, published by The New Press, New York, 1999.

Part Five

The USG Makes It Worse

42

The German Underground

Dear Chris,

Here is an interesting quote from the prestigious British journal, THE ECONOMIST:

As Mark Mazower points out in his book, DARK CONTINENT: EUROPE'S TWENTIETH CENTURY, the fighters for freedom and against fascism and racism in 1939-45 were rank hypocrites, since they were themselves running dictatorial empires in which racial superiority was a strong theme. No wonder that Mahatma Gandhi, when asked what he thought of western civilization, replied that it would be a good idea.[298]

The Germans were absorbed by the master race idea for about 15 years. The British embraced it for eight centuries. We have already spent several letters on the British "right" to conquer the world, let's look more at the Germans.

The Hollywood version of history says that the whole German nation went crazy and backed Hitler.

Many Germans did back Hitler, but many did not. In the 1932 election that brought Hitler to power, the madman got 42% of the votes, not 100%.

---

[298] THE ECONOMIST, September 11, 1999, p.9, survey article.

Those who opposed Hitler and fought against him are usually ignored because they keep us from seeing the war as a simple contest between good guys and bad guys.

This is similar to the Hollywood treatment of the French. We are told the invasion of Normandy "liberated" France. The fact is that many of the French backed the Germans and helped the Germans exterminate the Jews. They were not members of the Allies; they were Axis. The Allies did not liberate them; they were conquered.

In other words, there were French on both sides of the war. And there were Germans on both sides.

Chris, you should read a book about the German resistance called HITLER'S GERMAN ENEMIES by Louis L. Snyder.[299] Most Americans know about Colonel Claus von Stauffenberg's attempt to kill Hitler on July 20, 1944. This has been depicted in several movies. Stauffenberg planted a bomb in a conference room, but a thick table leg shielded Hitler. An aide was killed, and Hitler and a dozen others were injured, but survived.[300]

We have been led to believe this was the only German attempt to kill Hitler, but actually Stauffenberg's was the 40th known attempt.[301] The first was long before the war began, in January 1933. Another came in September 1938, and so on, with the number of attempts increasing year after year.[302]

In the summer of 1941, on the Eastern Front, German officers and troops were already disobeying Hitler's orders.

---

[299] HITLER'S GERMAN ENEMIES, by Louis, L. Snyder, Hippocrene Books, NY, 1990.

[300] WORLD ALMANAC AND BOOK OF FACTS 2000, World Almanac Books, Primedia Reference, Mahwah, NJ, 1999, p.246.

[301] "Old Scars, New Squabbles," NEWSWEEK, August 1, 1944, p.39.

[302] HITLER'S GERMAN ENEMIES, by Louis, L. Snyder, p.75.

They had been told to kill all Soviet political officers taken prisoner, and they were refusing to do so.[303]

The Allies knew about the opposition to Hitler[304] because German resistance leaders knew they needed the Allies' help and had contacted the Allies. Resistance leaders realized that after killing Hitler a period of confusion in Germany would be likely. They did not want the Allies to take this confusion as an opportunity to annihilate Germany. They contacted the Allies for an agreement that, if Hitler were killed, the Allies would not pounce.[305]

Allied rulers ignored them.

Many members of the resistance were religious. They were resisting the Nazis because they believed there is a Higher Law than any government's law.

A German Lutheran minister named Dietrich Bonhoeffer was assigned to contact the Allies and tell them of the plan to kill Hitler. Reverend Bonhoeffer enlisted the help of Dr. George Bell, the Bishop of Chichester in Britain. Bell had connections among Allied officials.

Bell and Bonhoeffer contacted Allied officials including Britain's foreign secretary Anthony Eden.

Eden and the others refused to help.[306] The resistance in other countries would be recognized and assisted, but not the resistance in Germany.

Allied leaders had decided that Germany would be seen as a unified whole, no distinction would be made between

---

[303] OUR CENTURY, A&E documentary series.

[304] UNCONDITIONAL SURRENDER by Anne Armstrong, Rutgers University Press, New Brunswick, 1961, p.27.

[305] HITLER'S GERMAN ENEMIES, by Louis, L. Snyder, Hippocrene Books, NY 1990, Chapter 1.

[306] HITLER'S GERMAN ENEMIES, by Louis, L. Snyder, p.16.

Nazis and anti-Nazis.[307] All Germans were enemies deserving of death.

This policy of painting all Germans with the same brush may have been connected to the fact that British bombers were conducting "area bombing" for the purpose of exterminating all Germans. If Allied leaders had acknowledged that some Germans were anti-Nazi and deserving of help, then how would they have explained that all Germans deserved to die?

A further problem for the German resistance was the Treaty of Versailles. Every German was afraid that if the Allies again overran Germany, the result would be the same as after World War I. Germans would again be saddled with all the blame, made to pay crushing reparations, and thrown into poverty.

Without a guarantee against another Treaty of Versailles, the growth of the German resistance was limited. Just before he died in 1987, former CIA director William Casey wrote in his memoirs that Franklin Roosevelt erred tragically in not backing the German resistance and helping them topple Hitler.[308]

However, even without the Allies' help, the German resistance did have a crippling effect on the Nazis. With each attempt to kill Hitler, the Nazis rounded up and murdered anyone they thought might be in the resistance. By this means, they gradually killed off the best and brightest, the people they needed most to help them win the war.

---

[307] "Resistance to Hitler, Doomed Chivalry," THE ECONOMIST, March 10, 1990, p.100.

[308] "Casey's Last Words," U.S. NEWS & WORLD REPORT, March 21, 1988, p.13.

The standout example was General Erwin Rommel, the "Desert Fox," who had made life awful for the Allies. Rommel was involved in the July 20, 1944, attempt to kill Hitler. Afterward he was forced to commit suicide. German forces were seriously handicapped by the loss of his leadership.

Chris, why did Allied leaders refuse to help the German underground kill Hitler? I doubt we will ever know for sure, we cannot read minds. Maybe they were afraid that if they tried to kill Hitler, he might try to kill them.

We will also never know if the German resistance would have succeeded if they had received help from the Allies. But, we do know the Allies not only refused to help remove Hitler, they took steps that made it almost impossible for the resistance to remove him. More in my next letter.

Uncle Eric

P.S. Why was the whole German population regarded as crazed killers? In my opinion, it was the propaganda from World War I. In order to rally the British people to the cause, and to persuade Americans to join with them, British officials in World War I launched a propaganda campaign that showed all Germans as monsters. For instance, in 1915, London issued the Bryce Report, which was almost a total fabrication. Among other things the report claimed that Germans were systematically torturing, mutilating, and burning helpless women and children.[309] Another British report, also a pack of lies, gave a grossly detailed report of Germans sending trainloads of dead bodies to a tallow factory where the

---

[309] THE PENGUIN BOOK OF LIES, edited by Philip Kerr, Viking Penguin, NY, 1990, p.294.

bodies were rendered into oil. The report even accused the Germans of using the bodies of their own troops for this purpose.[310]

It was all a complete fraud, but in those days people trusted their governments and the reports were believed. So, in 1939, the British and American people were already primed to assume all Germans were subhuman criminals deserving of any punishment.

Chris, here is an interesting question to research: How much of America's foreign policy has been created in London for the benefit of the rulers of Britain? A good place to start is the article, "The Medals of His Defeats," by Christopher Hitchens, page 118 of the April 2002 ATLANTIC MONTHLY. Among other things, Hitchens points out that a large part of the reason the USG got into the war was to save Britain from Hitler, but Britain never needed saving. The danger to Britain was mostly a fabrication to lure America in on Britain's side.

---

[310] THE PENGUIN BOOK OF LIES, edited by Philip Kerr, Viking Penguin, NY, 1990, p.301.

43

Unconditional Surrender

Dear Chris,

After a November 1943 meeting in Moscow, the chief Allied powers — Washington D.C., Moscow, London, and China — issued the Moscow Declaration. This said, among other things, that after the war the Germans would be forced to pay reparations again.[311]

This, of course, confirmed the worst fears of Germans who were thinking about joining the underground. If they killed Hitler and ended the war, they would be hit with another Treaty of Versailles.

As if this were not enough to prolong the war, the Allies had cooked up an even worse threat to those Germans who might try to kill Hitler. Chris, another book you really should read is UNCONDITIONAL SURRENDER by Anne Armstrong.[312] It is out of print, but you may find it at a library or used bookstore. Here is a brief look at the Unconditional Surrender story.

In October 1942, President Roosevelt had called for war crimes trials to punish Axis leaders for "innumerable acts of savagery."[313] This meant the Allies planned to hang Axis leaders.

---

[311] UNCONDITIONAL SURRENDER by Anne Armstrong, Rutgers University Press, New Brunswick, 1961, p.63.

[312] UNCONDITIONAL SURRENDER by Anne Armstrong, Rutgers University Press, New Brunswick, 1961.

[313] UNCONDITIONAL SURRENDER by Anne Armstrong, p.17-22.

It was no idle threat. When the war ended many were hanged.

The previous month, the Germans had attacked Stalingrad. This was the worst battle in all of human history. It lasted five months and killed 1.1 million people.

By January 1943, the German people knew the tide of war had turned. Officers at Stalingrad had been writing home making no effort to hide the seriousness of the situation — little Germany was clearly losing the war. Day after day, the German people and their leaders watched the Stalingrad meat grinder devour their sons by the tens of thousands.

The feeling throughout Germany, including among the generals, was that it was time to negotiate a peace settlement.[314] Field Marshall von Manstein and General Zeitzler attempted to resign, while many generals on the Eastern Front openly demanded that Hitler hand over command of the army to a professional soldier. Hitler refused, keeping the command for himself, and troops and officers began to whisper of revolt.[315] Intelligence reports told of whole streets in Germany plastered at night with signs reading "Down With Hitler" and "Stop The War."[316]

Then came the clincher. On January 24, 1943, one week before the Battle of Stalingrad ended, FDR made his famous call for Unconditional Surrender.

Unconditional Surrender sounded good but what did it mean?

---

[314] UNCONDITIONAL SURRENDER by Anne Armstrong, Rutgers University Press, New Brunswick, 1961, p.114-119.

[315] UNCONDITIONAL SURRENDER by Anne Armstrong, p.117.

[316] THE NEW DEALERS' WAR, by Thomas Fleming, Basic Books, NY, 2001, p.205.

Normally, surrenders are conditional. Leaders of the losing side contact the other side and say, we will lay down our arms if you promise not to harm us.

Note the condition: if you promise not to harm us. This is usually the primary condition and there may be others.

Unconditional surrenders are so rare they are almost unheard of. In an unconditional surrender, the losers are required to lay down their arms with no guarantees at all. They must simply put their fate in the hands of the winners, and the winners can do anything they please, including hang them.

The Treaty of Versailles had been an unconditional surrender. The Germans had not intended it that way, but that is how it turned out.

In October 1942, Roosevelt had announced war crimes trials, meaning Axis leaders would be executed. So, in demanding the famous Unconditional Surrender in January 1943, Roosevelt was saying, in effect, if you surrender, we will hang you.

Chris, would you have surrendered?

To the American public, who had not been educated about such things, Unconditional Surrender sounded like a fine thing. They wanted to see total defeat, and this is what Unconditional Surrender sounded like to them.

The demand for Unconditional Surrender was repeated many times for the rest of the war, and there was no mistaking its meaning to Axis leaders: if you give up, you die.

In a 1944 meeting between General Eisenhower and his Chief of Staff General Walter B. Smith, the two discussed the fate of the 3,500 officers they estimated to be part of the German leadership. Should the men be hanged or just imprisoned? Eisenhower and Smith said that punishment could be "left to nature if the Russians had a free hand."[317]

What did this mean?

Firing Squads. The Russians hated the Germans with a ferocity few Americans can imagine. At one of the official dinners in Iran, Stalin had raised his glass in a toast, proposing that 50,000 German prisoners be sent to firing squads. Stalin further proposed that four million Germans be sent to Russia as slaves.[318]

If you talk with any American veteran of the war who saw what the Russians did in Germany in 1945, you will know that the German fear of the Russians was well founded.

When the war was over, three million German prisoners of war were taken into the Soviet Union. Half were never seen again.[319] This is what Unconditional Surrender meant, and the Germans knew this is what it meant because they remembered how they had been treated at the end of the First World War.

Chris, in America, the phrase "let bygones be bygones" is common. Americans tend to look to the future, and they want old wounds to heal as soon as possible.

In the Old World, there is no such thing as a bygone. In 1940, the Germans forced the French to sign their surrender document in the same railroad car in which the French had forced the Germans to surrender in 1918. This is how strongly the Germans felt about the Treaty of Versailles, and they knew the demand for Unconditional Surrender meant they

---

[317] UNCONDITIONAL SURRENDER by Anne Armstrong, Rutgers University Press, New Brunswick, 1961, p.21-22.

[318] UNCONDITIONAL SURRENDER by Anne Armstrong, p.68.

[319] History Channel TV documentary "The Last Days of World War II."

were about to be subjected to this same kind of treatment again, and worse. That is how the Old World works, tit for tat; year after year, century after century, the hatred and retaliation never end.

American and British leaders tried to soften the threat of Unconditional Surrender by saying that only the German leadership would be punished. This did little good. The German people had no reason to believe it and a great deal of reason to consider it a lie because they remembered what had been done to them after World War I. And they knew what the Russians intended. In their minds, to surrender unconditionally was suicide. And, in fact, it was suicide. As mentioned earlier, when they finally did surrender unconditionally, three million were sent to Russia as slaves, and half were never seen again.

So just as the Germans were beginning to consider ending the war, at the end of the Battle of Stalingrad in January 1943, Roosevelt announced his demand for Unconditional Surrender. This galvanized the German army. After the war, German General Heinz Guderian wrote, "The effect of this brutal formula on the German nation and, above all, on the army was great. The soldiers, at least, were convinced from now on our enemies had decided on the utter destruction of Germany."[320]

The chief of British secret intelligence, General Sir Stewart Graham Menzies, said the demand for Unconditional Surrender would make the Germans fight "with the despairing ferocity of cornered rats."[321]

---

[320] PANZER LEADER by Heinz Guderian, Dutton, NY 1952, p.284, 285-87.

[321] THE NEW DEALERS' WAR, by Thomas Fleming, Basic Books, NY, 2001, p.174.

Chris, here is something that will help you understand how unusual, and how apocalyptic this demand for Unconditional Surrender was. One of Churchill's advisors, Lord Maurice Hankey, tried to find other historic cases of demands for Unconditional Surrender. He found only one, in the war between the Romans and the Carthaginians. The Romans entirely destroyed Carthage.[322]

It was quite reasonable for the Germans to believe that if they surrendered they would be completely wiped out. Remember the propaganda from World War I. An example was speeches by Newell Dwight Hillis who was a spokesman for an organization called Protestant America. Hillis had told Americans about "the duty of simply exterminating the German people," and he approved a proposal to sterilize Germany's entire 5-million man army."[323] Many Americans still believed this kind of rubbish, and the German people knew they believed it.

General Franz Halder was a member of the German underground. He reported that after FDR's announcement, it was no longer possible to recruit people to rise against Hitler. Even those who hated the dictator would say that "the same frightful fate awaited us with or without Hitler. ... The only thing to do was hold out until the end."[324]

British military historian B.H. Liddell Hart wrote, "The main obstacle in the Allies' path, once the tide had turned, was a self-raised barrier — their leaders' unwise and short-sighted demand for 'unconditional surrender.' It was the

---

[322] THE NEW DEALERS' WAR, by Thomas Fleming, p.174.

[323] THE NEW DEALERS' WAR, by Thomas Fleming, p.182.

[324] UNCONDITIONAL SURRENDER by Anne Armstrong, Rutgers University Press, New Brunswick, 1961, p.143.

greatest help to Hitler, in preserving his grip on the German people, and likewise to the War Party in Japan."[325]

After the war, General Hasso von Manteuffel wrote, "...we realized that the result of this foolish demand was that we must fight to the bitter end....The demand certainly lengthened the war."[326]

Manteuffel said that soldiers at the front often told him they had only begun to want to fight after they heard FDR's demand for Unconditional Surrender, and "The threat of inhuman punishment kindled renewed diligence in these people....The demand for Unconditional Surrender welded workers and soldiers together in a way which amazed me."[327]

The commander of the U.S. Eighth Air Force, General Ira C. Eaker, said,

> Everybody I knew at the time when they heard this said: 'How stupid can you be?' All the soldiers and the airmen who were fighting this war wanted the Germans to quit tomorrow. A child knew once you said this to the Germans, they were going to fight to the last man.[328]

The effect of Unconditional Surrender was fully understood by America's top military officers. In a February 1945 news conference, General Eisenhower admitted, "If you were

---

[325] HISTORY OF THE SECOND WORLD WAR, by B.H. Liddell Hart, Perigree Books, NY, 1982, p.712.

[326] UNCONDITIONAL SURRENDER by Anne Armstrong, Rutgers University Press, New Brunswick, 1961, p.144.

[327] UNCONDITIONAL SURRENDER by Anne Armstrong, p.144.

[328] THE NEW DEALERS' WAR, by Thomas Fleming, Basic Books, NY, 2001, p.175.

given two choices — one to mount the scaffold and the other to charge twenty bayonets, you might as well charge twenty bayonets."[329]

Pope Pius XII sent a message to Roosevelt saying that Unconditional Surrender was "incompatible with Christian doctrine."[330] The letter did little good, Roosevelt continued the demand, and because he was Commander-in-Chief of the armed forces, everyone went along.

Admiral Wilhelm Canaris was head of Hitler's intelligence service, the Abwehr, and is believed to have been a key leader in the attempt to get rid of Hitler. In 1940, the Abwehr had leaked Hitler's plans for the invasion of Holland, Belgium, and France to the Allies. (But the Allies ignored it.)

After Roosevelt's Unconditional Surrender announcement, Canaris told a friend, "The students of history will not need to trouble their heads after this war, as they did after the last, to determine who was guilty of starting it. The case is however different when we consider guilt for prolonging the war. I believe that the other side have now disarmed us of the last weapons with which we could have ended it."[331]

But Canaris would not give up. In June 1943, he contacted the Allies to say he could arrange an open door for the Allies to land in Western Europe if they would give up the demand for Unconditional Surrender. This was very likely a genuine offer, the head of Hitler's "Atlantic Wall" defenses was General Erwin Rommel, and Rommel was part of a plot to kill Hitler. It is reasonable to believe Rommel would have

---

[329] UNCONDITIONAL SURRENDER by Anne Armstrong, Rutgers University Press, New Brunswick, 1961, p.150.

[330] THE NEW DEALERS' WAR, by Thomas Fleming, Basic Books, NY, 2001, p.280.

[331] THE NEW DEALERS' WAR, by Thomas Fleming, p.176.

gone along with Canaris' offer to let the Allies land unopposed.

The head of U.S. secret intelligence, William ("Wild Bill") Donovan, flew to Istanbul to talk with the German rebels. Donovan was so impressed he returned to Washington D.C. and asked Roosevelt to agree to Canaris' offer. Roosevelt refused.[332]

So, Chris, Axis leaders were afraid to give up, and FDR would not back off his demand for punishment and Unconditional Surrender. So, instead of the war ending after the Battle of Stalingrad, the war dragged on two more years, with men, women, and children dying at the rate of a million a month.[333]

Let me emphasize that — dying at the rate of a million a month.

For two more years.

The Roosevelt demand for Unconditional Surrender may have killed more people than Hitler did.

Uncle Eric

P.S. It is important to remember, Chris, that the British and American armies were not on the European continent with overwhelming force until the invasion of Normandy, June 6, 1944. Until then, the most powerful army in Europe was that of Stalin.

If Germany's anti-Nazis had killed Hitler, triggering chaos in Germany, odds were high that Stalin would have quickly overrun Germany.

---

[332] THE NEW DEALERS' WAR, by Thomas Fleming, Basic Books, NY, 2001, p.204.

[333] WAR: A COMMENTARY BY GWYNNE DYER, PBS TV series.

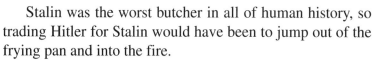

Stalin was the worst butcher in all of human history, so trading Hitler for Stalin would have been to jump out of the frying pan and into the fire.

In other words, Chris, if the anti-Nazis did not require that surrender be conditional — one condition being security from invasion by Stalin — then in killing Hitler they would very likely have been hurling Germany into mass suicide.

44

Why Did Roosevelt Do It?

Dear Chris,

You now have the evidence that leads me to believe America should never have entered World War II. By sending weapons and supplies to Stalin, by launching the invasion of Normandy to take pressure off Stalin, and by calling for Unconditional Surrender, President Roosevelt made the war much longer and much more bloody.

Why did he do it? We will never know, we cannot read his mind, but I can offer one suggestion.

Remember Churchill's remark to Roosevelt that I mentioned in an earlier letter: "I am half American and the natural person to work with you. It is evident that we see eye to eye. Were I to become Prime Minister of Britain we could control the world."[334]

America was protected by the two giant moats called the Atlantic and Pacific Oceans. There was no serious threat to American industry, while industries in all other major nations were being bombed, shelled, and burned.

My guess: Roosevelt realized that if he could keep the war going long enough, all the other major nations would pulverize each other, and he would end up emperor of the world.

---

[334] THE FINAL STORY OF PEARL HARBOR, by Harry Elmer Barnes, published by Left and Right, NY, 1968, p.15.

There is no way to know if this was his intention, all we can say is that this is how it did turn out. FDR died too soon to see it, but his successor, Harry Truman, achieved what Julius Caesar, Napoleon, and a host of other power junkies had striven for, emperor of the world. By 1945, Germany, Russia, and Japan were smoking ruins. Italy, France, Belgium, Holland, Yugoslavia, Austria, Poland, Czechoslovakia, Denmark, Luxembourg, and China were in better shape, but far from healthy. Britain's industry was worn out.

Hardly scratched, America was a giant standing tall and healthy on a battlefield littered with fallen rivals.

The dream of every power junkie since Alexander the Great had come true for Harry Truman. The owner of the only atomic bombs, plus the world's most lethal navy and air force, Truman was indisputably the most powerful man ever seen on earth.

For a person who has spent decades seeking political power, what could be more satisfying?

In my opinion, this is what Roosevelt was trying to achieve with his calls for Unconditional Surrender, and it worked.

It is interesting that after Roosevelt died, on April 12, 1945, Truman maintained the demand for Unconditional Surrender. He even went so far as to tell the Germans that they could not surrender only to the Americans and British; they must also surrender to the Russians.[335]

Germans fought on until the Russians eventually overran and massacred them.

---

[335] UNCONDITIONAL SURRENDER by Anne Armstrong, Rutgers University Press, New Brunswick, 1961, p.98.

But that massacre was not the end of World War II. The war in the Pacific was still raging.

Uncle Eric

P.S. Chris, in an earlier letter I mentioned that President Roosevelt had strong socialist leanings, and this probably explains his liking for "Uncle Joe" Stalin and the Union of Soviet Socialist Republics. This could be another reason FDR called for Unconditional Surrender.

Germany was the key bulwark against expansion of the U.S.S.R. By forcing the Germans to fight until they were exhausted and defenseless, FDR left Central and East Europe with no strong power to stand against Stalin.

Roosevelt's son, Elliot Roosevelt, reported that he was having lunch with his father when FDR came up with the idea of Unconditional Surrender. Elliot said his father's exact remark was:

> "Of course, it's just the thing for the Russians. They couldn't want anything better. Unconditional Surrender," he repeated, thoughtfully sucking a tooth. "Uncle Joe might have made it up himself."[336]

---

[336] ROOSEVELT'S ROAD TO RUSSIA, by George N. Crocker, Henry Regnery Company, Chicago, 1959, p.165.

45

Rarely Questioned

Dear Chris,

Before we move on to the war in the Pacific, do you remember the ten deadly ideas from my earlier letters about World War I? They are: the Pax Romana, fascism, love of political power, global protection, interests, cost externalization, Manifest Destiny, alliances, the glory of war, and the White Man's Burden.[337]

These ideas are the fundamental reasons the USG got into the two World Wars, and because the USG won those wars, the ideas are rarely questioned. Embedded in American culture, these ideas are today the reasons why the USG gets into so many wars in far corners of the globe.

Now that you have the rest of the story about the World Wars — the non-statist side — I hope you will consider the possibility that America's involvement not only was not necessary, it made the wars worse. Indeed, it made them *World* Wars.

Equally important, I hope you can see that there is good reason to suspect that when the USG gets into other people's wars today, it makes things worse.

---

[337] The ten deadly ideas that lead to war are discussed in Richard J. Maybury's book WORLD WAR I: THE REST OF THE STORY AND HOW IT AFFECTS YOU TODAY, published by Bluestocking Press, web site: www.BluestockingPress.com.

One of the many examples happened in 1999-2001 in the Balkans.

Balkans wars are medieval religious wars that go back a thousand years. I explained this to you in an earlier set of letters.[338] As you may recall, the three main groups in the Balkans are Catholics, Muslims, and Eastern Orthodox Christians.

In the 1990s, President Clinton got into the wars in Croatia, Albania, Kosovo, and Bosnia, professing his goal was to bring peace and goodwill to the three groups.

In 1999, the Orthodox Christians were persecuting the Muslims, so President Clinton sided with the Muslims, and the Muslims won.

Two years later, operating from U.S. protected safe areas, the Muslims were persecuting the Christians.

In the war in Macedonia in 2001, President George W. Bush was upset at the Muslims and began helping the Christians, but he continued helping the Muslims, too. He was afraid that if he didn't help the Muslims, the Christians would overrun them.

So, in the war in Macedonia, the USG ended up backing both sides.

This is the kind of insanity the ten deadly ideas lead to, yet they are rarely questioned because the U.S. won the World Wars. We will come back to the implications — they led directly to the destruction of the World Trade Center — after we look at the defeat of Japan.

Uncle Eric

---

[338] Uncle Eric is referring to Richard J. Maybury's book THE THOUSAND YOU WAR IN THE MIDEAST: HOW IT AFFFECTS YOU TODAY, published by Bluestocking Press, web site: www.BluestockingPress.com.

46

Why Was Nagasaki Bombed?

Dear Chris,

The Hollywood and U.S. Government versions of history contain two assumptions about the end of World War II:

1. Dropping atomic bombs on Hiroshima and Nagasaki was necessary because the only other way to defeat Japan was an invasion that could have cost a million American lives.

2. The Hiroshima bomb was the more important of the two.

That is the statist side of the story. The non-statist side holds that both these assumptions are wrong. A good way to start the non-statist investigation is to ask the question, why was Nagasaki bombed?

Nagasaki was destroyed on August 9, 1945, only 75 hours after Hiroshima had been hit.[339] With the destruction of communications between Hiroshima and Tokyo 450 miles away, this was surprisingly soon for another strike. Japanese rulers could not possibly gather enough information or expert advice to fully comprehend what had happened. A terrible new weapon, a single bomb, had destroyed an entire city.

---

[339] DAY ONE by Peter Wyden, Simon & Schuster, NY, 1984, p.xxiv & 300.

Chris, it helps to remember that the A-bomb was new. Until that time, most bombs were just 500 or 1,000 pounds of TNT. A very large bomb was 10,000 pounds. If it landed just right, it might destroy a dozen buildings.

The Hiroshima bomb flattened 50,000 buildings. To you and me this is not surprising, but in 1945 it was quite unbelievable. To expect Japanese rulers to gather enough data about it to grasp the importance within 75 hours was absurd.

Physicist John Jungerman, working on the Manhattan Project, was like many other scientists at the time. He did not question the use of the new weapon until Nagasaki was hit. "It didn't give the Japanese any time to react," he said. "They just hit them again. It drove home the fact that we scientists didn't have anything to say about it — it was a political and military decision."[340]

Indeed, on August 8th, Foreign Minister Togo and Emperor Hirohito had decided to ask the Japanese War Council to announce Japan's surrender.[341] Few Americans know this, or know why.

The conventional bombing had already demolished Japan. As an example, on March 9, 1945, an air armada of 279 B-29 bombers dropped a carpet of incendiary bombs on the Japanese capital of Tokyo. This hail of bombs destroyed 265,000 buildings and killed 185,000 Japanese,[342] more than were killed by the Hiroshima and Nagasaki atomic bombs combined. The cost to the Americans was 14 planes.[343]

---

[340] Interview of Jungerman published in the SACRAMENTO BEE newspaper, August 4, 1985, p.A24.

[341] DAY ONE by Peter Wyden, Simon & Schuster, NY, 1984, p. 300.

[342] HISTORY OF THE SECOND WORLD WAR, by B.H. Liddell Hart, Perigree Books, NY, 1982, p.691.

[343] HISTORY OF THE SECOND WORLD WAR, by B.H. Liddell Hart, p.691.

After the war, the Strategic Bombing Survey found that probably more people lost their lives in Tokyo in a six-hour period than in any similar length of time in all of history.[344] Another way to look at it is that in six hours, three times as many people died in Tokyo as the U.S. lost in the 15 years of the Vietnam War.

The fire was so intense that people who jumped into the canals were boiled alive. The American bomber crews reported they could smell flesh burning as they flew back from the raid.[345]

(Deaths from bombings are hard to calculate because so many bodies disappear in the flames and rubble. For immediate deaths from the Hiroshima bomb, I have seen estimates of between 60,000 and 100,000; from the Nagasaki bomb, 30,000 to 70,000. Thousands more died later from injuries and radiation. The Nagasaki bomb was more powerful but did less damage because parts of Nagasaki were protected by hills.)

This was happening all over Japan. The Japanese air force was so short of fighter planes and fuel that it could not stop the American bombers. The B-29s were able to come in at an altitude of only 7,000 feet instead of the usual five miles or more.[346] Nearly every Japanese city was going up in flames and, along with them, the factories and refineries that made their planes and fuel. Japan was being systematically demolished from the air months before the atomic bombs were used.

---

[344] "Tokyo's Firestorm, Worse Than Hiroshima," Peter McGill, WORLD PRESS REVIEW, August 1995, p.17.

[345] "Tokyo's Firestorm, Worse Than Hiroshima," Peter McGill, p.17.

[346] WHY THE ALLIES WON, by Richard Overy, W. W. Norton & Co., NY, 1995, p.126.

On August 9th, the Japanese War Council had just convened to discuss surrender when an officer walked into the room and said that Nagasaki had been obliterated.[347] Another city had been destroyed. At least 35,000 men, women, and children had been killed[348] for no purpose that has ever been clearly explained. So let's try to explain it.

Uncle Eric

---

[347] DAY ONE by Peter Wyden, Simon & Schuster, NY, 1984, p. 300.
[348] DAY ONE by Peter Wyden, p. 294.

47

105 Aircraft Carriers

Dear Chris,

The mystery deepens when we realize that by 1945 many American officials had come to believe that once Hitler had been defeated (on May 7th) there would no longer be any need for bloodshed. Navy Under Secretary Ralph Bard, for instance, was convinced the Allies could merely blockade Japan and wait for it to collapse.[349]

Remember, Chris, Japan is an island nation. The Japanese navy had been destroyed, which meant that with Germany's defeat and the capture of all remaining Axis ships, *nearly every warship on earth was available to surround Japan.*

By itself, the U.S. had 105 aircraft carriers, 18 battleships, 3 battle cruisers, 31 heavy cruisers, 48 light cruisers, 367 destroyers, 41 frigates, 200 submarines, and 4,100 other ships.[350]

By way of contrast, as I write this letter today, the U.S. has a total of about 300 ships, 12 of which are aircraft carriers,[351] and this is the most powerful navy in the world.

---

[349] DAY ONE by Peter Wyden, Simon & Schuster, NY, 1984, p.174-75, and Paul Galloway, "The Fateful Decision," SACRAMENTO UNION SUNDAY MAGAZINE, August 4, 1985, p.11.

[350] "The Navy's Second Wind," by John Lehman, WALL STREET JOURNAL, June 1, 1995, and JANE'S FIGHTING SHIPS OF WORLD WAR II, Crescent Books, NY, 1996.

[351] U.S. Navy web site.

The official explanation for dropping the atomic bombs was that the alternative was to invade, as in the invasion of Normandy, and this would cost a million American lives.

The figure of one million American deaths came from President Truman, not a military expert, and there has never been any evidence to support it.[352] Truman apparently made it up, and Americans today still believe it.

Stanford historian Barton Bernstein found that military planners estimated the number of American dead from an invasion of Japan at 40,000.[353]

The belief that an invasion was necessary, and the estimate of a million dead, must have been a smokescreen. Japan was entirely surrounded by Allied warships, cut off from the rest of the world. Its ships and industry had been destroyed.

Richard Overy is one of the few military historians to look at the economics of the war. He reports that, "Atomic weapons did not win the war, for they came far too late to affect the outcome. Japan was on the point of surrender by the time the two available bombs were used."[354]

Japan's economy had not been highly developed when the war began. By summer of 1945, it was barely above the Stone Age and no conceivable threat to anyone; 118 Japanese cities had been wrecked.[355]

There was no need to invade. With no natural resources except fish, timber, and water, and cut off from the rest of the

---

[352] "Why We Nuked Japan," by Gar Alperovitz, an article from TECHNOLOGY REVIEW reprinted in the SACRAMENTO BEE FORUM, August 19, 1990.

[353] "Why We Nuked Japan," by Gar Alperovitz, August 19, 1990.

[354] WHY THE ALLIES WON, by Richard Overy, W. W. Norton & Co., NY, 1995, p.242.

[355] DAY ONE by Peter Wyden, Simon & Schuster, NY, 1984, p. 331.

world, Japan could be kept in this near Stone Age condition forever, or until the Japanese surrendered.

Let me emphasize, Chris, by August 1945, there was no longer any need for killing or dying of any kind. The Japanese threat had been entirely erased. Japan was cut off from the rest of the world as if it had been sealed into a giant vacuum-packed coffee can.

As an example, on July 24, 1945, Allied aircraft carriers launched an attack on the Kure naval harbor area in Japan. The attacking planes numbered about 500. Against them the Japanese could send up only 21 planes, none of which were a match for the highly advanced American F4U Corsairs.[356]

The Japanese battleship *Yamato* — at 73,000 tons, the largest battleship ever built and the pride of the Japanese navy — had been sunk on April 7, 1945. It had been sent into the Battle of Okinawa with only enough fuel for a one-way trip.[357]

By August of 1945, the only requirement was to patrol the waters around Japan to keep the place isolated, and fly over occasionally to destroy factories if the Japanese tried to rebuild them. If the Japanese did not surrender, they could just slide back into the Stone Age and stay there, it was their choice.

The U.S. Strategic Bombing Survey after the war examined the question and concluded that, "Certainly prior to December 31, 1945, Japan would have surrendered even if the atomic bombs had not been dropped."[358]

[356] "Memoirs of a Japanese Fighter Pilot," by Ron Werneth, FLIGHT JOURNAL, April 2000, p.81.

[357] "Sinking of Great Japanese Battleship..." by T.R. Reid, WASHINGTON POST story in SACRAMENTO BEE, April 7, 1995, p.24.

[358] "Why We Nuked Japan," by Gar Alperovitz, an article from TECHNOLOGY REVIEW reprinted in the SACRAMENTO BEE FORUM, August 19, 1990.

Chris, now I am going to tell you something few Americans know, and few want to hear about, so be tactful with whom, as well as the manner in which, you share this information. Historians know it, but most don't talk about it.

In Europe, for the most part, Americans stuck to bombing military targets such as airfields, ports, and rail yards. They often missed and hit defenseless civilians, but the objective was not mass slaughter of civilians.

The Japanese, however, were of a different race than most Americans. Remember Anglo-Saxonism? The White Man's Burden[359]?

The USG did use "area bombing" on the Japanese.

Japanese homes were made of very light building materials, mostly small wooden beams and paper. This made them safer for earthquakes, which are a big threat in Japan, but the wood and paper homes burned like tinder.

The American air crews were ordered to drop incendiary bombs to burn the highly combustible Japanese homes.

By August, 1945, Japanese cities — and the men, women, and children in them — were being burned at the rate of one per day.

Japanese were systematically exterminated in much the same way that Hitler tried to exterminate Jews, except that the extermination device was not the gas chamber, it was the B-29 bomber and the incendiary bomb.

Chris, extermination was also what the British had been trying to do to the Germans using Lancaster and Halifax bombers for "area bombing." And, of course, Stalin's Soviet

---

[359] Discussed in Chapter 25 " The White Man's Burden and the Ugly American" of Richard J. Maybury's book WORLD WAR I: THE REST OF THE STORY AND HOW IT AFFECTS YOU TODAY, published by Bluestocking Press, web site: www.BluestockingPress.com.

Socialists had been murdering millions for years. The idea that Hitler was the only leader trying to massacre whole populations is wrong. All the top leaders in World War II seem to have been carried away by their power.

In fact, Chris, now that I think about it, I wonder if there was any nation in World War II that did not participate in systematic massacre of helpless civilians. A good research topic. Even the Canadians, Australians, and New Zealanders had air crews in the British area bombings.

I have only touched on the true extent of the American bombings of Japan. Another good research topic is to look at it in detail so that you can grasp the full picture. But you will need a strong stomach; it's not pretty.

You might be interested to know that five days after the Nagasaki bomb, even though U.S. leaders knew the Japanese were in the process of surrendering, the USG hit Japan again with a thousand bombers dropping incendiary bombs.[360]

Chris, now that you know what most Americans don't about the war, I think you can see that as the war dragged on, it became less about military strategy, and more about killing out of habit. Every leader's judgment went out the window.

The war had begun with a few thousand troops shooting at other troops. It ended with clouds of B-29 bombers destroying a city a day.

Americans had become the thing they were fighting.

Six months after the war ended, war correspondent Edgar L. Jones wrote in a magazine article:

---

[360] WHY THE ALLIES WON, by Richard Overy, W. W. Norton & Co., NY, 1995, p.127, and WORLD WAR II DAY BY DAY, by Donald Sommerville, Dorset Press, 1989, p.309,310.

What kind of war do civilians suppose we fought, anyway? We shot prisoners in cold blood, wiped out hospitals, strafed lifeboats, killed or mistreated enemy civilians, finished off the enemy wounded, tossed the dying into a hole with the dead, and in the Pacific boiled the flesh off enemy skulls to make table ornaments for sweethearts, or carved their bones into letter openers.[361]

The architect of the bombing of Japan, General Curtis LeMay, wrote that Japanese men, women, and children were "scorched and boiled and baked to death."[362]

General Bonner Fellers, an advisor to General MacArthur, wrote that the U.S. bombing of Japan was among "the most ruthless and barbaric killings of non-combatants in all history."[363]

It was as if there was an invisible force that was feeding off the death and destruction, enjoying it, and growing stronger with each million killed.

Uncle Eric

P.S. During the British area bombings, Roosevelt's Under Secretary of War for Air, Robert A. Lovett, wrote to a friend that he enjoyed looking at photos of the "obliteration" raid on the city of Essen with "sadistic barbarism."[364]

The phrase "drunk with power" comes to mind.

---

[361] "The Real War," by Benjamin Schwarz, ATLANTIC MONTHLY, June 2001, p.102.

[362] "The Real War," by Benjamin Schwarz, p.102.

[363] "The Real War," by Benjamin Schwarz, p.102.

[364] THE NEW DEALERS' WAR, by Thomas Fleming, Basic Books, NY, 2001, p.278.

48

Surrender Near

Dear Chris,

By 1945, Britain's economy was worn out producing war goods, and its empire was on the verge of breaking up. Exhausted Britain was well on its way to becoming a secondary power behind the U.S. and U.S.S.R. The President of the U.S. was the king of the world, and Unconditional Surrender was his call, no one else's.

British officials had long tried to steer U.S. foreign policy (and probably still do), but the war had dragged on too long and left Britain drained. London still had some influence in America, but no power on earth could come close to matching that of the USG.

In May 1945, Truman was already receiving reports that the Japanese were ready to surrender if the demand for Unconditional Surrender were dropped,[365] but he refused to drop it.

General Eisenhower, Commander of U.S. forces in Europe and later U.S. President, said he told Secretary of War Stimson, "my grave misgivings, first on the basis of my belief that Japan was already defeated and that dropping the bomb was completely unnecessary, and secondly because I thought that our country should avoid shocking world opinion by the use of a weapon whose employment was, I thought, no longer

---

[365] "Why We Nuked Japan," by Gar Alperovitz, an article from TECHNOLOGY REVIEW reprinted in the SACRAMENTO BEE FORUM, August 19, 1990.

mandatory as a measure to save American lives. ... It wasn't necessary to hit them with that awful thing."[366]

Winston Churchill later wrote, "It would be a mistake to suppose that the fate of Japan was settled by the atomic bomb. Her defeat was certain before the bomb fell, and was brought about by overwhelming maritime power. ... Her shipping had been destroyed."[367]

America's Chief of Staff, Admiral Leahy, said, "The use of this barbaric weapon at Hiroshima and Nagasaki was of no material assistance in our war against Japan. The Japanese were already defeated and ready to surrender because of the effective sea blockade and the successful bombing with conventional weapons."[368] He felt terrible about it. "My own feeling was that, in being the first to use it, we had adopted an ethical standard common to the barbarians of the Dark Age. I was not taught to make war in that fashion, and wars cannot be won by destroying women and children."[369]

British historian B.H. Liddell Hart wrote, "The Americans, however, were already aware of Japan's desire to end the war, for their intelligence service had intercepted the cipher messages from the Japanese Foreign Minister to the Japanese ambassador in Moscow. ... The use of the atomic bomb was not really needed to produce this result. With nine-tenths of Japan's shipping sunk or disabled, her air and sea forces crippled, her industries wrecked, and her people's food

---

[366] "Why We Nuked Japan," by Gar Alperovitz, an article from TECHNOLOGY REVIEW reprinted in the SACRAMENTO BEE FORUM, August 19, 1990.

[367] HISTORY OF THE SECOND WORLD WAR, by B.H. Liddell Hart, Perigree Books, NY, 1982, p.692.

[368] HISTORY OF THE SECOND WORLD WAR, by B.H. Liddell Hart, p.697.

[369] HISTORY OF THE SECOND WORLD WAR, by B.H. Liddell Hart, p.695.

supplies shrinking fast, her collapse was already certain — as Churchill said."[370]

Just before his death, Physicist Albert Einstein said, "I made one great mistake in my life — when I signed the letter to President Roosevelt recommending that an atomic bomb be made."[371]

Despite the fact that the blockade was working — Japan was sealed off from the rest of the world and the need for killing had ended — President Truman decided to stick to the demand for Unconditional Surrender and drop the atomic bombs anyhow.

Secretary Bard resigned.[372]

Chris, why were Americans not told that the blockade plan was working, and why were the atomic bombs used? Especially, why was the Nagasaki bomb used?

My next letter.

Uncle Eric

---

[370] HISTORY OF THE SECOND WORLD WAR, by B.H. Liddell Hart, Perigree Books, NY, 1982, p.694-96.

[371] DAY ONE by Peter Wyden, Simon & Schuster, NY, 1984, p. 342.

[372] DAY ONE by Peter Wyden, Simon & Schuster, 1984, p.174, and Paul Galloway, "The Fateful Decision," SACRAMENTO UNION SUNDAY MAGAZINE, August 4, 1985, p.11.

49

Fierce Fighters

Dear Chris,

Thanks for your letter. You ask a fair question. If the Japanese were so totally outclassed, why were they still fighting? Why had they not given up a long time ago?

After all, they were surrounded by aircraft carriers, not to mention thousands of bombers and other weapons they could not hope to cope with.

That question was, in fact, the support for the estimate that a million Americans would be killed in an invasion of Japan. The Japanese were completely beaten but were still fighting, so they must be crazy and would fight to the last man with knives and spears, Americans thought.

There was some truth in that assumption; the Japanese were fierce fighters, no doubt about it. But at this point in the war it did not count for much. The Japanese were stuck on their islands, cut off from the rest of the world, and no longer able to threaten anyone.

Remember my earlier letter about Unconditional Surrender? I believe the Japanese were still fighting because the leaders had been given the same demand for Unconditional Surrender as the Germans, and it apparently had the same effect. Chris, if someone said to you, if you surrender we will hang you, what would you do?

Back to the atomic bombs. As I said earlier, there was no need to use them or to do any more killing at all because

Japan's industry had been wrecked and the small island nation was sealed off.

So why were the bombs used?

In his book, DAY ONE, journalist Peter Wyden tells us several American officials had been in favor of using atomic bombs not to defeat the Japanese but as a demonstration to frighten the Russians.[373]

President Truman's personal journal discovered in 1979, and other documents that have come to light since the war, make it clear that the purpose of dropping the bombs on the Japanese was to overawe the Russians. Truman said, "If it explodes, as I think it will, I'll certainly have a hammer on those boys,"[374] meaning the Russians.

In RUSSIA AT WAR, former BBC[375] news commentator Alexander Werth writes, "The bomb, as is so clearly suggested by Truman, Byrnes, Stimson and others, was dropped very largely in order to impress Russia with America's great might. Ending the war in Japan was incidental (the end of this war was clearly in sight anyway.)"[376]

This desire to use atomic bombs to frighten the Russians was not new in 1945. The head of the Manhattan Project, General Leslie R. Groves, reported that in a July 22, 1943, meeting about atomic bomb development, Churchill expressed "vital concern" about the need to intimidate the Russians.[377]

---

[373] DAY ONE by Peter Wyden, Simon & Schuster, 1984, p.142.

[374] "Why We Nuked Japan," by Gar Alperovitz, an article from TECHNOLOGY REVIEW reprinted in the SACRAMENTO BEE FORUM, August 19, 1990.

[375] BBC: British Broadcasting Corporation

[376] RUSSIA AT WAR by Alexander Werth, Carroll & Graf Publishers, NY 1964, p.1042.

[377] NOW IT CAN BE TOLD by Leslie R. Groves, Harper Brothers, New York, 1962, p.132.

So, as early as 1943, Washington and London were beginning to face that fact that demolishing Germany would leave no counterbalance to Moscow.

Interesting, Chris, this was two years before the war ended, while "Uncle Joe" Stalin was still an ally of the U.S. and Britain, and receiving vast amounts of American help.

Despite the U.S.S.R.'s horrific brutality, the U.S. helped Stalin and his Soviet Socialists until May 12, 1945, when Truman halted Lend-Lease[378] aid to them. The next day, Churchill declared he would not let the Union of Soviet Socialist Republics take Western Europe.[379] It is probably fair to call that the beginning of the **Cold War**[380].

Chris, why did Washington D.C. and London help Stalin, the most brutal killer the world has ever seen? I have never seen any logical explanation. All I can suggest is that Stalin was socialist. Socialism was the popular new philosophy, and it could be that people who believed in it did not want to face the truth about it. Another part that seems likely is that Russia was farther from Britain than Germany was, and the British wanted the U.S. to destroy the Germans first.

Or, maybe political power is evil and it causes people to do evil things. Perhaps it is as simple as that. I don't know, Chris, what do you think?

In any case, thousands of Japanese were killed at Hiroshima and Nagasaki not to end the war but to demonstrate to the Russians that the USG was willing to use atomic bombs on cities full of men, women, and children.

---

[378] Lend-Lease: the weapons, ammunition, supplies and other aid given to Allied powers by the USG.

[379] CHRONICLE OF THE 20ᵀᴴ CENTURY, edited by Clifton Daniel, Chronicle Publications, Mount Kisco, NY 1987, p.592.

[380] Cold War: the half-century stand-off between Moscow and its allies, and Washington and its allies.

My point is that this explains why the Nagasaki bomb was dropped so quickly. Its purpose, like that of the Hiroshima bomb, was not to defeat Japan but to create fear in Russia. The interval between the drops was unimportant.

In fact, it is probably fair to suggest that the Nagasaki bomb was dropped so quickly because American officials were afraid the Japanese would surrender before the Russians had been sufficiently frightened. The evidence for this is strong.

General Groves writes that prior to the July 16th **Trinity**[381] test of the bomb, when the scientists only expected the yield to be somewhere between 0.7 and 5.0 kilotons,[382] [383] the second drop was scheduled for August 20th, two weeks after the first. But to everyone's surprise, the Trinity yield turned out to be an astounding 20 kilotons.[384] Groves moved the Nagasaki drop up to August 11th. Then he moved it up again, to August 9th, despite scientists' warnings that shaving off two more days would cause so much rush and disruption that something might go wrong.[385]

Chris, why else would Groves be in such a hurry to drop the second bomb if this were not to do so before the Japanese could surrender?

When Truman called for surrender ten days after the Trinity test, he not only repeated the demand that the surrender

---

[381] Trinity: code name for the first test of the Atomic bomb in New Mexico on July 16, 1945.

[382] NOW IT CAN BE TOLD by Leslie R. Groves, Harper Brothers, New York, 1962, p.269.

[383] Kiloton: equal to a thousand tons of TNT.

[384] DAY ONE by Peter Wyden, Simon & Schuster, 1984, p.194.

[385] NOW IT CAN BE TOLD by Leslie R. Groves, Harper Brothers, New York, 1962, p.341-42.

be unconditional, he did it with great emphasis. "There are no alternatives," he said.[386]

If you surrender, we will hang you.

Even after the Nagasaki bomb was dropped, the Japanese war council remained understandably reluctant to give up, but fortunately the Emperor overrode them despite the fact that he, too, was in danger of being hanged.[387]

Was the USG using Unconditional Surrender as a means to keep the Japanese in the fight so that the Japanese could be a demonstration for the atomic bombs? Chris, it seems likely to me, and it is an interesting topic for a research report. If you do it, I'd like to see it.

Were it not for the Emperor's amazing courage, millions more Japanese could have been killed in the effort to frighten the Russians. Another 48 atomic bombs were scheduled for production — seven per month — and Groves had been ordered to drop them all.[388]

Chris, in researching the war for more than 30 years, I have been struck over and over by the feeling that no human could be this evil. But there it is. Each time U.S. rulers had a chance to end or lessen the war, they instead took the route that would make it worse. It was as if they were in the grip of something that was enjoying this war very much and did not want it to end.

They were burning a city a day.

As I said in an earlier letter, Chris, war changes what we are.

---

[386] DAY ONE by Peter Wyden, Simon & Schuster, 1984, p.226.

[387] DAY ONE by Peter Wyden, p.298-307.

[388] DAY ONE by Peter Wyden, p.15-17.

I am sure you find all this quite shocking, but it is only the tip of the iceberg. In my next letter I will give you more of the non-statist side of the story.

Uncle Eric

P.S. In early 1943, about the same time as the Unconditional Surrender demand was issued, VICTORY MAGAZINE ran an article titled, "Roosevelt of America, President, Champion of Liberty, United States Leader in the War to Win Lasting and Worldwide Peace."[389]

Chris, as Senator Hiram Johnson said in 1917, "The first casualty when war comes is truth."

I am sure it is a common experience among veterans that not until years after the war is over do they learn that they were deceived, led into something no honorable person could be proud of.

There is an old joke: What is the battle cry of the Italian army?

We have been betrayed!

---

[389] THE NEW DEALERS' WAR, by Thomas Fleming, Basic Books, NY, 2001, p.201.

50

The Russians React

Dear Chris,

The official explanation for the atomic bombing — to avoid the need for invasion of Japan — might have been believable if only one bomb had been used and if Japan had not already been sealed off from the rest of the world. But the Nagasaki bomb was clearly overkill and it demonstrated an eagerness on the part of American officials to use their new weapon.

This eagerness, coupled with President Truman's tough rhetoric toward the Russians, produced exactly the effect U.S. officials had hoped for. British journalist Alexander Werth lived in Russia throughout the war and observed the Russian people's reaction toward the atomic bombs: "Everybody there [in Moscow] fully realized that the atom bomb had become an immense factor in the world's power politics, and believed that, although the two bombs had killed or maimed a few hundred thousand Japanese, their real purpose was, first and foremost, to intimidate Russia."[390] This had a "deeply depressing effect" on the Russians, Werth wrote.[391]

---

[390] RUSSIA AT WAR by Alexander Werth, Carroll & Graf Publishers, NY 1964, p.1044.

[391] RUSSIA AT WAR by Alexander Werth, , p.1038.

The terrible influence of this on our way of life for a half-century afterward and on our way of life today becomes clear when we understand a bit more of Russian history.

It is also the reason for September 11, 2001.

Here is the story.

In 1917, the Russian people had been suffering under the czars for centuries, and they had attempted one uprising after another with little success. They were poorly armed.

During the Cold War era (1945-1990), Americans were led to believe that the Soviet people were so beaten down by centuries of slavery that they were sheep who would never dream of resisting. Nothing could be further from the truth.

During the centuries that the Russians lived under the czars, rebellions and assassinations became national sports. The first four years of the reign of Czar Nicholas I, for instance, in 1825-29, saw 41 peasant uprisings. Between 1830 and 1849, there were 378 uprisings. The last five years of Nicholas' reign brought an annual average of 27 uprisings.[392] The army was exhausted trying to bring the peasants under control, and any Russian official who died of old age was lucky.

I know of no other culture with such a strong heritage of violent rebellion.

Then came the First World War. This war was so huge that millions of Russians were sent to fight against the Germans.

For the first time, millions of Russians had modern weapons.

They decided they would rather use them against the Czar than against the Kaiser, and the Czar was overthrown and killed. This was the 1917 Russian Revolution.

---

[392] ENCYCLOPEDIA BRITANNICA, 1950, under "Russia," p.700.

Through an unfortunate turn of events, socialists came to power and transformed Russia into a police state renamed the Union of Soviet Socialist Republics.

Chris, as I pointed out in an earlier letter, socialism requires government planning for nearly all economic activity (all production and trade). Socialism therefore always leads to the question, what do we do with people who refuse to follow the plan?

The answer is, throw them in prison, and when the prisons are full, shoot them.

To achieve their socialist goals, the new rulers began a two-decade slaughter of millions of their fellow countrymen. Persons who refused to follow the government's Five-Year Plan were called "wreckers."[393] Historians estimate that Stalin had 14.5 million of them murdered.[394]

And, as we have seen, Stalin had millions of others murdered for other reasons, or for no reason. His total body count, according to R.J. Rummel in DEATH BY GOVERNMENT, was 42.6 million. The total body count for all Soviet Socialist regimes eventually totaled 61.9 million, as nearly as Rummel could calculate it.[395]

When World War II came around, it was reasonable to expect a repeat of the 1917 uprising. The Soviet people had been rearmed with modern weapons and they would again turn on their tyrannical rulers.

What happened? Next letter.

Uncle Eric

---

[393] STALIN, by Albert Marrin, Penguin Books, NY, 1988, p.137.

[394] STALIN, by Albert Marrin, p.115.

[395] DEATH BY GOVERNMENT, by R.J. Rummel, Transaction Publishers, New Brunswick, NJ, 1994, Chapter 4.

51

The Soviet Uprising

Dear Chris,

The rebellion began immediately. When the Germans invaded, they were often *welcomed* by the Lithuanians, Latvians, Estonians, Ukrainians and other Soviet people as — believe it or not — *saviors!*[396] That is how awful Stalin and his Soviet Socialists were.

Werth reports that by 1945 resistance to Soviet rule had either broken out or was threatening to break out among the Kalmuks, Chechens and Balkarians, to name only a few.[397]

As early as 1943, up to 20,000 Soviet Cossacks had joined the Germans in combat against their own government,[398] and Cossacks had always been the most loyal of Russian groups.

Historians estimate that eventually 400,000 Soviet citizens would join the German army to fight against Stalin and his Soviet Socialists.[399] The German army's crack Waffen SS had a whole division, called the Galicia Division, of Soviet men who had switched sides to fight Stalin.[400]

Chris, try to imagine it. How much would you need to hate your government for you to join an enemy that had

---

[396] RUSSIA AT WAR by Alexander Werth, Carroll & Graf Publishers, NY 1964, P.145.

[397] RUSSIA AT WAR by Alexander Werth, p. 574-81.

[398] RUSSIA AT WAR by Alexander Werth, p.574-81.

[399] STALIN, by Albert Marrin, Penguin Books, NY, 1988, p.178.

[400] "Red Empire," in THE TIME MACHINE series, A&E Network, 1992.

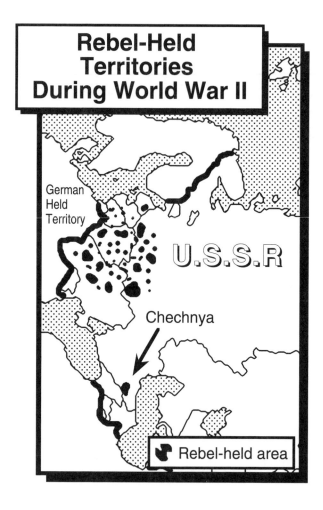

During World War II, the Soviet people again acquired modern weapons and began to turn on their Soviet rulers, as they had on their Russian rulers during the first world war. They began to capture large swaths of territory, and by 1945 it appeared they might overthrow Stalin.

invaded your homeland and was slaughtering your own countrymen? That is how much Russians hated Stalin and his government.

Incidentally, the choice faced by these Russians — to join either the Soviet army or the Nazi army — tells us much about the Old World. Liberty is rarely an option, and it was not in World War II. Mostly it was a choice between socialism and fascism.

During his 29-year reign (1924-1953), Stalin was sent, on average, two "death lists" per week. These lists contained the names of individuals or groups the police suspected of being "enemies of the people." Stalin would scan the lists, and then make notes such as "arrest everyone," or "no need to check, shoot them all."[401]

It is natural to expect that when the war was over and the German threat gone, the Soviet people, now heavily armed, would rally to exterminate Stalin and his Socialist regime.

Instead, the new uprising began to fade at the end of the war. Some pockets of Estonian resistance lasted until 1947,[402] and Ukrainian till 1952,[403] but after 1945, popular support failed to spread. The 1917 revolt was not repeated, and Stalin and his brutal Soviet Socialist government survived.

For almost another half century, the Soviet people suffered under the rule of the Soviet Socialists while the whole world lived in fear of nuclear war between Moscow and the USG.

---

[401] STALIN, by Albert Marrin, Penguin Books, NY, 1988, p.125.

[402] EUROPEAN RESISTANCE MOVEMENTS by Trevor Nevitt Dupuy, Franklin Watts, Inc., NY 1965, p.71.

[403] EUROPEAN RESISTANCE MOVEMENTS by Trevor Nevitt Dupuy, Franklin Watts, Inc., NY 1965, p.74.

The fear may still be reasonable. As I write this letter, Russia is reported to have thousands of nuclear missiles ready to fire.

Chris, we will never know the innermost thoughts of the Soviet rebels of 1945. But it certainly does appear the reason their uprising dwindled away was the Nagasaki bomb. Such obvious overkill, coupled with President Truman's tough rhetoric toward Russia, left the Russian people no choice. They realized the only thing standing between them and the U.S. Government was the Soviet government, and they would be fools to destroy their only shield.

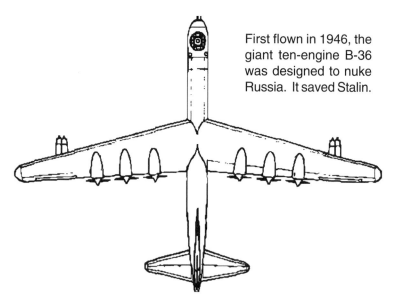

First flown in 1946, the giant ten-engine B-36 was designed to nuke Russia. It saved Stalin.

The B-36 was so big the Wright brothers could have made their first flight on its wings with a hundred feet to spare. The plane had ten engines and could fly from the U.S. to Russia, drop atomic bombs, and return. The Soviet people's only defense against the B-36 was the Soviet government, so attempts to overthrow the Soviet government, vigorous during World War II, faded away.

A likely contributing reason the uprising faded was the Allies' Operation Keelhaul. At war's end, captured Soviet rebels in German uniforms were not set free; they were turned over to Soviet authorities. Scores of Soviet rebels held in the U.S. at the Fort Dix **POW**[404] camp had tried to commit suicide rather than be handed over, but Keelhaul was continued anyhow.[405]

The total Soviet rebels in Europe turned over to Stalin by Allied governments, to be immediately executed or imprisoned, is estimated at two million.[406] Chris, imagine how demoralizing Operation Keelhaul must have been to Soviet rebels still fighting.

In short, the evidence strongly suggests not only that the nuclear death and destruction rained on Japan in 1945 was not necessary, it rescued the Soviet government from the wrath of the Soviet people. It kept the Soviet Socialists in power, and thereby gave the world the nuclear arms race and Cold War in which two generations of children grew up waiting to be vaporized by nuclear bombs.

Chris, the horrible threat of nuclear war was caused by the irresponsible use of language. Officials in the USG insisted on seeing "the Soviets" as a single unified group, just as they saw "the Germans" as a single unified group. They saw no difference between the governments and the people. In 1945, they decided to use atomic bombs to frighten "the Soviets," and they succeeded spectacularly. They completely ignored the fact that no one had more to gain

---

[404] POW: Prisoner of war.

[405] WALL STREET JOURNAL, September 29, 1987, p.28.

[406] THE FAILURE OF AMERICA'S FOREIGN WARS, edited by Richard Ebeling and Jacob Hornberger, The Future of Freedom Foundation, Fairfax, VA 1996, p.211.

from the demise of the Soviet government than the Soviet people did.

Instead of trying to frighten "the Soviets" in 1945, U.S. officials should have been smuggling them sniper rifles. Stopping a tyrant does not require an arsenal of million-dollar atomic bombs, it only requires a ten-cent bullet. The Soviet people would have been happy to fire these bullets if American officials had not frightened them so badly.

For a half century, the message of the Hiroshima and Nagasaki bombs was, the USG was willing to do this to Japanese cities full of civilians, and the USG is willing to do it to Soviet cities full of civilians.

Of course, the Cold War is over now. By 1990, the U.S. had gone 45 years without destroying the U.S.S.R., and the Soviet people had apparently come to believe the USG had lost the will to do it.

In other words, I think that in the 1990s, the Soviet people rebelled against the Kremlin because they finally felt safe in destroying their shield against nuclear attack.

The triggering event was the 1979-1989 war in Afghanistan. Soviet troops invaded Afghanistan in 1979, and, in one of the most vicious wars ever fought, were eventually defeated by Afghan Muslims (called "freedom fighters" by the West). The victory by the Afghan Muslims galvanized people in the Soviet Empire. The mighty Kremlin was not so mighty after all. In February 1989, the Soviets fled Afghanistan, and in November 1989, crowds in Germany began tearing down the Berlin Wall, beginning the breakup of the Soviet Empire.

Today that depraved empire is a mere shadow of its former self, but the effects of the Cold War live on, in the wreckage of the World Trade Center. In my next letter I will explain how.

Chris, it is important to remember that a million Afghan Muslims died in the ten-year war to defeat the Union of Soviet Socialist Republics. The world owes the Muslims who fought this worst empire the world has ever known a great debt of gratitude. Franklin Roosevelt saved the Soviet Empire, making it a superpower, and the Afghan Muslims shattered it.

Uncle Eric

P.S. At the end of World War II, the USG had the world's most powerful army, navy, and air force, including the world's only atomic bombs. U.S. officials could do anything they pleased and the rest of the world would have been helpless to stop them. In an apparent continuing attempt to keep Stalin in power, they granted him the privilege of taking East Europe. He promptly stole factories and vast amounts of other resources and shipped them back to the Soviet Union. The total value has been calculated at $14 billion (in 1945 dollars).[407] U.S. officials could just as easily have threatened to nuke the Kremlin if Stalin did not get out of East Europe, but they did not. This lends credence to the belief that their aim was to threaten the Soviet people, not Soviet leaders, thereby keeping the Soviet Socialist elite in power.

---

[407] "Fortieth Anniversary of Yalta Conference Finds Soviets Uneasy," by Frederick Kempe, WALL STREET JOURNAL, February 8, 1985, p.1.

Part Six

Effect
On Us Today

52

Arm Any Gangster

Dear Chris,

In order to stop Hitler, the USG kept Stalin in power and made a habit of it. With U.S. help, Stalin crushed the Germans and then crushed the Russian rebels who were trying to overthrow him.

The U.S. direct assistance to Stalin stopped with the end of the war in 1945, but by then it was too late. Joseph Stalin, the worst tyrant in all of human history, who murdered 42.7 million,[408] emerged from the war as the most powerful man in the Old World. He directly controlled a sixth of all the land on earth, and threatened everything else.

After 1945, with Hitler out of the way, Americans began to worry about Stalin. When he got the atomic bomb in 1949, they panicked.

The USG adopted a policy of giving money, weapons, and military training to anyone who claimed to be anti-Soviet. This was the so-called Truman Doctrine, decreed by President Truman in 1947 and embraced by every President afterward until the collapse of the Soviet Empire in the 1990s.

Other statements of the USG's intention to create a global empire followed the Truman Doctrine. Perhaps the most noteworthy was National Security Council Document number 68, dated April 14, 1950. NSC-68 had two main goals. First, it said the USG must "contain" the Soviet Union. This would

---

[408] DEATH BY GOVERNMENT, by R.J. Rummel, Transaction Publishers, New Brunswick, NJ, 1994, p.8.

become the policy of "containment" designed to keep Stalin's Empire from expanding.

Second, NSC-68 said "the absence of order among nations is becoming less and less tolerable," and the USG must use its power to straighten out the world. The tactics could involve "any means, covert or overt, violent or nonviolent."

Toward this end, said NSC-68, the USG should "Strengthen the orientation toward the United States of the non-Soviet nations; and help such of those nations as are able and willing to make an important contribution to U.S. security, to increase their economic and political stability and their military capability."

NSC-68 did not say U.S. money and weapons should go only to governments that permit freedom, it said only that they should go to those that are on the side of the U.S.[409]

Chris, of the more than 200 countries in the world, not more than 20 have governments limited enough that an American would feel comfortable living there without the escape hatch of a U.S. passport. Any American living under the unlimited regimes with only the legal rights of the native people would feel as if he were living in Nazi Germany.

Stalin is long dead, and the Soviet Empire splintered in the early 1990s, but the USG still provides money, military training, or other assistance to more than 100 governments. This means more than 80 of its allies are tyrants, crooks, and gangsters.

These thugs have included, believe it or not, Osama bin Laden in Afghanistan, Fidel Castro in Cuba, Saddam Hussein in Iraq, President Diem of Vietnam, the Shah of Iran,

---

[409] NSC-68 can be found by searching the Internet for "NSC-68." An explanation of the document's ramifications can be found in Chapter Eight of EMPIRE AS A WAY OF LIFE, by William Appleman Williams, Oxford University Press, NY, 1980.

General Zia ul-Haq in Pakistan, Marcos in the Philippines, Manuel Noriega in Panama, Mobutu in the Congo, Chiang Kai-Shek in Taiwan, General Park Chung-hee in Korea, and Suharto and Habibie in Indonesia.

If you do not believe it, check into the biographies of these outlaws, all received help from the USG — even Osama bin Laden.

The Shah of Iran and his secret police terrorized Iranians for 25 years with the backing of the USG.

Frequently, after these thugs have gotten all they can from the USG, they turn on us and stab us in the back.

All this began at the end of World War II when the USG decided to begin fighting the Soviet Socialist tyranny it had helped rescue and strengthen during the war. In the effort to "prevent the rise of another Hitler," the USG formed alliances with anyone who claimed to be anti-Soviet and pro-American. Chris, remember the ten deadly ideas that lead to war, especially the idea of alliances?[410]

The USG has continued this practice, backing cutthroats who claim to be pro-American.[411] By the year 2000, the U.S. "sphere of influence," meaning the U.S. Empire, comprised more than 100 countries. It was the largest empire the world has ever known, a powerseeker's dream come true.

None of the victims of these U.S.-backed gangsters have much good to say about America and some are getting revenge. This is the root cause of the so-called terrorism that worries us today.

More in my next letter.

Uncle Eric

---

[410] The ten deadly ideas that lead to war are discussed in Richard J Maybury's book WORLD WAR I: THE REST OF THE STORY, published by Bluestocking Press, web site: www.BluestockingPress.com.

[411] "In Pharaoh's Kingdom," WALL STREET JOURNAL, January 2, 2001.

53

September 11th

Dear Chris,

Americans have never quite grasped the importance of the fact that the Bill of Rights stops at the border.

Inside the U.S., powerseekers face severe limitations.

Beyond U.S. borders, they can do anything.

You have read my original set of letters about THE THOUSAND YEAR WAR IN THE MIDEAST[412] so you know that what happened on September 11, 2001, at the World Trade Center and Pentagon was no surprise. The USG's support for tyrants around the world left millions of victims with grudges, so it was only a matter of time until these victims found a way to begin striking back in ways that would get the undivided attention of the American people.

Chris, foreigners are fond of Americans as individuals, and for the most part they like America's private companies and products. However, they hate and fear the U.S. Government which meddles in every corner of the globe.

Much of the meddling is secret, but an example came to light in 2001. As mentioned in my previous set of letters about World War I, the National Security Archive at George

---

[412] Uncle Eric is referring to Richard J. Maybury's book THE THOUSAND YEAR WAR IN THE MIDEAST: HOW IT AFFECTS YOU TODAY, published by Bluestocking Press, web site: www.BluestockingPress.com.

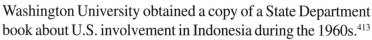

Washington University obtained a copy of a State Department book about U.S. involvement in Indonesia during the 1960s.[413]

Publication of the untitled book was banned by the State Department but the book was posted at www.nsarchive.org. It may still be there.

The formerly secret book reveals that during a rebellion against the Indonesian dictatorship, the State Department supplied the dictator's military units with money and intelligence information about rebel groups.

The Indonesian dictator claimed to be anti-Soviet and pro-American.

The USG's aid to him led to the deaths of more than 100,000 suspected rebels.

The key word is "suspected." The Indonesian government has never been very big on legal technicalities such as evidence and juries — nor are most of the other governments that the USG supports.

With money, weapons, military training, or some other kind of aid, the USG helps the governments of Russia, Egypt, Macedonia, Romania, Kazakhstan, Uzbekistan, Saudi Arabia, Chad, Nigeria, and Columbia, to name but a few. No rational American would want to live under any of these governments.

Two months after September 11th, in an attempt to understand how the U.S. Government operates abroad, the WALL STREET JOURNAL ran a front-page story titled, "A C.I.A.-Backed Team Used Brutal Means To Crack Terror Cell."[414]

The story describes foreign police and military units trained and financed by the USG using torture to extract

---

[413] "Book on US Role..." CHICAGO TRIBUNE, 29 Jul 01, p.6.
[414] WALL STREET JOURNAL, November 20, 2001, p.1.

information from persons who may be totally innocent. For instance, one suspect, who had not been found guilty of anything, was hung by his wrists while electrical wires were applied to various parts of his body.

Your tax dollars at work.

Inside the United States the government is forbidden to behave this way, but the Bill of Rights stops at the border. Outside the country the government does pretty much anything it wants, and it has been doing this for more than a hundred years.

It is anyone's guess how many innocent people the American taxpayer is forced to help terrorize, torture and murder, but the number is certainly in the millions.

Each of these victims has family and friends who love him or her very much, and these people are not the least bit happy with the USG.

President Clinton had an easy opportunity to break out of this pattern when the Soviet Empire fell apart in the early 1990s. He could have ended aid to crooks and tyrants, but he did not. Refusing to give up his empire, he continued supplying money, arms, and training to any thug who claimed to be pro-USG.

Instead of putting a halt to the meddling, Mr. Clinton sent aid to the Kremlin when Russian troops were massacring the Muslim Chechens.

But that was only the tip of the iceberg. We will come back to Mr. Clinton shortly.

                                    Uncle Eric

54

Blowback

Dear Chris,

In the 1950s, Iranians and other victims of the USG's aid tried to call attention to their plight. Americans would not listen.

Most of us attend schools that are owned or controlled by government agencies. As we grow up studying history, we rarely hear anything critical of the U.S. Government.

We develop a trust in the government's foreign policy and few of us have any interest in it, preferring to leave it to the "experts."

By the mid-1960s, it was becoming apparent to the victims of the USG's aid that the American people were not going to listen. Victims realized they needed to do something to grab our attention. Americans were focused entirely on the Soviet threat and could not have cared less about the USG's behavior in Iran or anywhere else.

The victims of U.S. aid to foreign tyrants did not like killing innocent people, but their own families were dying at the hands of USG-backed regimes; so, in desperation, some decided to act. In the Central Intelligence Agency (CIA), the victims' retaliation is called **blowback**.

In 1968, when Presidential candidate Robert Kennedy promised to send fifty F-4 Phantom jet fighters to Israel, a Palestinian named Sirhan Sirhan killed him.

Americans did not want to hear the reason for this blowback; they just wanted revenge.

In subsequent years, more blowback:

- 1973 brought the first Arab oil embargo against the U.S. Again, Americans did not ask the reason for this blowback, they just got angry.

- 1979 brought the Iranian hostage crisis. Americans did not want to hear explanations; they just wanted to hit back.

- 1983 brought the bombing of the marine barracks in Beirut, killing 241 marines. Still, Americans did not ask why, they just rallied behind their leaders and demanded revenge.

- In 1988, Pan Am flight 103 was blown up over Scotland. No one asked, "Why do they hate us?"

I could list dozens of examples but you get the point. Not even the 1993 bombing of the World Trade Center was enough to make the American people question their government's foreign policy.

- 1996 brought the bombing of the Khobar towers in Saudi Arabia, killing 19 Americans.

- 1998 brought the bombing of two embassies in Africa, killing 224.

Still not enough. Americans had been taught to trust their government's judgment in foreign affairs, so they assumed the attacks were unprovoked. They did not want to hear the reasons for the blowback. Nor were they told.

Then President Clinton poured gasoline on the fire.

Like every other President of the 20th century, Mr. Clinton had carte blanche to do anything he pleased outside the country. The Bill of Rights stops at the border, it does not protect people in other lands.

Chris, you may remember reading about Mr. Clinton's friend Monica Lewinsky. The President was married but was spending a lot of time behind closed doors with Miss Lewinsky and probably other women, too.

As the President's scandals began to surface, he tried to divert attention. Embracing foreign intervention with a vengeance, he began firing what came to be called "Monica missiles" into Serbia, Iraq, Sudan and Afghanistan.

We will never know how many innocent people died under the hail of Mr. Clinton's Monica missiles, but we can be certain their families and friends were not happy about it.

If someone killed a person you love in order to draw attention from his scandals, how would you feel? What would you do?

What would be your attitude toward the people he represents when they refused to do anything about him?

Summarizing, it was FDR's insane rescue of Stalin that led to the equally insane policy of aiding any tyrant who claimed to be anti-Soviet. Each of these dozens of tyrants has hurt thousands, sometimes millions, and now the victims are looking for revenge.

After the fall of the Soviet Empire in the early 1990s, President Clinton had an easy opportunity to end this insanity, but instead he (and Congress) continued aiding foreign tyrants, and then he fired hundreds of "Monica missiles" to divert attention from his scandals.

Apparently, the Monica missiles were the last straw, and on September 11, 2001, the massive retaliation began.

Unsurprisingly, the tough and resourceful people who defeated the Soviet Empire led the retaliation. Muslims.

Chris, political power corrupts the morals and the judgment, history teaches no clearer lesson. The root cause of what happened on September 11, 2001, was the belief that Hitler was the worst evil in history and America must do whatever it takes to prevent the rise of another Hitler, including support any gangster who claims to be pro-American.

There is an unbroken chain of events that runs directly from people such as Theodore Roosevelt and Admiral Alfred Thayer Mahan, who taught a hundred years ago that the USG has the right and duty to meddle in other countries, to the two World Wars, Korea, Vietnam, and a host of other conflicts, and then to the destruction of the World Trade Center.

In short, what happened on September 11th was blowback from the ideas that became popular in the USG a century ago.

This is one reason I always emphasize that I love my country and would not want to live anywhere else, but the country and the government are not the same thing.

Chris, if someone said to me, in the final analysis the World Trade Center was destroyed by Teddy Roosevelt and his cronies, I would have a hard time disagreeing.

Uncle Eric

"We have torn up 150 years of traditional foreign policy. We have tossed Washington's Farewell Address into the discard. We have thrown ourselves squarely into the power politics and power wars of Europe, Asia, and Africa. We have taken the first step upon a course from which we can never hereafter retreat."

— Senator Arthur Vandenberg
on the passage of Lend-Lease in March 1941

Blowback

The term "blowback," which officials of the Central Intelligence Agency first invented for their own internal use, is starting to circulate among students of international relations. It refers to the unintended consequences of policies that were kept secret from the American people. What the daily press reports as the malign acts of "terrorists" or "drug lords" or "rogue states" or "illegal arms merchants" often turns out to be blowback from earlier American operations.

It is now widely recognized, for example, that the 1988 bombing of Pan Am flight 103 over Lockerbie, Scotland, which resulted in the deaths of 259 passengers and 11 people on the ground, was retaliation for a 1986 Reagan administration aerial raid on Libya that killed President Muammar Khadaffi's stepdaughter. ...

One man's terrorist is, of course, another man's freedom fighter, and what U.S. officials denounce as unprovoked terrorist attacks on its innocent citizens are often meant as retaliation for previous American imperial actions. Terrorists attack innocent and undefended American targets precisely because American soldiers and sailors firing cruise missiles from ships at sea or sitting in B-52 bombers at extremely high altitudes or supporting brutal and repressive regimes from Washington seem invulnerable. As members of the Defense Science Board wrote in a 1997 report to the undersecretary of defense for acquisition and technology, "Historical data show a strong correlation between U.S. involvement in international situations and an increase in terrorist attacks against the United States."[415]

— Chalmers Johnson
BLOWBACK, Published in 2000

[415] BLOWBACK, by Chalmers Johnson, Henry Holt & Co., NY, 2000, p.8-11.

55

MAD

Dear Chris,

Blowback has not been the only effect of the USG's meddling in the World Wars.

After Soviet rulers got the atomic bomb in 1949, they began to threaten America in the same way that the USG had been threatening the U.S.S.R. Both sides threw themselves into an arms race, each trying to build more and bigger bombs.

This horrific situation continues to this day. Both sides keep an arsenal of thousands of nuclear weapons.

This is called Mutually Assured Destruction, or **MAD**. The theory is that war between the two nuclear powers will not happen because if it does, both countries would be destroyed. Indeed, much of the world would be destroyed.

In the Southern Hemisphere, mass destruction is less likely because Russia and the U.S. are in the Northern Hemisphere. I have heard New Zealanders and Australians speak of the Northern Hemisphere as "the splatter zone."

Chris, you are too young to remember how frightening MAD was before the Soviet Empire began to break up in 1989. Here is an example.

In 1961, during the Berlin Wall Crisis, the Kremlin wanted to frighten America. In Siberia, as a demonstration of what they could do to America, Soviet rulers detonated the largest bomb in history.

This was an H-bomb, a hydrogen bomb, far more pow-erful than an A-bomb or atomic bomb.

The Soviet H-bomb produced a blast of 50 megatons, meaning it was equal to 50 million tons of conventional ex-plosives.

How much is 50 million tons?

It is equal to one million railroad boxcars full of explo-sives.

Or, it is 2,500 times as powerful as the A-bomb that de-stroyed Hiroshima.

The leg of the mushroom cloud was six miles wide, and the cloud reached 40 miles above the earth's surface. This is seven times as high as commercial airliners fly.

The shock wave broke windows in Norway and Finland 700 miles away.[416]

The next year, 1962, brought the Cuban Missile Crisis. President Kennedy learned that the Kremlin was moving nu-clear-tipped missiles to Cuba, which is only 90 miles from the U.S.

The USG had nuclear-tipped missiles in Turkey, right on the border of the U.S.S.R., but President Kennedy said the Kremlin had no right to keep missiles near America. He threat-ened to invade Cuba to remove the missiles by force if the Kremlin did not remove them.

The Kremlin backed down.

Decades later, Americans were told the rest of the story.

Unknown to President Kennedy, nuclear weapons were already in Cuba, armed and ready for use. These weapons had no combination locks or other safety features. Like any

---

[416] "The Cold War: The Strangelove Factor," History Channel documentary.

other weapon, they could be fired entirely at the discretion of their crews.

And their crews had been told by the Kremlin to fire if the Americans invaded.

It was only luck that the Kremlin contacted Kennedy and backed down before Kennedy picked up the phone and gave the order to attack. If the Kremlin had delayed, or if for some reason the phone line between Moscow and Washington D.C. had been out of service, your parents and I would be radioactive dust and you would never have existed.

That is just one of the many awful crises that grew out of the USG's support for Stalin during World War II.

In my next letter, more about terrorists.

Uncle Eric

56

Police Officers of the World

Dear Chris,

Victory in the World Wars has led the USG to assume it has some kind of right to use America's soldiers, sailors, and airmen as police officers of the world.

An example of the result happened in 1999. U.S. aircraft were flying over Iraq to prevent Iraqi aircraft from entering the "no fly" zones[417] over Iraqi territory. President George H. W. Bush had decreed these zones after the 1990-91 Iraq-Kuwait War. They were a way of punishing Saddam Hussein and thwarting his efforts to take back Iraq's share of the Persian Gulf oil fields. (Iraq and Iran owned the Persian Gulf for more than 2,000 years until London and Washington took it away from them during the 20th century.)

Sometimes pilots flying fast jets thousands of feet in the air have a hard time identifying objects on the ground. In 1999, pilots of U.S. warplanes mistook a sheep-watering trough for a missile launcher in Iraq. They dropped a three-thousand-pound bomb on a group of shepherds and their families.[418]

Chris, if someone from the other side of the world did that to your family, would you be willing to forgive and forget?

---

[417] No fly zone: an area where one power forbids another power to fly its planes.

[418] "The Unvanquished," by Jon Lee Anderson, THE NEW YORKER, December 8, 2000, p.81.

Would you accept the claim that we had good intentions but we made a mistake?

Maybe you would, but it does not work that way in the Mideast. Those dead men, women, and children all had relatives and friends who cared about them. I think it is entirely likely that one or more of these relatives or friends are now looking for ways to get revenge against America.

Humans are not perfect; they make mistakes, and when they make them in someone else's country, the victims are not likely to be very broad-minded about it.

Another example.

In 1998, the USG mistakenly fired missiles at a pharmaceutical plant in Sudan.

That same year they fired missiles at suspected "terrorist" camps in Afghanistan.

How many innocent people did they kill? We do not know, but it is a safe bet the families and friends of the victims will not forgive or forget.

I could go on, but you get the point. Americans have been taught that Hitler was something unusual, the most evil person the world has ever known, and he was only stopped, narrowly, by America's participation in World War II. They believe the U.S. armed forces must be used to prevent new Hitlers from arising, and they are willing to pay the price of killing innocent people to do that.

They do not realize that people like Hitler are not the least bit unusual in the Old World.

In 1999, when President Clinton sent U.S. troops into Kosovo in Europe, he said he was doing it because, "World War II taught us that America could never be secure if Europe's future was in doubt."[419]

---

[419] "Clinton Outlines Kosovo Strategy," by Sandra Sobieraj, Associated Press story in the SACRAMENTO BEE, February 14, 1999, p.A25.

With each U.S. attack on foreign lands, in the name of stopping another Hitler, more innocents are killed and more "terrorists" are created.

In my opinion, the "terrorism" will continue escalating until Americans know the rest of the story about the World Wars. The USG's role as global cop in those wars did not make things better, it made them worse. And the USG's role as global cop today is making things worse.

Geopolitics is never so simple as Hollywood's good guys versus bad guys model.

In any country, the government is one group and the people are another.

Governments also break down into various **factions**, and the people are usually split into many more factions. Each faction has its own history, its own way of thinking, and its own way of judging right and wrong.

Who are the good guys? Usually there is no way to know.

This is why for centuries the Swiss have had a policy of heavily armed neutrality. The whole male population serves in the militia, and, as I write this letter, the militia has never been sent into other countries during modern times.

The Swiss are in the exact center of Europe, surrounded by nations that periodically go crazy and slaughter each other. Swiss know how complex each nation and each rivalry is, and they know war is almost never a case of good guys against bad guys.

In most cases, it is bad guys against bad guys.

In my opinion, the best policy for America is to copy the Swiss system of defense that I explained in my previous set of letters on World War I. Be friendly with everyone, visit them and do business with them, but no political connections and no foreign wars.

Notice that this is not a policy of **isolationism**. For centuries, the Swiss maintained a policy of political neutrality, but remained fully involved in Europe and the rest of the world. Theirs has been one of the most open societies on earth. The Swiss held the policy that I believe America should have: stay politically neutral and keep your powder dry.

Uncle Eric

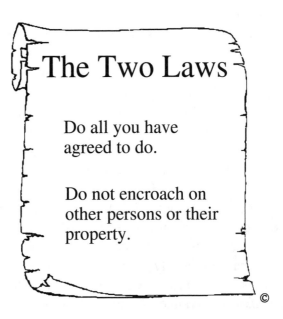

The Two Laws

Do all you have
agreed to do.

Do not encroach on
other persons or their
property.

©

P.S. Chris, in my opinion, the only way to make the world better — to reduce the tyranny, bloodshed and poverty — is to *teach* the two legal principles that make peace, liberty and prosperity possible.

I explained these principles in my previous set of letters to you on the subject of justice.[420] The two principles are, do all you have agreed to do — this is the basis of contract law — and do not encroach on other persons or their property — this is the basis of tort law and some criminal law.

These are the laws on which all religions agree.

Where these laws are widely violated, life gets worse, and where they are widely obeyed, life gets better.

Chris, I am sometimes asked what I would do about foreign wars if I were President. I would have a simple rule. When someone advised me to get into someone else's war in places such as Kosovo or the Persian Gulf, I would ask myself, is this something I would be willing to die for? If the answer is no, then I would not send someone else to die for it.

But no President has had this policy in at least a hundred years, so America has been in one foreign war after another, making enemies by the millions. On September 11, 2001, the enemies found a way to make every one of us begin to pay the price, to feel fear and sorrow.

There is no way to stop paying this price without obeying the two laws. Any attempt to achieve peace must begin with the two laws as the foundation of U.S. foreign policy.

U.S. officials must announce that they will never again meddle in other countries. Then we can begin working toward real peace and liberty.

---

[420] Uncle Eric is referring to Richard J. Maybury's book WHATEVER HAPPENED TO JUSTICE? published by Bluestocking Press, web site: www.BluestockingPress.com.

57

Summary

Dear Chris,

Repeating from an earlier letter, here is a summary of the story generally accepted by Americans for how the USG got into World War II.

* Bad men rose to power in Germany, Italy, and Japan (the chief Axis powers) with the intention of taking over the world by force.

* The rulers of Britain, France, the Soviet Union, and America (the chief Allied powers) had no such intention. They believed in liberty and justice for all.

* The most evil, dangerous person in history was Adolph Hitler.

* The Allies delayed intervention in Axis plans until it was too late to nip the problem in the bud.

* The Allies were outgunned by the Axis and by the fall of 1941, they were losing.

* The U.S. entered the war on December 7, 1941, with the Japanese attack on Pearl Harbor. This was a

tragedy but in the long run it was for the best because the U.S. saved the world.

• Victory was a near thing. The good rulers in Britain, France, and the Soviet Union had little chance of beating the bad rulers in Germany, Italy, and Japan without the help of America.

• If the U.S. had not saved the day, our world would now be in the grip of fascism and we would all be slaves. Everyone in the U.S. would be forced to speak German, Italian, or Japanese.

• The lesson of World War II is that America must intervene early and often in disputes in every corner of the world to keep these conflicts from becoming a global bloodbath like that of the 1940s.

• More importantly, America must intervene to keep another Hitler from coming to power.

Summarizing the view taught to most Americans, World War II was a battle of good versus evil, and good triumphed only by the skin of its teeth. To prevent another such catastrophe in which we might not be so lucky, the U.S. must have military forces that are global police officers, ready to go to any corner of the globe to fight evil.

Chris, now that you know the rest of the story, the non-statist side, I think you can see that this widely believed explanation is not supported by the facts.

I am convinced there was simply no reason for America to be involved in the war. America's participation made the war much longer and far more bloody — it surely added ten million to the final body count, and probably a lot more.

The USG's aid to the U.S.S.R. made the aftermath of the war — the nuclear arms race with the brutal Soviet Union — the most dangerous condition humans have ever faced. And it led to the "terrorism" we face today.

It would have been far better for America to have taken George Washington's advice and remained neutral, and let the German Nazis and Soviet Socialists pound each other to dust on the Eastern Front.

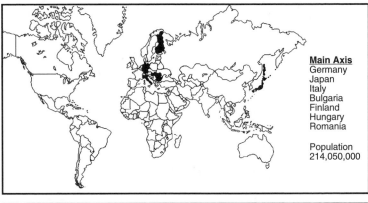

Main Axis
Germany
Japan
Italy
Bulgaria
Finland
Hungary
Romania

Population
214,050,000

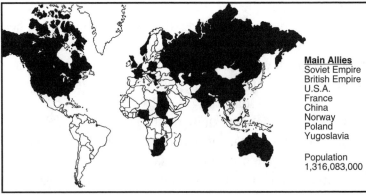

Main Allies
Soviet Empire
British Empire
U.S.A.
France
China
Norway
Poland
Yugoslavia

Population
1,316,083,000

Does it really seem plausible that the Axis almost won?

In other words, the Eastern Front was not a problem; it was the solution. On September 12, 1941, when the first snow fell on German soldiers in Russia, that should have been the beginning of the end of the war.

I think there is a 99 percent probability it would have been if the USG had let the war run its course.

But the USG did not stay out, so the worst of all the evils in the war — the worst evil the world has ever known, the Soviet Empire — survived, and survived with enough strength to recover, then threaten the world with nuclear annihilation.

Chris, if you are one of the millions of Americans who still feel loyalty to Britain and would want to have seen the USG get into the war on the side of London, let me suggest an alternative, a four-point plan:

The USG should have said to London:

1. Set your colonies free and bring your army, navy, and air force home to seal England off from the continent.

2. English citizens in the colonies who are afraid of the natives or of the Axis can catch a ride home with the navy.

3. Sit with us in the grandstand and watch the contest on the playing field. Root with us for the cutthroats in Tokyo, Berlin, Moscow, and China to hammer each other into rubble.

4. If one of the cutthroats survives the war strong enough to threaten us, we can pounce on him together at that time, after he has been weakened

by war with the others. In no case should we help any of these cutthroats, and certainly not help the worst of them, Stalin.

Reread item #1, Chris. Notice the **premise** of what I am saying. The U.S. participation in the war was, among other things, a way of relieving London of the need to free its conquered peoples.

The USG saved both the British Empire and the Soviet Empire, neither of which was worth so much as one American life.

Britain today is a different country than it was in 1940. Today it is one of the best, but in 1940, London was sitting atop an empire that was the result of eight centuries of conquest.

Again, Chris, no war is ever so simple as white hats against black hats.

Uncle Eric

Part Seven

Final Thoughts
About War

58

The Needless Deaths of 35 Million

Dear Chris,

When I was your age, I had been raised on a steady diet of films, books, and articles showing war as a contest between good guys and bad guys. Especially the World Wars.

I wanted to be a hero, a man, so when the Vietnam War came along and I received my draft notice, I joined the Air Force.

I nearly got killed several times,[421] and some of my friends did get killed. This made me start to wonder what it was all for.

Chris, I began to research war and have never stopped. Now I have been at it for more than 30 years and have found war to be nothing like the good guys versus bad guys stories that influenced me so much when I was your age.

These letters have given you facts that I am sure you will not find anywhere else, at least not easily. They are the facts that I wish someone had given me when I was your age.

When it comes to defending my family and my homeland, you will never meet a more intense warhawk than me. But when it comes to getting into other people's wars in far corners of the globe, I have never seen a case where I would do it knowing the history of those people.

Here is a summary of how I see the 20th century.

---

[421] Although not in Vietnam, Richard Maybury was involved in covert warfare in Central America.

- As the century dawned, the Spanish-American War and massacre of Filipinos had given Americans a taste for blood and empire.

- This war fever led the USG to intervene in World War I on the side of the British and French.

- The addition of U.S. power gave the British and French a mighty advantage. It destroyed any chance of a fair settlement for the Germans, and lengthened the war.

- The U.S. intervention in World War I therefore led to the Treaty of Versailles, which impoverished and humiliated the Germans.

- The German hunger for revenge became the Second World War.

- President Roosevelt's call for Unconditional Surrender in World War II lengthened that war, too.

- The bombings of Hiroshima and Nagasaki frightened Russians so much that their attempt to overthrow the Kremlin — which was their only shield against the U.S. — evaporated and would not be revived for almost a half century.

- The survival of the Kremlin after 1945 led to the Cold War and nuclear arms race, and several close calls with Armageddon in incidents such as the 1962 Cuban Missile Crisis.

- The USG's method of fighting the Cold War — by backing any regime that claimed to be anti-Soviet and pro-U.S. — led to the imprisonment, torture, and murder of uncountable innocent people, probably millions, and thereby to the "terrorist" blowback that threatens us today.

A key point: like its predecessor, World War II did not become a world war until the U.S. got into it. Until then it was just another typical European and Asian bloodbath, the same thing that has been going on in the Old World for thousands of years and is still going on today.

So, Chris, all this leads me to the following conclusion:

The U.S. intervention in World War I lengthened that war and produced World War II and its Cold War aftermath. This means the USG's participation in the Old World's vendettas led to the needless deaths of at least 35 million people.

Chris, as you learned from my previous set of letters about World War I, the two World Wars grew out of the mindset adopted by Americans in the Spanish-American War.

Actions have consequences, which leads me to consider this question: Was the September 11th attack just the latest chapter in the Spanish-American War?

Uncle Eric

P.S. Chris, ever since the movie SAVING PRIVATE RYAN, there has been an upsurge in interest about World War II. The men and women who fought that war are again being recognized for their sacrifice and painted as heroes that young people like yourself should try to emulate.

This worries me greatly. To acknowledge the horrific hardship and suffering of the World War II veterans is a fine thing. After all, their hearts were in the right place. They did it because they thought it was the right thing to do. They were bombarded with war propaganda like that in Frank Capra's WHY WE FIGHT films.

But to make them into heroes that young people should emulate is begging for trouble. Such movies can persuade another generation of fine young men and women to blindly march off to war: 1) before fully understanding the opponent's point of view and, 2) before seeing a mountain of evidence that the war is for an extremely good reason.

We have returned to the spirit of the 1950s and '60s, when hero worship for the World War II veterans persuaded many from my generation to fight in the Vietnam War.

Chris, if your country is genuinely in danger, then by all means do whatever you can to defend it. I know I will. But make sure you have the full story before you commit your life to the road the government wants you to travel.

59

The Normal Condition of Humans

Dear Chris,

> The history of Europe and Asia is long and violent.
> Tenacious emotions and habits are associated with it.
> Can the American people, great and ingenious though
> they be, transform those traditions, institutions,
> systems, emotions and habits by employing treasure,
> arms, propaganda, and diplomatic lectures? Can they,
> by any means at their disposal, make over Europe and
> Asia, provide democracy, a bill of rights, and economic
> security for everybody, everywhere, in the world? ...
>
> Yet we do know that the present war did not spring
> out of a vacuum, nor merely out of the Versailles
> Treaty. Its origins, nature, and course are rooted in
> the long history of the Old World and the long conflicts
> of the great powers.

Those are the words of historian Charles A. Beard in testimony before the Senate Foreign Relations Committee in
1941.[422] Beard turned out to be right; America's intervention
was a waste. In fact, it made things worse.

Chris, many veterans of Korea and Vietnam suspect their
lives were risked for nothing. Most veterans of World War II

---

[422] FRANKLIN D. ROOSEVELT AND THE WORLD CRISIS, 1937-1945, edited
by Warren F. Kimball of Rutgers University, D.C. Heath & Co.,
Lexington, Mass. 1973, p.9.

are much different. For a half-century, the World War II generation has been told they are heroes who saved the world.

If you suggest there is any other side to the story about the World Wars, the veterans of Korea and Vietnam may listen with an open mind. However, this might not be the case with World War II veterans. So be tactful when approaching the subject of war.

Perhaps the best approach is to simply ask a veteran to tell you everything he or she can about the reasons for their government being involved in the war. Be a listener. Learn from them what they know, and what they don't know.

Chris, war has been the normal condition of humans for at least 6,000 years. There have been more than 14,000 wars. The vast majority have been in the Old World, and they have killed an estimated 3.6 billion.[423]

Americans do not appreciate this because they live in the New World where major wars have been rare; and the news media do not cover most wars in the Old World.

So, not knowing about all those foreign wars, many Americans assume peace is the normal condition of humans and they do not object to U.S. troops being used abroad as world cops to "keep the peace" — a peace that does not and never has existed.

The people of the Old World hold grudges, long, long grudges. We Americans find this hard to understand. America is so unusual. In most parts of the world, bygones are not bygones. Wars rarely spring from fresh causes, most are just resumptions of previous wars.

The Korean and Vietnam wars grew out of World War II. World War II grew out of World War I. World War I grew out of the 1870 Franco-Prussian war. The Franco-Prussian war grew out of the Napoleonic wars in 1803-1815.

[423] DIRTY LITTLE SECRETS, by James F. Dunnigan and Albert A. Nofi, Quill/William Morrow, 1990, p.419.

Yugoslavia's wars in the 1990s can be traced back eighteen centuries to the ancient Roman wars.

Who threw the first punch? In most cases we will never know. There is no way any judge will ever sort out who owes whom, or who has what rights to which piece of land.

When people ask me for advice about how to deal with a dispute in the Old World, I say, stay out of it. In the long run, intervention will only make it worse because each of those people is an individual with his own feelings and we cannot do anything about those feelings.

Helping any given government will only make us enemies of that government's enemies.

The best advice I can give to people who live in the Old World is, always be ready to pack your bags and get out of Dodge.

America's Founders understood this. In 1796, George Washington warned us about the Old World, saying we "should have with them as little political connection as possible." In 1823, Thomas Jefferson warned:

> I have ever deemed it fundamental for the United States never to take active part in the quarrels of Europe. Their political interests are entirely distinct from ours. Their mutual jealousies, their balance of power, their complicated alliances, their forms and principles of government, are all foreign to us. They are nations of eternal war.

Chris, this is not an argument for isolationism. It is an argument for neutrality and **nonintervention.**

When we suggest nonintervention, people accuse us of isolationism.

America has never been isolationist. This country is where the clipper ship was invented. It's where the airplane was invented — and the steamboat and telephone. Americans were quick to adopt all these, plus television, radio and the Internet. The purpose of all of these technologies is to reach out to people in distant places, to talk with them, visit with them, and do business with them.

Americans are probably the least isolationist people in the world, except possibly for the Swiss, and this is a fine thing.

I argue only for staying neutral and for having no political or military connections. No alliances. We can learn from the Swiss, but we must study the Swiss example now before the Swiss are pressured into giving it up, and it becomes a history lesson rather than a current event — they have been gradually dismantling it.

Chris, another point about language. When talking about the World Wars we tend to say "Japan did this," or "Germany did that." Always bear in mind that we are not talking about the Japanese people or the German people, we are talking about their governments. As in America, the typical citizen in these countries had no idea what their governments were doing in secret, and could not have done much about it if they had known. Governments do as they please; in most cases it is quite impossible for the citizens to do much about it.

A German or Japanese soldier did not want to stop a bullet any more than an American did. Nor did their mothers or wives want to go to their funerals any more than American mothers or wives did.

Wars are between governments, not between the people ruled by these governments. To jump to the conclusion that, for instance, the German government was evil and so all the German people were evil is to mislead yourself drastically.

What about U.S. aid to other nations?

Chris, the U.S. Government represents everyone in the country. When it helps someone, it commits the entire country to that cause.

Enemies of the country that have been helped then feel they have a legitimate reason to attack *all* of America. That's why I caution you not to fall into the same trap. Separate the people from their governments.

All governments have enemies. Any aid to any government is a slap in the face to that government's enemies.

It may not be an exaggeration to say all aid to any government is military aid. Even something as harmless appearing as a million dollars worth of food and blankets to a government to distribute to earthquake victims is really military aid. It is a million dollars the recipient government does not need to spend on food and blankets, so it is a million dollars saved — a million dollars that can be spent on bullets and bombs.

Money is **fungible**. One dollar can substitute for any other dollar, so a dollar saved on one thing can be spent on another. Virtually all foreign aid can work in this fashion, so foreign aid is a key component of the USG's efforts to keep its puppet regimes in power. Few Americans understand fungibility, so they do not understand what is happening. To them, blankets and food appear to be only blankets and food.

If private citizens want to donate to private organizations such as the Red Cross to help others in need, this is fine. Private individuals and groups represent only themselves. If the Red Cross makes a mistake, this mistake will not likely jeopardize the lives of people who work in New York office buildings.

Chris, in your last letter you said that you "now better understand why we provided help to Stalin so that he could win the war in the East."

Be careful with the word "we," Chris. The war ended long before you were born. When you use the word "we," you are accepting responsibility for what others have done. If you intend to do that, fine, but do you?

Uncle Eric

P.S. Chris, while reading my previous set of letters about World War I, you asked if I was "against" America's armed forces. I should repeat my answer here.

No, of course I'm not against the armed forces. It isn't that we should not have armed forces; it is that we have the *wrong kind.*

We have the kind designed to "project power," which means get into other people's wars. And our armed forces do this very well. In fact, they have done it so well for so long that on September 11, 2001, the foreign wars they have been sent into followed them home to American soil. You are aware of this because you have read my original set of letters about the thousand year war in the Mideast.[424]

We need the kind of armed forces deemed necessary by the Second Amendment — a "well-regulated militia," trained and equipped with the latest and best weapons, to fight as guerrillas who can make the country impossible for an enemy to occupy and who can find and kill the enemy's leaders. A defensive force; like a porcupine. This is how we can protect our homeland without meddling in other countries and without being a threat to other countries.

---

[424] Uncle Eric is referring to Richard J. Maybury's book THE THOUSAND YEAR WAR IN THE MIDEAST: HOW IT AFFECTS YOU TODAY, published by Bluestocking Press, web site: www.BluestockingPress.com.

60

The Cause of War

Dear Chris,

By the end of World War II, the USG had been so swept away by the routine slaughter that it was burning a city a day.

I have written many times that the World Wars were not about good versus evil. So what were they about?

Some would say economics. There is a widespread belief that all human behavior is, at bottom, about the quest for wealth, and war is one of the ways nations seek wealth.

This may explain some wars but, in my opinion, very few. War is the most expensive thing humans do, any alternative is cheaper, so economics always argues against war.

I think World War II and the vast majority of all wars are about political power: either the thrill of using political power or the quest for more power.

It is very difficult for wealth seekers to understand the motives of powerseekers. A wealth seeker tries to improve his condition by, we hope, producing goods or services of value to trade for what he wants. This process of production and trade is satisfying in itself, and it moves the wealth seeker in the direction he wishes to travel.

The powerseeker is willing to trade his wealth for the privilege of forcing others to bend to his will. If you watch closely in every election, you will see people investing thousands or millions of their own dollars for campaigns to acquire political jobs paying small salaries that can never repay the investment.

Are these people trying to get government jobs to get rich? Or are they after something else, for the ability to impose their plans on others?

If you are not a powerseeker, war is just a big waste. (Unless you are an arms maker.) But war is the most thrilling and, therefore, most satisfying expression of political power. If you are a powerseeker, war is nirvana.[425]

Very important: war is not the route to nirvana; it is nirvana. War is the end in itself, the big payoff.

Walk around any school yard and watch the bullies tormenting their victims. Are the bullies doing it to grow rich? Or are they doing it for the thrill of inflicting pain, of forcing someone to bend to their will, of intimidation — the joy of power?

Why is it that humans, and especially those of the Old World, are continually at war with each other?

Actually, they aren't. We have no evidence that warfare is an inherent compulsion in individuals. But we have plenty that it is inherent in governments.

America contains Germans, English, French, Serbs, Muslims, Croats, Russians, Chinese, Japanese and probably immigrants from every other country.

Unlike in the Old World, these people do not build fortifications and try to massacre each other. Why?

When they came here, they did not bring their governments with them.

Governments attract people who want political power. After these people have spent their entire adult lives trying to acquire power, they naturally want to use it on someone. Military force is the most exciting and satisfying use of political

---

[425] A state of perfection and happiness; paradise.

power, so the powerseekers stir up their populations, spreading war fever.

Chris, I do not know of anything on this planet that is more evil than political power.

This is not to say that if you want to go into politics to try to alter the government's course, you should not do it, but be aware of what you are getting into. It is rather like the question, what should we do about the runaway bulldozer? Should we stand by and watch it demolish the town, or should we try to climb up into the driver's seat and turn off the ignition?

Naturally, we want to turn it off, but let's be very clear about the fact that once we are in the driver's seat the incredible power of the machine will tempt us to go on a joy ride. We must resolve ahead of time that we will not yield to the temptation.

Uncle Eric

P.S. Chris, I hope you took the time to examine the footnotes in this set of letters. As I said early on, you will find the research is not from esoteric sources that you cannot check. It's from material that has been freely available to the general public and to historians for years.

All I have done is rearrange and highlight the facts according to the two laws explained in my previous set of letters on law[426]— especially, Do not encroach on other persons or their property. This causes the facts to paint a picture much different than the one commonly accepted.

---

[426] Uncle Eric is referring to Richard J. Maybury's book WHATEVER HAPPENED TO JUSTICE?, published by Bluestocking Press, web site: www.BluestockingPress.com

61

Minor League to Emperor of the World

Dear Chris,

In these letters I have tried to give you the rest of the story, the non-statist side, about the World Wars and how they affect us today.

For the rest of your life you will be meeting people who believe the Hollywood version of the wars. Some of them will be veterans of World War II. The last thing these veterans want to hear is that it was all for nothing and that they were, in fact, fighting on the side of the worst of the two groups of gangsters.

If their minds are not open to new points of view, there is not much you can do except listen politely to their stories or change the subject.

For persons who do have open minds, you cannot remember everything you have found in my letters, so here is a single paragraph that tells the story:

President Franklin Roosevelt sided with the Allies, the most important of which was the enormous Soviet Union. The Allies also included China. *The number of innocent men, women, and children murdered by Allied regimes was at least twice those murdered by Axis regimes.* The complete body counts are in R.J. Rummel's book DEATH BY GOVERNMENT.

Note, Chris, we are talking here not about soldiers or civilians killed in battle, we are talking about innocent men, women and children murdered, as Hitler murdered the Jews. The Allies murdered at least twice as many as the Axis. By this measure, the Allies were twice as evil as the Axis.

Chris, why is the rest of the story about World War II not widely known? We cannot be certain, but my best guess is that there are two reasons.

First, Americans generally assume the government and the country are the same thing. If the government did something evil, they think America did it. They don't want to hear it.

Second, Franklin Roosevelt is widely regarded as one of America's greatest Presidents. To most Americans, if Roosevelt did so many evil things, then no President can ever be trusted.

For a non-statist this is no big deal, a no-brainer.

For statists, who comprise most of the United States population, the inability to trust any President is a highly disturbing thought; it produces ideological whiplash.

In 1940, the USG was a second-rate power. Its industrial strength was the greatest ever known, but in the military and geopolitical sense — which is the sense most important to statists — it was minor league. Its empire was nothing like that of London or Moscow.

Five years later, Franklin Roosevelt and his cronies had achieved what Alexander the Great, Julius Caesar, Genghis Kahn and Napoleon had failed to do. Roosevelt died in 1945, but his successor, Harry Truman, had become the undisputed emperor of the world.

Minor league to emperor of the world in just five short years. Amazing.

The people who inhabit the 6.6% of the earth that is Europe have spent thousands of years trying to conquer each other as well as those who inhabit the other 93.4% of the earth. The mess they left behind could take as long to clean up. The hatreds and vendettas are endless.

America can help by teaching the two fundamental laws, but I do not think there is much else we can do except stay neutral and keep our powder dry.

If this had been the USG's foreign policy during the 20th century, I am sure the World Trade Center would still be standing.

Uncle Eric

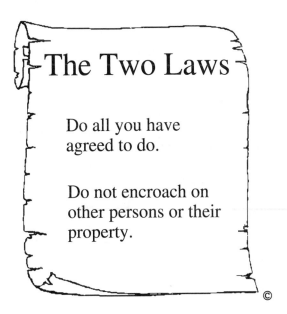

The Two Laws

Do all you have agreed to do.

Do not encroach on other persons or their property.

The two laws that make civilization possible.

Spread the Word!

Bibliography
and Suggested Reading
(Top picks are asterisked)

- *ATLAS OF RUSSIAN HISTORY, by Martin Gilbert, Dorset Press, Great Britain, 1972

- AND I WAS THERE, by Commander Edwin T. Layton, 1985

- BETRAYAL AT PEARL HARBOR, by James Rusbridger & Eric Nave, Summit Books, NY, 1991

- *DAY OF DECEIT, by Robert B. Stinnett, The Free Press (Simon & Schuster), NY, 2000

- DAY ONE, by Peter Wyden, Simon & Schuster, NY, 1984

- *DEATH BY GOVERNMENT, by R.J. Rummel, Transaction Publishers, New Brunswick, NJ, 1994

- *EMPIRE AS A WAY OF LIFE, by William Appleman Williams, Oxford University Press, NY, 1980. A history of Anglo-Saxonism and the U.S. Government's conquest of other nations. Explains why so many people hate America. Contains an excellent list and short descriptions of U.S. foreign interventions. Leftist but highly revealing and useful.

- FAILURE OF A MISSION, by Sir Nevile Henderson, G.P. Putnam's Sons, NY, 1940

- GREAT BRITAIN, GREAT EMPIRE, by W. Ross Johnston, University of Queensland Press, NY, 1981

- GREAT TERROR, by Robert Conquest, Macmillan Company, NY 1968

- *HISTORY OF THE SECOND WORLD WAR, by B.H. Liddell Hart, Perigee Books, NY, 1982

- *HITLER'S GERMAN ENEMIES, by Louis, L. Snyder, Hippocrene Books, NY, 1990

- THE NEW DEALERS' WAR, by Thomas Fleming, Basic Books, NY, 2001

- NO CLEAR AND PRESENT DANGER, by Bruce M. Russett, Westview Press, Boulder, CO, 1977

- THE OTHER VICTIMS, by Ina R. Friedman, Houghton Mifflin Co., Boston, MA, 1990

- PERPETUAL WAR FOR PERPETUAL PEACE, by Harry Elmer Barnes, Greenwood Press, NY, 1953

- RISE AND FALL OF THE THIRD REICH, by William L. Shirer, Simon and Schuster, NY, 1960

- RUSSIA AT WAR, by Alexander Werth, Carroll & Graf Publishers, NY, 1964

- *RUSSIAN VERSION OF THE SECOND WORLD WAR, edited by Graham Lyons, Facts on File Publications, NY, 1976

- STALIN, RUSSIA'S MAN OF STEEL, by Albert Marrin, Puffin Books, NY, 1988

- *SUPPLYING WAR, by Martin van Creveld, Cambridge University Press, 1977

- *UNCONDITIONAL SURRENDER, by Anne Armstrong, Rutgers University Press, New Brunswick, 1961

- *WHY THE ALLIES WON, by Richard Overy, W. W. Norton & Co., NY, 1995

- *WORLD WAR II DAY BY DAY, by Donald Sommerville, Dorset Press, 1989

Suggested Listening

- WORLD WAR II, Knowledge Products audio history, distributed by Bluestocking Press, Placerville, CA. www.BluestockingPress.com, Ph: 800-959-8586.

- THE IRISH TENORS, who are John McDermott, Anthony Kearns and Ronan Tynan. The following selections are highly recommended: "Only Our Rivers Run Free," "Grace," and "The Town I Loved So Well."

- WORDS AND MUSIC OF WORLD WAR II by Sony. (2 music CDs) The producers of this package have attempted to recapture the mood of the WW Two period via broadcasts and popular music of the time, linked together by commentary. Includes broadcasts by Edward R. Murrow; Pearl Harbor Attacked broadcast; FDR declaring war; Mary Anderson, Director of the Women's Bureau, Dept. of Labor, on Women's Value to the War Effort; On the Spot Account of American Forces Landing on Iwo Jima; Truman Announces the Dropping of the First Atomic Bomb over Hiroshima. Tokyo Rose Broadcasts to the American Troops in the Pacific. Songs: A Little Old Church in England, Any Bonds Today, This Is the Army, Mr. Jones, Stars and Stripes of Iwo Jima, Atom and Evil, You're a Sap, Mr. Jap, and much more. Highly recommended.

Suggested Viewing

Although movies generally give the government's official view of the World Wars, there are exceptions, and even some of the most statist movies can paint enlightening pictures of real events.

U.S. foreign and military policy today, in the 21ˢᵗ century, is still largely determined by the emotions generated by World War II movies. As I write this, the government and the country as a whole are now led by baby boomers, and the boomers were raised on a steady diet of World War II films. Screen images and music are so powerful they can overwhelm facts.

— Richard Maybury

- BLACK HAWK DOWN starring Tom Sizemore & Sam Shepard. (2002) Rated R for extremely authentic violence. Horrifically accurate account of the Battle of Mogadishu, which killed 18 Americans and somewhere between 1,000 and 10,000 Somalis. The United Nations wanted tribal warlords eliminated and a U.N.-approved government installed in Somalia. U.S. troops were sent to do the job and were attacked by Somali guerrillas. The catastrophe traumatized the Pentagon; the desire to avoid a repeat has been a top priority of U.S. foreign policy ever since.

- BRAVEHEART starring Mel Gibson (1995). Rated R. 13ᵗʰ century Scottish warrior William Wallace who rebels against the tyranny of English King Edward I.

- COMMAND DECISION starring Clark Gable (1948). Not Rated. Gripping, tense story about decision-making by air commanders in World War II.

- DAS BOOT starring Jurgen Prochnow (1981). Rated R. Except for its submarines, the German navy did not amount to much and was quickly sunk or incapacitated. This highly realistic picture of German submarine warfare shows the hopelessness of Germany's war at sea.

- DOCTOR ZHIVAGO starring Omar Sharif and Julie Christie (1965). Rated PG-13. Russian Revolution. A good visual example of Russian winters.

- ENEMY AT THE GATES starring Jude Law and Ed Harris (2001). Rated R. If wars were mountains, the Eastern Front clash between Hitler and Stalin was the Himalaya of world history, and everything else in World War II was foothills. In terms of the number killed, the Eastern Front was equal to a thousand Iwo Jimas. To know what the Eastern Front was like, see this movie about the Battle of Stalingrad. This was the worst battle in all of human history. It killed as many people as the U.S. has lost in all the wars it has ever fought.

- "History vs. Hollywood: Sand Pebbles," from the History Channel.

- KHARTOUM starring Charlton Heston (1966) – British defeat in Northern Africa by Arab tribesman circa 1885. Enlightening look at the British Empire vs. Muslims.

- THE LONGEST DAY starring John Wayne (1962). Rated G. Epic story of the invasion of Normandy. Re-creation of historic events on a grand scale. As you watch, remember that the invasion was done primarily to take the pressure off Stalin.

- MEMPHIS BELLE starring Matthew Modine (1990). Rated PG-13 for profanity and violence. Story of the first B-17 crew to survive 25 missions over Germany.

- "Modern Marvels: Kaiser," from the History Channel. About Henry J. Kaiser's amazing feat of mass producing 10,000 ton ships in World War II the way he mass-produced cars on an assembly line.

- QUIGLEY DOWN UNDER starring Tom Selleck (1990). Rated PG-13. American cowboy travels to Australia in the 1860s where he has been hired to protect a British rancher's property, which Quigley discovers means murdering the land's aborigines.

- THE SAND PEBBLES starring Steve McQueen (1966). Rated PG-13. American warship is stationed off China in 1926, cruising the Yangtze River.

- SAVING PRIVATE RYAN starring Tom Hanks (1998). Rated R for violence. The opening 20-minute depiction of the D-Day assault is very graphic, but, according to soldiers who were there, does a commendable job of helping an audience understand what troops were up against on that day.

- THE SOUND OF MUSIC starring Julie Andrews (1965). Rated G. Story of Maria, a novice at the Abby, who falls in love with widower Baron von Trapp and his children. Set during the Nazi occupation of Austria, shows how World War II Germans have typically been depicted in films, reinforcing World War II propaganda.

- THEY WERE EXPENDABLE starring John Wayne (1945). Rated PG. Probably the best World War II propaganda movie. Any young man who can see this and not run right down to the nearest recruiting station has amazing self-control.

- THIRTEEN DAYS starring Kevin Costner (2000). Rated PG-13. Realistic depiction of the 1962 Cuban Missile Crisis in which the White House and Kremlin nearly went head-to-head in a nuclear war.

- TWELVE O'CLOCK HIGH starring Gregory Peck (1949). Perhaps the best movie ever made about the bombing of Germany.

- VICTORY AT SEA produced by Henry Salomon (1954). TV documentary series about the Allied fight during World War II.

- WHY WE FIGHT. An Oscar-winning wartime series created and directed by Frank Capra. Includes American newsreels, United Nations films, and captured-enemy motion pictures.

- ZULU starring Michael Caine (1964). Not Rated. For Older Students. True story of undermanned British forces trying to defend themselves against thousands of Zulu warriors in 1879 South Africa.

Glossary

(Other names can be found in the Cast of Characters.)

ANCILLARY. Subordinate or less important.

ALLIES. Enemies of the Axis, led by Britain, United States, Russia.

AREA BOMBING. A British term from World War II. The bombing of civilian housing areas for the purpose of killing and terrorizing civilian men, women, and children. Done mostly by the British to Germans, but also done to some extent by Americans to Germans, and to a greater extent by Americans to Japanese.

AXIS. Enemies of the Allies, led by Germany, Italy, Japan.

BAILIWICK. Domain.

BERLIN WALL. The wall between West Berlin and East Berlin erected in 1961 by the Kremlin. The wall was designed to keep Germans in Soviet-controlled East Germany from escaping to the West. The Berlin Wall became a symbol of Soviet tyranny, and when it was torn down in 1989, this triggered a domino effect that led to the collapse of the entire Soviet Empire.

BLACK HOLE. A star so massive that its gravity prevents anything from escaping, not even light. Hence the star is black. Nothing that goes into a black hole can come back out. To say Russia is a black hole for invaders is to say an invader that goes into Russia is doomed.

BLITZ. The German bombing of England. The meaning is often restricted only to the German bombing of London in 1940.

BLITZKRIEG. Lightning war. A German term meaning a swift, powerful strike spearheaded by tanks and aircraft.

BLOWBACK. A Central Intelligence Agency term, means retaliation by victims of Washington's foreign interventions.

CENTRAL PLANNING. Government bureaucrats directing the work, production, and trade of the people.

CENTRAL POWERS. In World War II, consisted of Germany, the Austro-Hungarian Empire, Turkey, and Bulgaria.

COLD WAR. The half-century standoff between Moscow and its allies, and Washington and its allies.

CONCENTRATION CAMP. A prison, often just an open area surrounded by barbed wire and guard towers, in which political dissidents, members of ethnic minorities, and other innocent persons are kept, usually under harsh conditions.

DIVISION. Generally, six brigades. An infantry division is about 10,000 troops. An armored division, about 600 tanks. Typically, but not always, there are nine troops in a squad, three squads to a platoon, four platoons to a company, six companies to a battalion, two battalions to a brigade, and six brigades to a division.

EASTERN FRONT. The war in East Europe. Mostly involving Russia and Germany.

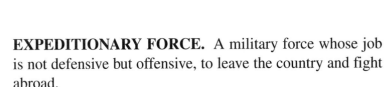

EXPEDITIONARY FORCE. A military force whose job is not defensive but offensive, to leave the country and fight abroad.

FACTION. A group of people within a larger group, working together against other groups or against the main body.

FASCES. A bundle of rods bound with an ax or spear. The bound rods symbolized all the people of all the provinces "unified" under a single government. The ax or spear symbolized what happened to anyone who did not obey this government.

FASCISM. The political philosophy that is no philosophy at all. Do whatever appears necessary. It is derived from the law of the Roman Empire.

FREEZE. To hold assets and prevent the owner from having access to them.

FUNGIBLE. Transportable and of uniform characteristics, so that one unit of the item can substitute for any other unit, as one gallon of pure water can substitute for any other gallon of pure water.

GENOCIDE. The systematic killing of a whole national or ethnic group.

ISOLATIONISM. Having no political or economic relations of any kind with other countries.

JEWISH HOLOCAUST. The systematic murder of Jews by Hitler and his followers during World War II.

LABOR CAMP. A prison camp in which the inmates are used as slave labor. Often inmates are worked to death.

MAD. Mutually Assured Destruction. Nuclear policy of Washington and the Kremlin.

MOBILIZED. To prepare for war. To arm troops and move them near expected areas of fighting.

NAPALM. Jellied gasoline that erupts in an inferno when it hits the ground.

NEUTRALITY. Not aligned with, supporting, or favoring any side in a war or dispute.

NONINTERVENTION. Similar to neutrality. Refusal to meddle in the affairs of another nation, or in a dispute or war.

POW. Prisoner of war.

PREMISE. The basis or starting point of an argument.

PROTOTYPE. An early experimental or demonstration version, not a mass production version. Usually, prototypes are hand made.

SOCIALISM. An economic and political system under which virtually everything and everyone is owned and controlled by government agencies.

SS. Schutzstaffel. The elite military unit of the Nazi party. Noted for ruthlessness and lack of ethics, the SS served as Hitler's personal guard and as a security force in Germany and occupied areas.

STRATEGIC. Planning, maneuver and placement of forces — not *what* the forces are, but *where* they are and *how* they are used.

TRINITY. Code name for the first test of the Atomic bomb in New Mexico on July 16, 1945.

TRUE BELIEVER. One who is highly dedicated, to the depths of his soul. The belief may have been so ingrained in his personality for so long — perhaps taught in school at a young age — that he may not realize it is a belief, to him it as unquestionable as the existence of air.

USG. United States Government.

U.S.S.R. Union of Soviet Socialist Republics. The Russian Empire. Headquarters, the Kremlin in Moscow.

VARMINT. Variation of vermin. An unwanted animal or person who is hunted as a pest.

WESTERN FRONT. The war in West Europe. Mostly involving Britain, France, Germany, and the United States, and mostly land and air battles.

WHITE HATS AGAINST BLACK HATS. An expression from early western movies in which the good guys wore white hats and the bad guys wore black hats.

About Richard J. Maybury

Richard Maybury, also known as Uncle Eric, is a world renowned author, lecturer and geopolitical analyst. He consults with business firms in the U.S. and Europe. Richard is the former Global Affairs editor of MONEYWORLD and widely regarded as one of the finest free-market writers in America. Mr. Maybury's articles have appeared in THE WALL STREET JOURNAL, USA TODAY, and other major publications.

During the 1960s, in the U.S. Air Force 605th Air Commando Squadron, Mr. Maybury was an aircrew member on AC-47, C-47 and C-46 aircraft, and was involved in covert warfare operations in Central America. He saw, in his own words, "real politics, up front and personal, and it isn't anything like what most Americans think it is."

Richard Maybury has penned eleven books in the Uncle Eric series. His books have been endorsed by top business leaders including former U.S. Treasury Secretary William Simon, and he has been interviewed on more than 250 radio and TV shows across America.

He has been married for more than 35 years, has lived abroad, traveled around the world, and visited 48 states and 40 countries.

He is truly a teacher for all ages.

Index

"...the entire [Uncle Eric] series should be a required, integral, component of the social studies curriculum in all public and private schools. This would bring a quantum leap upward in the quality of citizenship in this country in a single generation."

—William P. Snavely
Emeritus Professor of Economics
George Mason University

Study Guides and / or Tests available (or forthcoming)

for the Uncle Eric books

Each study guide will include some, and at times all, of the following:

1) Chapter-by-chapter comprehension questions

2) Research activities

3) A list of films

4) Thought questions

5) Final exam

Order from your favorite book store or direct from the publisher:

Bluestocking Press
www.BluestockingPress.com

(See contact information
on the last page of this book.)

Bluestocking Press

Bluestocking Press publishes the following:

1) Richard J. Maybury's Uncle Eric books (and the accompanying student study guides for the Uncle Eric books)

2) Karl Hess' CAPITALISM FOR KIDS

3) Kathryn Daniels' COMMON SENSE BUSINESS FOR KIDS

4) ECONOMICS: A FREE MARKET READER

5) LAURA INGALLS WILDER AND ROSE WILDER LANE HISTORICAL TIMETABLE

Visit the BLUESTOCKING PRESS CATALOG online at
www.BluestockingPress.com

To order by phone, contact Bluestocking Press
(See contact information
on the last page of this book.)